Edmund Spenser's *The Faerie*

Reading Guides to Long Poems

Published:
John Milton's Paradise Lost: *A Reading Guide*
Noam Reisner
Hbk: 978 0 7486 3999 1
Pbk: 978 0 7486 4000 3

Edmund Spenser's The Faerie Queene: *A Reading Guide*
Andrew Zurcher
Hbk: 978 0 7486 3956 4
Pbk: 978 0 7486 3957 1

Homer's Odyssey: *A Reading Guide*
Henry Power
Hbk: 978 0 7486 4110 9
Pbk: 978 0 7486 4109 3

Forthcoming:
Elizabeth Barrett Browning's Aurora Leigh: *A Reading Guide*
Michele Martinez
Hbk: 978 0 7486 3971 7
Pbk: 978 0 7486 3972 4

Alfred Lord Tennyson's In Memoriam: *A Reading Guide*
Anna Barton
Hbk: 978 0 7486 4135 2
Pbk: 978 0 7486 4134 5

Edmund Spenser's
The Faerie Queene
A Reading Guide

Andrew Zurcher

Edinburgh University Press

© Andrew Zurcher, 2011

Edinburgh University Press Ltd
22 George Square, Edinburgh

www.euppublishing.com

Typeset in 10.5/13 Sabon
by Servis Filmsetting Ltd, Stockport, Cheshire, and
printed and bound in Great Britain by
CPI Antony Rowe, Chippenham and Eastbourne

A CIP record for this book is available from the British Library

ISBN 978 0 7486 3956 4 (hardback)
ISBN 978 0 7486 3957 1 (paperback)

The right of Andrew Zurcher
to be identified as author of this work
has been asserted in accordance with
the Copyright, Designs and Patents Act 1988.

Contents

	Preface: How to read *The Faerie Queene*	vi
	Series Editors' Preface	viii
1.	Mapping and Making	1
2.	Selections from the Poem	16
3.	Contexts and Reception	162
4.	Teaching the Text	195
5.	Resources for Study	209
	Index	214

Preface: How to read *The Faerie Queene*

There are many battles in Edmund Spenser's *The Faerie Queene* but the first battle of the poem is that of the reader. From the opening stanzas, the poem is swashbucklingly pacy, full of magic and mischief, and often weirdly beautiful. On the other hand, it is long and it may seem difficult, even intimidating. Should you plunge right into an unannotated edition, trusting yourself to get the hang of it as you go along? Or should you invest in a densely commented copy, and pick your painful way through its minutely charactered pages? Spenser anticipated questions like these – no doubt he had asked them of himself, when considering how to read Ovid and Virgil – and in the opening episode of the first canto he offers us some guidance on how to read the poem. Three people – a knight, a princess and a dwarf – get lost in a wood. In the centre of this wood, they discover a cave, inhabited by a fabulous monster, half-woman, half-snake, called Errour. The knight of holiness, Redcrosse, is all for charging headlong into the cave and taking his chances. Believing that his native valour will illuminate his reading of the situation, he tells Una, the princess, that 'vertue giues her selfe light, through darkenesse for to wade' (I.i.12.9). Una is not so sure. She counters, 'yet wisedome warnes, whilest foot is in the gate, I To stay the steppe, ere forced to retrate' (I.i.13.4–5). Both 'errour' and 'retrate' – through its Latin root *tractum*, 'writing' – are words closely connected with reading and interpretation, which suggests that Redcrosse's headstrong rashness may offer readers not only an ethical warning, but a caution about how they read – even, how they are reading this particular poem. To 'stay' a step is to interrupt or check it; but in the sixteenth century the verb could also mean 'to support, strengthen'. Una may be telling her champion to pause, but she may also be telling us, the readers, to tread carefully and securely along the path ('gate') of a text that will weave, ply and knot in mystifying, even dangerous ways. Redcrosse, then, wants to get on with it, while Una wants him to (t)read more carefully. Meanwhile, the dwarf wants nothing to do with the poem at all: 'Fly, fly (quoth then I The fearefull

Dwarfe:) this is no place for liuing men' (I.i.13.8–9). But he is a dwarf for a reason, and the heroes of the poem ignore him. So should you.

The purpose of this *Guide* is to offer readers new to Spenser a 'stay' for their first steps in *The Faerie Queene*, and the immediate purpose of this introductory discussion to prepare them for the poem itself, selections from which follow in the next section. Like Spenser, I think of readers of this poem as heroes, but prudent ones: full of might and courage, but ready to resort to offered aid. The *Guide* thus tries to steer a course between letting readers get on with reading, and helping them to 'retrate' – to back up, to re-read, to get a picture (Italian *ritratto*) of the poem. First of all, a brief introduction (Chapter 1, 'Mapping and Making') offers an account of Spenser's life and career, both as a secretary in Elizabethan Ireland and as a poet, which places the genesis of *The Faerie Queene* in the various literary, intellectual, social and political contexts that shaped Spenser's writing life. The introduction also offers a summary map of the poem as a whole, which will help the reader to form an overview of this massy work, and position the selections that appear in the next chapter. These selections (the 'Reading Guide') are themselves, in turn, lightly annotated in two ways; glosses for archaic and hard words appear in the margin, while a spare commentary at the foot of each page indicates the major historical, literary and other resonances of particular words, lines and passages. In the two chapters that follow the poem selections ('Contexts and Reception' and 'Teaching the Text'), readers will find discussion and thinking plans designed both to unlock the pastness of *The Faerie Queene*, and to demonstrate its philosophical vitality as a poem for modern readers. These sections address sixteenth-century preoccupations with literary allusiveness and imitation, history, theology and philosophy, as well as more modern responses to Spenser's work – from criticism focusing on gender and sexuality, to psychological topics like visual reading, and political concerns such as law and empire. In a final chapter ('Resources for Study'), the *Guide* summarises the scholarly and critical resources, both print and electronic, available to readers of the poem. In every section of this guide, the aim is the same: to help the reader to understand, and to enjoy understanding, this long poem, and to incite her to a life of repeated and fruitful engagements with it.

Series Editors' Preface

The form of the long poem has been of fundamental importance to Literary Studies from the time of Homer onwards. The *Reading Guides to Long Poems Series* seeks to celebrate and explore this form in all its diversity across a range of authors and periods. Major poetic works – *The Odyssey, The Faerie Queene, Paradise Lost, The Prelude, In Memoriam, The Waste Land* – emerge as defining expressions of the culture which produced them. One of the main aims of the series is to make contemporary readers aware of the importance of the long poem for our literary and national heritage.

How 'long' is a long poem? In 'The Philosophy of Composition' Edgar Allan Poe asserted that there is 'a distinct limit, as regards length, to all works of literary art – the limit of a single sitting'. Defined against this, a long poem must be one which *exceeds* the limit of a single sitting, requiring sustained attention over a considerable period of time for its full appreciation. However, the concept of poetic length is not simply concerned with the number of lines in a poem, or the time it takes to read it. In 'From Poe to Valéry' T. S. Eliot defends poetic length on the grounds that 'it is only in a poem of some length that a variety of moods can be expressed. . . . These parts can form a whole more than the sum of the parts; a whole such that the pleasure we derive from the reading of any part is enhanced by our grasp of the whole.' Along with Eliot, the Series Editors believe that poetic length creates a unique space for a varied play of meaning and tone, action and reflection, that results in particular kinds of reading and interpretation not possible for shorter works. The *Reading Guides* are therefore concerned with communicating the pleasure and enjoyment of engaging with the form in a range of ways – focusing on particular episodes, tracing out patterns of poetic imagery, exploring form, reading and re-reading the text – in order to allow the reader to experience the multiple interpretative layers that the long poem holds within it. We also believe that a self-awareness about *how* we read the long poem may help to provide the modern reader with a necessary fresh perspective upon the genre.

The *Reading Guides to Long Poems Series* will engage with major works in new and innovative ways in order to revitalise the form of the long poem for a new generation. The series will present shorter 'long poems' in their entirety, while the longest are represented by a careful selection of essential parts. Long poems have often been read aloud, imitated, or even translated in excerpts, so there is good precedent for appreciating them through selective reading. Nevertheless, it is to be hoped that readers will use the *Guides* alongside an appreciation of the work in its entirety or, if they have not previously done so, go on to read the whole poem.

Ultimately the *Edinburgh Reading Guides to Long Poems Series* seeks to be of lasting value to the discipline of Literary Studies by revitalising a form which is in danger of being marginalised by the current curriculum but is central to our understanding of our own literature, history and culture.

Sally Bushell with Isobel Armstrong and Colin Burrow

Chapter 1
Mapping and Making

Spenser's writing life

Very little can be said with certainty of the particulars of Edmund Spenser's life; no reliable contemporary account survives, so any picture must be compiled from meagre and scattered evidence. He was born to a family of modest means in London, in or around 1552, and matriculated at the new Merchant Taylors' School some time shortly after its foundation in 1561; in 1569 he departed London for Pembroke College, Cambridge. In this year, too, Spenser published his first poetry, translations from French and Italian poems for Jan van der Noodt's *A Theatre for Worldlings*. Between 1569 and 1576 Spenser appears to have remained mainly resident in Cambridge, for he took degrees in 1573 (BA) and again in 1575 (MA).[1] He finally left Pembroke as private secretary to its departing Master, John Young, who had been appointed Bishop of Rochester. But by 1580, immediately after the publication of his first masterpiece, *The Shepheardes Calender* (1579), Spenser claimed to have been living under the roof of the Earl of Leicester in London. The capacity in which Spenser served Leicester is not clear,[2] but whatever his position, it did not last long; in August 1580 he departed for Dublin as the personal secretary to the newly appointed Lord Deputy of Ireland, Arthur Lord Grey of Wilton, a post he would hold until Grey's recall two years later.[3] Spenser spent the better part of his life's remainder in the 'New English' service in Ireland, first as a private secretary, and later as a planter or 'undertaker' on the Munster plantation near Cork. While he was certainly in London for the printing of *The Faerie Queene* in 1590 (Part 1) and in 1596 (Part 2),[4] and perhaps at other times, too, Spenser appears to have lived primarily at his plantation estate at Kilcolman, in Munster, between about 1587 and the outbreak of the Munster revolt in 1596. This period coincides with an enormously productive decade of poetic composition: not only the first and second halves of his ambitious romance epic, but a short book of *Complaints* (1591), a sonnet sequence and marriage hymn (*Amoretti and Epithalamion*, 1595), and a series of court, anti-court and occasional poems. When the war finally came to Kilcolman, Spenser fled Ireland, possibly carrying urgent letters from the besieged townspeople of Cork. He died in London in 1599, according to both William Camden and Ben Jonson in penniless circumstances.[5]

To his London origins and, above all, to the Merchant Taylors' School and its first headmaster, Richard Mulcaster, Spenser owed his rigorous humanist education. Though little evidence survives of his career at the school, we know a good deal about Mulcaster's teaching methods, largely from his own publications on education.[6] Boys were admitted to the school at about the age of 10, when they could read and write in English, and knew their catechism in English or Latin. Many of them were poor or from guild backgrounds, and were the first in their families to receive a formal education; as Mulcaster writes in *Positions*, 'the parentes and freindes [of Merchant Taylors' pupils] with whom I haue to deale, be mostwhat no latinistes.'[7] Lessons focused on intensive training in Latin and Greek language, which culminated in yearly examinations in which external visitors rigorously questioned the boys on linguistic, rhetorical and poetical matters. In 1571, for example, school records show that the boys in the highest form were examined on one of Horace's odes (in Latin), on the poetry of Homer (in Greek), and on the psalter (in Hebrew).[8] In addition to Horace and Homer, students would likely have studied Terence, Ovid, Seneca, Virgil, and above all Cicero; it is no doubt during his schooling that Spenser first developed a thorough knowledge of the *Iliad* and the *Odyssey*, and of Virgil's poetic *rota* ('wheel', or poetic career), which moves from the pastoral poetry of his *Eclogues* to the martial and imperial verse of the *Aeneid*. Standards at Merchant Taylors' were exacting; Bishop of London Edmund Grindal commended Mulcaster after the examinations of 1562 for bringing the Merchant Taylors' pupils to as high a level as the scholars of any school in the realm.[9] But, as his writings show, Mulcaster also placed substantial emphasis on the arts; in addition to the traditional exercises in double translation and Latin composition that typified humanist school learning in the sixteenth century, Mulcaster's pupils also danced, drew, wrote poetry and acted in plays.[10]

Spenser matriculated at Pembroke Hall, Cambridge as a 'sizar' (or poor scholar) in the spring of 1569. His placement at Pembroke may reflect ongoing support from Grindal, who had recently served as (absentee) Master of the college. Grindal was sharply critical when, almost immediately after Spenser's arrival in Cambridge, a fierce doctrinal dispute erupted in Cambridge, centring on Thomas Cartwright, a fellow of Trinity appointed Lady Margaret Professor of Divinity in 1570.[11] Cartwright's appointment had been a victory for young, radical, anti-establishment Protestants, and he immediately began using his lectures as a vehicle for Puritan ideas. The Regent Masters – the fellows of the university's colleges, assembled in Senate House – leaned as a group toward these radical ideas, whereas the heads of the colleges, along with the university's officers (including Lord Burghley, the Chancellor), took a more conservative view on church government, and on other points of contention such as the use of vestments and ceremonies. The 1570 altercation between Cambridge's Regent Masters and its heads of house was so violent that Cartwright was ejected from his chair, while the new Master of Trinity, John Whitgift, hastily redrafted the university's statutes in order to give the authorities the upper hand. Spenser's immersion in this heated dispute, only months after his initial arrival at the university, must have occupied him body and mind, and traces of its influence are obvious in his major works, *The Shepheardes Calender* (1579) and *The Faerie Queene* (1590, 1596). The controversy exposed fiercely fought faultlines within the Elizabethan settlement, and pushed Grindal and his fellow bishops into an uncomfortable middle ground – neither 'hot' Protestants like Cartwright, nor reactionary conservatives, like the Queen herself. It was a middle ground that may have appealed to Spenser.

In addition to this immediate and thorough exposure to radical Cambridge Protestantism, Spenser quickly discovered at Cambridge the literary friendships and patronage connections that would determine the course of his later career. His friend and tutor during these years, Gabriel Harvey, was a client of the celebrated diplomat and philosopher Sir Thomas Smith. Like Harvey and Smith, Spenser probably read widely while at Cambridge in classical and Italian republican history, in Protestant theology and in poetry – above all in the verse romances of Matteo Boiardo (*Orlando Innamorato*, left unfinished in 1494), Ludovico Ariosto (*Orlando Furioso*, 1516–32) and Torquato Tasso (*Gerusalemme Liberata*, 1574), all of which would prove major influences on *The Faerie Queene*. With Harvey Spenser must also have studied logic and metaphysics, two central components of the university curriculum. Spenser's work doubtless impressed the Master of Pembroke, John Young, who employed him as his private secretary when he resigned the mastership to be consecrated Bishop of Rochester in 1578. Factional patronage connections continued to define Spenser's own bumpy career. His 1580 appointment as personal secretary to Lord Grey appears to have been at the advice of the Earl of Leicester – *the* great patron of the Protestant radicals – and, perhaps, Leicester's nephew Philip Sidney, with whom Spenser claims, again in a letter to Harvey, to have been on close terms.[12] Once in Ireland, Spenser's association with Grey no doubt led to advantages – lucrative offices, estates in his master's gift, close partnership with other Grey clients like his fellow secretary Lodowick Bryskett – but it also led to enmities; above all, Spenser probably attracted the censure of William Cecil, Baron Burghley, over many years effectively head of Elizabeth's government.[13] Still, Spenser's active participation in the 'New English' community of Protestant English administrators and military men in Ireland brought him wealth and status. He acquired a vast estate in Munster and the style of a gentleman, and in 1598 secured the Privy Council's nomination as sheriff of Cork. Spenser's savvy manipulation of factional and patronage politics, over the whole course of his life, is everywhere in evidence in his poetry, most visibly in its dedications and other paratexts, but also in its content, and particularly in its shrewdly topical historical allegory.

The office of an Elizabethan secretary demanded acute political sensitivity and probity, as the secretary enjoyed special access to most, if not quite all, of his master's most intimate and secret dealings.[14] Spenser was charged with writing some letters, copying others, and certifying other documents – the work of other secretaries, as well as transcripts, accounts and other official papers. He acted as paymaster to the messengers who, in the days before a postal system, carried these letters both within Ireland and across the seas, and as paymaster almost certainly also supervised intelligence for the Lord Deputy. Before writing or sealing his first letter, a secretary had to master the complex language of courtesies and codes that governed diplomatic post, from the various scripts or 'hands' in which he wrote, to forms of address and subscription, and even to complicated ciphers. Spenser's experience in the post prepared him well for the complex regional politics of the Munster plantation, where he schemed to obtain an estate in 1587, and later fought off attempts by Viscount Roche of Fermoy, his neighbour, to crush his interests there. Spenser may have served as an administrator in the New English colonial government, but he was never far from the brutal and repressive violence of Elizabeth's military campaigns in Ireland. He was present at Lord Grey's victory at Smerwick in the autumn of 1580, when at least 600 Spanish and Papal troops surrendered and were summarily massacred. He later accompanied Lord Grey on similarly brutal campaigns in Wicklow and Wexford, and he must have seen – and perhaps done – terrible things during the war that slowly engulfed Ireland after the revolt of the Earl of Tyrone in 1594, a revolt that burned Spenser out of his Kilcolman estate, eventually driving him to his death in London. It has long been claimed that the violence of these colonial experiences informed Spenser's composition of the later parts of *The Faerie Queene*, in particular Books V and VI. Whether for good or ill, there can be no doubt that Elizabethan Ireland exerted a strong influence on Spenser's mature imagination, and on the moral scheme of the latter part of his masterwork.

The Faerie Queene grew out of the encounters both human and literary that shaped Spenser's life: the classical humanism of his education, the doctrinal strife that engulfed his years at Cambridge, the factional politics that governed preferment and policy in England and Ireland, the harsh realities of colonial occupation. But the poem is also much more than the combination of these factors, and Spenser's achievement much greater than a simple response to them. *The Faerie Queene* wears proudly its indebtedness to the great medieval English romance writers – not only to Chaucer (Spenser's 'well of English vndefyled') and his romance *Troilus and Criseyde*, but to the works of John Lydgate, William Langland and John Skelton, and to Sir Thomas Malory's *Morte d'Arthur*. Spenser's archaic language seemed to his contemporaries so Chaucerian that some of them (especially Ben Jonson) ridiculed him, but in reviving this tradition Spenser seems to have been creating, almost single-handedly, a canon of English literary giants whose enduring glories he might crown. To write a chivalric romance in imitation of the famous Italians Ariosto and Tasso was to put English, as a civilised and philosophical literary language, on a par with the leading vernacular tongue of Europe; to give this romance poem epic pretensions was to challenge for the prestige of Virgil; to give it allegorical complexity was to emulate the best of Ovid and, in the Christian tradition of Biblical allegoresis, Dante. But Spenser managed in *The Faerie Queene* to accomplish all of this within the larger framework of a thoroughly English idiom, one that built on native folk and literary traditions, and that shadowed in its historical allegory the tumultuous events of recent Tudor political and religious history. At the time of its first publication, it was without rival the longest, most sophisticated and most ambitious English literary work ever printed in England. Spenser's emergence as 'England's Arch-Poët' thus marked not only his own success, but the birth of a literary English ready to receive the impression of Shakespeare, Marlowe, Jonson, Donne, Milton and many others.

A map of *The Faerie Queene*

The most straightforward way to map the contents of *The Faerie Queene* is simply to epitomise it, as in the summary that follows. Such a summary can only capture the outlines of Spenser's verse and his poetic vision, but it will help to make sense of the extracted passages that follow in the next section (distinguished by *italic face* in this summary), and as an overview it clearly reveals the patterns of linear quest and romance dilation from which Spenser's narrative is constructed. In each of Books I, II, V and VI, for example, it is clear that the patron knight sets off on a quest, is diverted, and finds his way back to his mission through the offices of some intermediary – usually Prince Arthur. Books III and IV – which largely concern the female knight Britomart in her quest for Artegall, and the subsidiary (or projected) narratives of the maidens Florimell and Amoret – work by a different, more medieval logic. Britomart never fights a monster or defeats a tyrant; instead, her proxies Florimell and Amoret overcome their own psychological and ethical obstacles in their journeys toward faithful love, making it possible for Britomart and Artegall to plight their faith to one another.

This summary also makes clear the overall (incomplete) moral project of the poem, the full title of which should always be borne in mind: *The Faerie Queene. Disposed into twelue books, Fashioning XII. Morall vertues.* Book I concerns holiness, Book II temperance and Book III chastity. The second part of the poem, which readers have long tended to consider more public and political in its preoccupations, deals with friendship (Book IV), justice (Book V) and courtesy (Book VI), while the *Two Cantos of Mutabilitie* (published ten years posthumously) appear to concern constancy. However Spenser conceived the relation between private and public virtue, it is certainly true that the poem never takes an outright didactic approach to moral instruction, but prefers to illustrate and exemplify, analyse and synthesise. *The Faerie Queene* does not contain answers to moral or political problems, but the experience of reading it may help a reader (to use Spenser's word) to 'fashion' such answers.

The Faerie Queene. Disposed into twelue bookes, Fashioning XII. Morall vertues.

Book I: The Legend of the Knight of the Red Crosse, or Of Holinesse

We learn in Spenser's 'Letter of the Authors . . . to Sir Walter Raleigh' that a young princess – Una – has come to Gloriana's court seeking a champion who might liberate her parents' kingdom from the ravages of a terrible dragon. She provides a suit of armour, and Gloriana grants the quest to an unproved yokel, thereafter called the Red Crosse Knight, or Redcrosse. *Along the way, Redcrosse and Una ('oneness', Truth) meet with a number of perils: the monstrous serpent Errour and her brood, whom Redcrosse defeats (I.i); the enchanter Archimago ('arch-mage', or 'arch-imager', also known as Hypocrisie), who succeeds in dividing the knight from his lady (I.i–ii); and Duessa ('twoness', duplicity), a shrivelled witch disguised as the winsome young beauty Fidessa (I.ii ff.).* Orgoglio, the embodiment of pride (I.vii–viii), eventually defeats Redcrosse and imprisons him. Meanwhile Redcrosse also battles the 'sarazin' or pagan knights Sans foy, Sans loy and Sans joy ('faithless', 'lawless' and 'joyless' – I.ii–v), and visits the palace of the proud Queen Lucifera (I.iv–v), while Una is captured by satyrs (I.vi). They are ultimately reunited by Prince Arthur, who delivers Redcrosse from Orgoglio (I.vii–viii) only to leave him defenceless against Despaire (I.ix). Under Una's guidance, though, Redcrosse escapes to the House of Holinesse (I.x) – the 'allegorical core' of the book – where he receives absolution and education under the tutelage of Contemplation, and is granted a vision of the New Jerusalem. It is here, too, that Redcrosse discovers his real identity: no faery knight, but England's patron saint, St George. With renewed confidence, he assails the dragon that has tyrannised Eden, and after three days, triumphs (I.xi). In the final canto of the book (I.xii), Una and Redcrosse are betrothed, in the process seeing off a late legal challenge to their union by Archimago and Duessa. Bound for a certain term to serve Gloriana, Redcrosse departs, but promises to return to fulfil the union.

Book II: The Legend of Sir Guyon, or Of Temperance

Early in the book Sir Guyon, travelling with a Palmer (a Christian pilgrim), hears the cries of a dying woman (II.i). By the time they reach her side, Amavia is nearly dead, but she has just time enough to reveal how both she and her knight Mordant – whose body lies beside her – were killed by the hand of an enchantress called Acrasia, who with Circean charms seduces knights in a pleasure garden called the Bower of Bliss. Guyon takes up their child, whom he names Ruddymane ('bloody hands') because the infant bears the indelible stain of his mother's gore; he swears that he will avenge the child's loss upon Acrasia. Guyon subsequently passes through a number of discrete adventures in which he learns about the nature of temperance. First he visits the house of Medina ('mean'), whose sisters Elissa and Perissa ('too little' and 'too much', respectively) vie in their animosity for her (II.ii). Afterwards he falls in with the squire Phedon (II.iv), who has killed his faithless mistress and her lover, and now requires redemption from his tormentors, the villains Furor and Occasion. No sooner have Guyon and the Palmer released and healed Phedon, but they receive a new lesson in extremity, now in an allegorical vein, by the knights Pyrochles ('fiery temper') and Cymochles ('watery temper'). Pyrochles falls prey to Furor and Occasion (II.v), while Cymochles succumbs to the wanton nymph of the Idle Lake, Phaedria (also known as 'Mirth'). Guyon resists the fate of both (II.vi), but when he travels to the house of Richesse with Mammon (II.vii), he only narrowly evades Mammon's tempting lures, both of money and of worldly honour, and reaches solid ground in a coma, barely alive. It is left to Prince Arthur, who happens upon his apparently lifeless body, to defend Guyon from Pyrochles and Cymochles (II.viii), and when Guyon regains consciousness, the two knights travel together to the house of Alma (II.ix). Alma's castle furnishes the 'allegorical core' of the book and, as a transparent allegory for the embodied soul, her house occasions a series of lessons in temperate thought and regimen. Throughout the book, Spenser's account of temperance has frequently touched on the troubled relation between humble pursuit of the mean, on the one hand, and the heroic ambition proper to chivalric knights, on the other. In canto x, Arthur and Guyon visit the tower room of Eumnestes, Alma's historian, and read the chronicles: Arthur those of Briton kings, and Guyon those of Faery. Their newfound understanding of their own places in their respective histories enables them to realise heroic destinies. Arthur defeats Maleger, the intemperate captain whose hordes are besieging Alma's castle (II.xi); *while Guyon, reunited with the Palmer, sails across the Idle Lake to Acrasia's bower and, at length resisting her many enticements, roughly pulls the whole beautiful paradise to the ground.*

Book III: The Legend of Britomartis, or Of Chastitie

The structuring quest of the third book is not one assigned by Gloriana. Instead, we follow the adventures of the female knight Britomart, who has taken up arms in a bid to find her destined husband, Artegall. In the opening canto of the book, Britomart meets Redcrosse, Guyon, Arthur, and Arthur's squire Timias, but the group is immediately dispersed when they observe a beautiful maiden rush by, chased by a lecherous forester. Arthur and Guyon pursue Florimell, while Timias chases the forester; Britomart and Redcrosse, by contrast, make their way to the Castle Joyeous. There she defeats many knights and fights off the amorous Malecasta ('false chastity') when, thinking Britomart a man, she slips by night into her bed. To Redcrosse Britomart then recounts her history (III.ii–iii): how she first saw Artegall in a magic mirror and, unable to shake off her love for his image, coaxed a prophecy from the sorcerer Merlin, and set off with her maid, Glauce, to seek Artegall through the world. When Redcrosse leaves her, Britomart encounters and summarily unseats Marinell (III.iv), the knight of the Rich strond (or shore) and an emblem of isolationist chastity. Marinell's wounds are grievous, and his sea-nymph mother goes to the gods for help. As we reach the middle of the book, the separate narrative strands fray and multiply. Florimell takes refuge with a witch, is freed by Satyrane, but ends up being chased by a flesh-eating hyena and is ultimately seized by Proteus, who locks her in his watery dungeon (III.vii). Meanwhile Timias has been seriously wounded by the forester and his brothers (III.v), but is nursed back to health by the virgin huntress Belphoebe, whose birth in the Garden of Adonis is recounted at length in canto vi. Sir Satyrane, losing Florimell, rescues the Squire of Dames from the incestuous giantess Argante, and hears of his love for the lady Columbell (III.vii). Following Florimell's escape, the witch creates a false

Florimell to entertain her clod son (III.viii), but Braggadocchio passing by soon steals her away, and in turn loses her to Sir Ferraugh. In the final four cantos, Britomart has two adventures that probe chastity's ethical relation to destructive jealousy. First she visits the house of Malbecco ('jealousy'), whose wife Hellenore absconds with all his gold in the company of the lustful knight Paridell (III.ix–x). Paridell eventually casts her off among some rutting satyrs, but Malbecco – who attempts to enlist the help of Braggadocchio and his squire Trompart – fails to win her back. *Britomart does not find Artegall, but instead helps the despairing knight Scudamour to recover his lady, Amoret, from imprisonment in the house of the enchanter Busirane (III.xi–xii). Taking up Scudamour's quest, she penetrates Busirane's castle, views his Ovidian tapestries and witnesses the masque of Cupid, before finally compelling Busirane to undo his enchantments and release Amoret. In the 1590 conclusion to the book, Britomart returns Amoret to Scudamour; in the revised text of 1596, Scudamour has already departed by the time Britomart and Amoret finally escape from Busirane's castle.*

Book IV: The Legend of Cambel and Telamond, or Of Friendship

While Book IV continues many of the narrative strands and allegorical preoccupations begun in Book III, its first publication in 1596 also sets it distinctively apart from the first three books of the poem. Britomart's adventures continue, and it is in this book that we learn of Amoret's early history with Scudamour, and see Marinell at last united with Florimell; but this book also marks a shift in Spenser's moral vision toward more social preoccupations – away from the 'privacy' of holiness, temperance and chastity, and toward the more political ideals of friendship, justice and courtesy. The book opens, accordingly, with a revision of Britomart's visit to Malecasta's castle, the first episode of the preceding book (IV.i, reprising III.i); here, at the castle of couples, Britomart permits a social but not intimate alliance when she consents to act as the lady of a stranger knight, thus preventing his expulsion. In the ensuing two cantos (IV.i–ii), we see a similarly social emphasis on knights challenging for, taking and losing ladies, but in a more burlesque style. Blandamour and Paridell, riding with Duessa and the goddess of discord, Ate, challenge Scudamour and Ferraugh, winning the False Florimell. From the Squire of Dames they learn that Satyrane has proclaimed a tournament, at which the fairest lady will win Florimell's girdle, and the stoutest knight the lady. As the company travels to the tournament, they meet another two knights and their ladies: Cambel, Triamond, Canacee and Cambina. In a long digression that occupies most of canto ii and all of canto iii, Spenser completes Chaucer's unfinished Squire's Tale, relating how Triamond and his brothers challenged Cambel in a tournament for the hand of his sister Canacee, a mortal battle only concluded when Cambina (Triamond's sister) intervened, bearing the narcotic drink Nepenthe, and compelled the four of them to intermarry in a loving tetrad (IV.iii). At the tournament (IV.iv), the Knights of Friendship triumph on the second day (under Cambel), but the Knights of Maidenhead take the prize on the first day (under Satyrane) and on the third day (under Britomart), and Britomart is eventually adjudged the victor. The False Florimell wins the girdle (IV.v) but it will not fit her; it fits Amoret but she will not have it. Meanwhile Artegall has developed a jealous enmity for the knight who defeated him at the tournament – the beavered Britomart – and joins forces with Scudamour to defeat her (IV.vi). In one freak stroke of their inevitable battle, he shears off her helmet, and the two instantly recognise, and love, one another. Cantos vii and viii reprise the Timias and Belphoebe narrative from the preceding book. Here Timias succours Amoret when she is attacked by Lust (IV.vii); Belphoebe misconstrues his solicitude as betrayal and spurns him; Timias grows wild with grief in the woods, but a chance encounter with Belphoebe later causes her to relent and the two are reunited (IV.viii). It is left to Prince Arthur, though, to resolve the fates of Amoret and her fellow captive Aemylia. After passing a night with them in the house of Sclaunder (IV.viii), he delivers the squire Placidas from the tyrant Corflambo, reforms Corflambo's house, and creates another loving tetrad by marrying Placidas to Corflambo's daughter, Poeana, and Aemylia to her own lover, the squire Amyas – Corflambo's prisoner (IV.ix). When Arthur and Amoret then chance on Scudamour and Britomart, the meeting occasions Scudamour's relation of his original 'ravishment' of Amoret from the Temple of Venus – the subject of canto x and, in its formal, emblematic detail, surely one of the allegorical centres of the book. Although we never learn that Scudamour and Amoret have been reunited – instead she simply disappears from view – in the final two cantos of the book we do witness the union of Marinell and Florimell. Attending on his mother at the wedding of the Thames and Medway, held in Proteus hall, Marinell passes canto xi by watching a spousal procession of the sea-gods, accompanied by all the British and Irish rivers. Excluded from the wedding feast because of his mortal nature, he kills time wandering by Proteus dungeon, where he hears the complaints of Florimell (IV.xii). He loves her instantly, and his mother once more intervenes to petition Neptune for her release.

Book V: The Legend of Artegall, or Of Justice

The long proem to Book V emphasises the decay of justice – as evidenced by astronomical variation and irregularity – since ancient times. The depar-

ture from the world of Astræa, goddess of justice, occupies the opening of the first canto; in her place she has left Artegall, who thus begins his quest somewhat hamstrung, a deputy delivering the justice of a god, perhaps with merely human results. He is accompanied throughout his journeys by Astræa's page, the iron automaton Talus, whose executive function in Artegall's judgments suggests a distinction between the philosophical rigour of what is right and fair (Artegall) and what passes for justice in practice (Talus). Artegall's eventual aim is the liberation of the lady Irena (from the Greek for 'peace', with a nod at Éire, the Irish name for Ireland) from the tyrant Grantorto ('great wrong'). Along the way he must dispatch a docket of other cases, all of which seem to challenge fundamental assumptions about the nature or right exercise of justice: he adjudicates between Sir Sanglier and a squire, who both challenge property in a lady (V.i); he defeats the toll-collecting magnate, Pollente ('powerful') and his daughter Munera ('bribe, gift'), before debating the nature of justice with a demagogic giant, and eventually ordering his execution (V.ii). After attending Marinell's and Florimell's wedding (V.iii) – at which Guyon recovers his horse and Florimell her girdle, and Braggadocchio is punished for his impostures – Artegall settles a contested inheritance between two brothers, Amidas and Bracidas (V.iv). By canto v, though, the limits of Artegall's understanding of justice are becoming exposed, as he accedes rashly to a set of conditions proposed in a combat with the Queen of the Amazons, Radegund (V.v). When he is defeated, Radegund sets him to work carding wool, and Talus must bring Britomart to his rescue (V.vi). Along the way Britomart evades an assassination attempt from Dolon, the father of one of Artegall's early victims (V.vi), and must pass the night in the church of Isis (V.vii), one of the book's two allegorical centres. Here Britomart has a dream which, interpreted, reveals the true nature of equitable justice, and allows her to overcome Radegund in single combat (V.vii). Thereafter Artegall, enlarged, meets Prince Arthur, and the two of them save a maiden, Samient, from an assault by Adicia ('injustice') and her husband, the Souldan (V.viii). After a visit to the other of the book's two allegorical centres, the court of Mercilla ('mercy') – at which they witness the trial and execution of Duessa (V.ix) – Arthur and Artegall complete parallel quests; in a transparently historical allegory, Arthur liberates the lady Belge and her sons from Geryoneo and his monster (V.x–xi), while Artegall finally reaches the salvage island and similarly liberates Irena from Grantorto (V.xi–xii). But before he can institute lasting reformations to Irena's commonwealth, Artegall is recalled to Gloriana's court, the victim of the two hags Envy and Detraction, who attack and molest him with the Blatant Beast.

Book VI: The Legend of Sir Calidore, or Of Courtesy

The structure of Book VI follows that of most of the earlier books, in its broader contours as well as its local details. The first two cantos of the book show the courteous knight, Calidore, revisiting the first two episodes of Artegall's quest in Book V, in all but name. First he reforms an abusive toll-bridge, defeating Crudor and enticing him to marry his lover, Briana (VI.i, reprising V.ii). In the second canto, Calidore pronounces judgment on the woodman Tristram, who has killed a knight he saw abusing a lady; discovering Tristram's hidden gentility and the rightness of his action, Calidore absolves him of the crime and dubs him knight (VI.ii, reprising V.i). These two episodes suggest how courtesy might improve upon justice; Calidore deals justly, but also acts well. In the following two episodes, though, Calidore begins to show the cracks in his grasp of courtesy. First he resorts to deceit in order to save the wounded Aladine and protect the reputation of his lover Priscilla (VI.iii), and then he barges awkwardly into a love tryst between Calepine and Serena – occasioning Serena's capture by the Blatant Beast (VI.iii). Though Calidore saves her, she has been seriously wounded, and as Calidore charges off after his epic quarry, the narrative instead follows the two blighted lovers. Calepine is rudely refused at Turpine's castle in canto iv, and is only saved from Turpine's discourteous and unequal assaults by a savage man. When Calepine disappears into the woods, following a bear carrying a baby between its jaws, the savage man becomes Serena's faithful attendant. Together they meet Prince Arthur and Timias (VI.v), who has also been wounded by the Blatant Beast; while Timias and Serena receive medical and ethical attention from a skilled hermit, Arthur and the savage man defeat and baffle Sir Turpine (VI.vi–vii). Immediately thereafter (VI.vii–viii) Arthur and the savage man encounter the lady Mirabella, attended by Scorn and Disdain, who have already captured Timias. Refusing Arthur's offered help, Mirabella explains how Cupid imposed jailors upon her in punishment for her crimes against love. Though Arthur frees Timias from Scorn and Disdain, Serena has already fled into the mountains, where she is captured by cannibals. Her last moment has nearly arrived when Calepine appears and delivers her (VI.viii). The final four cantos of the book revert to Calidore's quest to subdue the Blatant Beast, whom he follows in canto ix to a pastoral retreat. *There, slacking his quest, he falls in love with the shepherdess Pastorella, and during an afternoon of rambling discovers Venus' favoured haunt on Mount Acidale, where he views the Graces dancing (VI.x). In this allegorical set-piece, Calidore is instructed in the philosophy of courtesy by no less a figure than Colin Clout – Spenser's own poetic persona – but the interlude ends unhappily when Pastorella is captured by brigants, her community razed, her fellows executed, and she herself nearly sold into slavery. With the help of the shepherd Coridon, Calidore delivers her from the brigants (VI.xi).* In the final canto he discovers that she is truly the lost daughter of his friends, the knight Bellamoure and his lady Claribell (VI.xii). In this post-pastoral world, Calidore rapidly runs the Blatant Beast to ground and muzzles it, but the book concludes with the narrator's admission that the beast has again got free.

Two Cantos of Mutabilitie

The printer of the 1609 edition of *The Faerie Queene*, Matthew Lownes, supposed that the *Cantos* had originally been intended as part of the 'next' book of the poem, possibly concerning the virtue of constancy. The provenance of the manuscript, like the manuscript itself, is long lost, and many readers have disputed Lownes's claim, preferring to see the *Cantos* as a discrete and complete para-poem, composed in the style of *The Faerie Queene*, which functions as a kind of coda or epilogue to the rest. In the first canto (VII.vi), the titaness Mutabilitie challenges Cynthia (Diana) for the kingdom of the moon, and then threatens Olympus itself. Jove calls a council of the gods, but ultimately all agree to refer the matter to Dame Nature, who appoints a trial to be held on Arlo Hill, a low mountain near Spenser's estate at Kilcolman in the south of Ireland. The remainder of this canto relates, in an Ovidian digression, Diana's reasons for transforming this once-beautiful *locus amoenus* into a wild and barbarous wasteland; the woodgod Faunus, wishing to sea Diana naked, suborned the river nymph Molanna to assist him, in return for which he promised her the love of the River Fanchin. In the end Diana discovered Faunus and punished him, but he kept his word and the Fanchin and the Molanna were nonetheless combined. In the final canto (VII.vii), the scene of the great trial is revealed and Mutabilitie presents her case, a huge pageant illustrating the pervasiveness of change in sublunary as well as divine affairs. Notwithstanding Mutabilitie's manifest influence in all things, Dame Nature finds for Jove, and the poem concludes – in two stanzas labelled, since Lownes, as 'The VIII. Canto, vnperfite' – with an apparently sincere prayer for divine revelation.

Paratexts

At its original printing in 1590, *The Faerie Queene* was accompanied by a substantial collection of 'paratexts', or ancillary matter printed on both sides of the volume. In addition to the title page and a dedication to Queen Elizabeth, both printed at the front of the book, the poem was accompanied by (i) 'A Letter of the Authors ... to Sir Walter Raleigh', a long letter explaining the narrative origins of the poem and giving some (interesting but probably facetious) instructions in how to read the allegory; (ii) a set of commendatory verses written by Ralegh, Spenser's friend Gabriel Harvey, and others; and (iii) seventeen dedicatory sonnets addressed by Spenser to various potential patrons, ranging from Lord Burghley and Sir Francis Walsingham, to 'all the gratious and beautifull Ladies in the Court'. Some copies of the 1590 text exist with only ten dedicatory sonnets, which may suggest that, for some reason, Spenser added seven during the printing. Most of these paratexts appeared at the back of the book, and were largely not reprinted in the 1596 edition of the poem.

Notes

1. See J. A. Venn, *Alumni Cantabrigienses* (Cambridge: Cambridge University Press, 1922–54), Pt 1, vol. 4, p. 132.
2. Spenser claims in a 1579 letter to Harvey that he is shortly to leave on business for the Earl of Leicester, 'to employ my time, my body, my minde, to his Honours seruice'; see the *Three Proper, Wittie, and Familiar Letters* and *Two Other, very commendable Letters* (London: Henry Bynneman, 1580), pp. 60–1.
3. For an account of Spenser's experience in Ireland in these years, see Christopher Burlinson and Andrew Zurcher, eds, *Edmund Spenser: Selected Letters and Other Papers* (Oxford: Oxford University Press, 2009), pp. xv–xxx.
4. See Frank B. Evans, 'The Printing of *The Faerie Queene* in 1596', *Studies in Bibliography*, 18 (1965), 49–67; and Andrew Zurcher, 'Printing *The Faerie Queene* in 1590', *Studies in Bibliography*, 57 (2004–5), 115–50.
5. See Camden, *Annales Rerum Anglicanarum et Hibernicarum regnante Elizabetha* (London: William Stansby for Simon Waterson, 1615), p. 171; and Jonson, *Conversations with William Drummond of Hawthornden*, ed. G. B. Harrison (London: John Lane, 1923), pp. 8–9.
6. See Richard Mulcaster, *Positions, wherin those primitiue circumstances be examined, which are necessarie for the training vp of children* (London: Thomas Vautrollier, 1581), and *The first part of the elementarie which entreateth chefelie of the right writing of our English tung* (London: Thomas Vautrollier, 1582). In the teaching of older boys, Mulcaster probably used methods similar to those described by Roger Ascham, tutor to Elizabeth I, in his treatise *The Scholemaster* (London: John Daye, 1571): grammatical and rhetorical analysis of Latin passages, translation into English, and 'double translation' of English passages, once translated, back into Latin.
7. Mulcaster, *Positions*, p. 3.
8. H. B. Wilson, *The History of Merchant-Taylors' School From Its Foundation to the Present Time*, 2 vols (London, 1812), I, pp. 38–40.
9. Wilson, *History of Merchant-Taylors' School*, I, p. 32.
10. Along with reading and writing, Mulcaster includes dancing, drawing and playing as three of the five branches of 'elementarie' study for young pupils; see *The first part of the elementarie*, p. 5. Boys were encouraged to write verses in Latin, and probably English, to be presented to the school's examiners each year.
11. The best account of the Cartwright controversy is Patrick Collinson's, in *The Elizabethan Puritan Movement* (Oxford: Clarendon Press, 1967); see also his

biography, *Archbishop Grindal 1519–1583: The Struggle for a Reformed Church* (London: Jonathan Cape), pp. 167–83.
12. See the *Two Other, very commendable Letters* (London: Henry Bynneman, 1580), p. 54, where Spenser reports to Harvey that 'for the two worthy Gentlemen, Master *Sidney*, and Master *Dyer*, they haue me, I thanke them, in some vse of familiarity.'
13. Spenser mentions the criticism of a 'rugged forehead', and a 'mighty Peres displeasure' in *The Faerie Queene*, IV.Pr.1 and VI.xii.41. These references have traditionally been thought to be to Burghley, who may also have taken offence at a lampoon in Spenser's short satirical poem, *Mother Hubberds Tale* (1591).
14. On Spenser's position as secretary within the Dublin and Munster secretariats, see Burlinson and Zurcher, *Edmund Spenser: Selected Letters and Other Papers*, pp. xv–lxiv.

Chapter 2
Selections from the Poem

THE FAERIE
QVEENE.

Disposed into twelue books,

Fashioning

XII. Morall vertues.

1. Book I, proem and cantos i–ii

The first selection comes from the opening of the poem. In these two cantos, we see the knight of the Red Crosse (or, Redcrosse, the knight of holiness) and his companion, Una (oneness, 'Truth'), setting off on a quest to defeat the dragon and liberate Una's parents in Eden. That great battle will take place in canto xi (see summary in Chapter 1). Here, Redcrosse faces another dragon: the monster Errour, half-woman, half-snake, whose endless serpentine folds threaten to overwhelm him. The fight with Errour in part represents a meditation on the nature of this epic romance poem itself, for 'error' (from Latin *errare*, 'to wander, digress'), according to Renaissance genre theory, is the defining principle of romance narrative. In Redcrosse's fight with the monster, we also see Spenser's first use of a highly visual, emblematic style of writing, the descriptive details of which suggest the wide range of dangers – moral, political, metaphysical – that Errour may represent. For example, Spenser compares Errour's barking brood to the fertile flood of the Nile, indicating that Errour, in turn, should be read as a fundamental principle of generation, not only a threat to moral truth but also a very force of nature. Following his apparent victory over Errour, Redcrosse is immediately deceived by the enchanter Archimago (an arch-mage, or arch-imager), whose skill at creating false visions separates Redcrosse from Una and leaves him vulnerable to the deception of a new lady, Duessa (twoness, duplicity). Redcrosse's success against Errour, followed by his immediate susceptibility to Archimago and Duessa, shows one of the key advantages of a long poem: Spenser can repeat the same basic moral danger again and again, varying its mode of presentation (now pictorial, now narrative) and its details (now martial, now sexual; now explicit, now subtle) in order to sharpen the reader's understanding. Like Errour herself, the long poem works by folds and layers.

THE FIRST
BOOKE OF THE
FAERIE QVEENE.

Contayning

THE LEGENDE OF THE
KNIGHT OF THE RED CROSSE,

Or

OF HOLINESSE.

1

Lo I the man, whose Muse whilome did maske,
   As time her taught in lowly Shepheards weeds,
   Am now enforst a far vnfitter taske,
   For trumpets sterne to chaunge mine Oaten reeds,
   And sing of Knights and Ladies gentle deeds;
   Whose prayses hauing slept in silence long,
   Me, all too meane, the sacred Muse areeds
   To blazon broad emongst her learned throng:
Fierce warres and faithfull loues shall moralize my song.

whilome before *maske* go disguised
As time her taught as befitted the time
weeds dress, garments

meane lowly, unworthy
areeds instructs, advises
blazon broad publish (the praises)
moralize give moral meaning to

2

Helpe then, ô holy Virgin chiefe of nine,
   Thy weaker Nouice to performe thy will,
   Lay forth out of thine euerlasting scryne
   The antique rolles, which there lye hidden still,
   Of Faerie knights and fairest *Tanaquill*,
   Whom that most noble Briton Prince so long

Nouice apprentice, initiate
scryne chest (as of records or relics)

    1.4 trumpets sterne . . . Oaten reeds] *trumpets* and *reeds* are metonymies for epic and pastoral poetry, respectively.
    1.1–5 Lo I . . . gentle deeds] Spenser here echoes the spurious opening lines of the medieval text of Virgil's *Aeneid*: *Ille ego, qui quondam gracili modulatus avena carmen . . . at nunc horrentia Martis* ('I am that man, who once composed a song upon a slender pipe . . . but now (I sing) of the fearful (arms) of Mars'). The fifth and ninth lines, by contrast, echo the opening stanza of Ludovico Ariosto's *Orlando Furioso*: *Le donne, i cavallier, l'arme, gli amori . . . io canto* ('I sing of ladies, knights, of arms and loves').
    2.1 holy Virgin chiefe of nine] Either Clio, muse of history, or Calliope, muse of epic poetry; the ambiguity is probably deliberate.
    2.5 Tanaquill] The name of the wife of Tarquinius Priscus, the first of the Tarquins, kings of ancient Rome. See Livy, *Ab urbe condita*, 1.34–5. Here the name appears to be an epithet for Gloriana, Queen of Faeries; see I.i.3.2n., below, and Arthur's description of his love for Gloriana at *FQ* I.ix.9–15.
    2.6 that most noble Briton Prince] Arthur, son of Uther, fabled king of ancient Britain. The 'matter of Britain' – or of Arthur, his round table and the quest for the grail – was one of the standard themes of medieval chivalric romance.

Sought through the world, and suffered so much ill,
That I must rue his vndeserued wrong:
O helpe thou my weake wit, and sharpen my dull tong.

3

And thou most dreaded impe of highest *Ioue*,	*impe* scion, offspring
Faire *Venus* sonne, that with thy cruell dart	
At that good knight so cunningly didst roue,	*roue* shoot about
That glorious fire it kindled in his hart,	
Lay now thy deadly Heben bow apart,	*Heben* ebony
And with thy mother milde come to mine ayde:	
Come both, and with you bring triumphant *Mart*,	
In loues and gentle iollities arrayd,	
After his murdrous spoiles and bloudy rage allayd.	*spoiles* plunders, destructions

4

And with them eke, ô Goddesse heauenly bright,	*eke* also
Mirrour of grace and Maiestie diuine,	
Great Lady of the greatest Isle, whose light	
Like *Phœbus* lampe throughout the world doth shine,	
Shed thy faire beames into my feeble eyne,	*eyne* eyes (archaic plural form)
And raise my thoughts too humble and too vile,	
To thinke of that true glorious type of thine,	*type* figure
The argument of mine afflicted stile:	*argument* subject, theme
The which to heare, vouchsafe, ô dearest dred a-while.	*stile* pen (L *stylus*); register, manner of writing *vouchsafe* condescend, deign to grant

Canto I.

The Patron of true Holinesse,
Foule Errour doth defeate:
Hypocrisie him to entrape,
Doth to his home entreate.

    2.7 suffered so much ill] A translation of the opening lines of the *Odyssey*, where Homer notes that Odysseus μάλα πολλά πλάγχθη ('suffered many evils') on his return from Troy.
    3.1–2 dreaded impe . . . sonne] Cupid.
    3.3 that good knight] Arthur.
    3.7 triumphant Mart] Mars, god of war.
    4.4 Phoebus lampe] The sun.
    4.1–4 ô Goddesse . . . doth shine] Whether this address is to Queen Elizabeth as a reader, or to Gloriana, presiding Queen of Faery land, is left unclear – again, probably deliberately.
    ***Arg.1* Patron**] A significant but difficult word for the poem as a whole. 'Patron' could mean 'protector' or 'defender', but also 'sponsor' or even, in this period, 'patron saint'; compare also the related word 'pattern', in the sense of 'model, exemplar'.

1

A Gentle Knight was pricking on the plaine,   *pricking* spurring (his horse)
    Ycladd in mightie armes and siluer shielde,   *ycladd* dressed
    Wherein old dints of deepe wounds did remaine,   *dints* dents (a 'dint' is properly a 'blow')
    The cruell markes of many' a bloudy fielde;
    Yet armes till that time did he neuer wield:
    His angry steede did chide his foming bitt,   *chide* resist, chew at
    As much disdayning to the curbe to yield:
    Full iolly knight he seemd, and faire did sitt,   *iolly* handsome, gallant, trim (Fr *joli*)
As one for knightly giusts and fierce encounters fitt.   *giusts* jousts

2

But on his brest a bloudie Crosse he bore,
    The deare remembrance of his dying Lord,   *remembrance* souvenir, token; also
    For whose sweete sake that glorious badge he wore,   'heraldic device' (c15)
    And dead as liuing euer him ador'd:
    Vpon his shield the like was also scor'd,   *scor'd* incised, painted
    For soueraine hope, which in his helpe he had:
    Right faithfull true he was in deede and word,
    But of his cheere did seeme too solemne sad,   *sad* serious
Yet nothing did he dread, but euer was ydrad.   *ydrad* dreaded

3

Vpon a great aduenture he was bond,   *bond* bound, sworn
    That greatest *Gloriana* to him gaue,
    That greatest Glorious Queene of *Faerie* lond,
    To winne him worship, and her grace to haue,   *worship* honour, reputation
    Which of all earthly things he most did craue;
    And euer as he rode, his hart did earne   *earne* long, yearn
    To proue his puissance in battell braue   *puissance* strength or force (trisyllabic)

    1.2 mightie ... shielde,] In his letter to Ralegh, Spenser calls Redcrosse's armour 'the armour of a Christian man specified by Saint Paul v. Ephes[ians]'; see *Ephesians* 6.11–17.
    1.1–7 A Gentle ... to yield:] John Upton – an eighteenth-century scholar who produced the first edited text of *The Faerie Queene* – was the first to point out that Redcrosse appears to be 'pricking' (or spurring) his horse at the same time that he is 'curbing' him with the bit; naturally, the beast 'foams' at his inexperienced rider.
    1.8 seemd] Redcrosse's merely apparent suitability for his quest is focused by this important verb, which recurs – generally in connection with the allegory's villains – throughout the book.
    2.1 bloudie Crosse] The traditional badge of St George, patron saint of England, was a red cross on a white field.
    3.1 great aduenture] We learn in the letter to Ralegh that Una, daughter to 'an ancient King and Queene' who 'had bene by an huge dragon many years shut vp in a brasen Castle', petitioned the Queen of Faeries for a champion to liberate them. Redcrosse, a 'clownish person' who was in the court, asked to be granted the quest and was allowed it, on condition that he wear a suit of armour and carry weapons brought for that purpose by Una.
    3.2 *Gloriana*] The name of the Queen of Faery derives from L *gloria*, 'fame, glory'.

Vpon his foe, and his new force to learne;
Vpon his foe, a Dragon horrible and stearne.

4

A louely Ladie rode him faire beside,
   Vpon a lowly Asse more white then snow,
   Yet she much whiter, but the same did hide
   Vnder a vele, that wimpled was full low,   *that wimpled was* so that it (her
   And ouer all a blacke stole she did throw,   whiteness) was veiled; *or* that was
   As one that inly mournd: so was she sad,   folded, rippled *inly* within, privately
   And heauie sat vpon her palfrey slow;
   Seemed in heart some hidden care she had,
And by her in a line a milke white lambe she lad.

5

So pure an innocent, as that same lambe,
   She was in life and euery vertuous lore,
   And by descent from Royall lynage came
   Of ancient Kings and Queenes, that had of yore
   Their scepters stretcht from East to Westerne shore,
   And all the world in their subiection held;
   Till that infernall feend with foule vprore
   Forwasted all their land, and them expeld: *forwasted* utterly spoiled
Whom to auenge, she had this Knight from far compeld.   *compeld* obliged, required

6

Behind her farre away a Dwarfe did lag,
   That lasie seemd in being euer last,
   Or wearied with bearing of her bag
   Of needments at his backe. Thus as they past,   *needments* necessary items
   The day with cloudes was suddeine ouercast,
   And angry *Ioue* an hideous storme of raine
   Did poure into his Lemans lap so fast,   *Lemans* lover's
   That euery wight to shrowd it did constrain,   *wight* person *shrowd* take cover
And this faire couple eke to shroud themselues were fain.   *were fain* were glad, were forced

---

4.1–2 A louely ... lowly Asse] Una: first named at 45.9. Her lowliness, spotlessness, modesty and unknowability make her an icon of religious truth in the poem, while the veil and lamb are conventional elements of the legend of St George. Upton, again, was the first to notice the implausibility of the poem's opening image: a mounted knight in full career, a lady riding on an ass and an encumbered pedestrian dwarf cannot travel together for more than an instant.
    5.3–6 And by descent ... subiection held;] English Protestant reformers claimed they were restoring Christian belief and practice to its ancient, 'primitive' form – an early Christianity predating (alleged) papal corruption.

7

Enforst to seeke some couert nigh at hand,   *couert* shelter *nigh at hand* nearby
  A shadie groue not far away they spide,   *spide* saw
  That promist ayde the tempest to withstand:
  Whose loftie trees yclad with sommers pride,
  Did spred so broad, that heauens light did hide,
  Not perceable with power of any starre: *perceable* able to be pierced, penetrable
  And all within were pathes and alleies wide,
  With footing worne, and leading inward farre: *footing* walking, treading
Faire harbour that them seemes; so in they entred arre.

8

And foorth they passe, with pleasure forward led,
  Ioying to heare the birdes sweete harmony,
  Which therein shrouded from the tempest dred,
  Seemd in their song to scorne the cruell sky.
  Much can they prayse the trees so straight and hy,   *can* did, may
  The sayling Pine, the Cedar proud and tall,
  The vine-prop Elme, the Poplar neuer dry,
  The builder Oake, sole king of forrests all,
The Alpine good for staues, the Cypresse funerall.

9

The Laurell, meed of mightie Conquerours   *meed* reward
  And Poets sage, the Firre that weepeth still,
  The Willow worne of forlorne Paramours,
  The Eugh obedient to the benders will,   *Eugh* yew
  The Birch for shaftes, the Sallow for the mill,   *Sallow* a low-growing, bushy willow
  The Mirrhe sweete bleeding in the bitter wound,
  The warlike Beech, the Ash for nothing ill,
  The fruitfull Oliue, and the Platane round,   *Platane* plane tree (L *platanus*)
The caruer Holme, the Maple seeldom inward sound.   *Holme* holm oak

10

Led with delight, they thus beguile the way,
  Vntill the blustring storme is ouerblowne;
  When weening to returne, whence they did stray,   *weening* thinking, planning

    7.2 A shadie groue] See the *selva oscura* at the beginning of Dante's *Inferno* (1.1–3), and the forest within which Aeneas and Dido take amorous shelter in Virgil, *Aeneid*, 4.114–72.
    8.5–9.9 Much can . . . inward sound.] Spenser's catalogue of trees is based on that of Chaucer, *The Parlement of Foulys*, ll.176–82. Each tree has its associations: the pine good for ships' masts, the cedar a Biblical emblem of pride, the elm often encumbered with ivy, the poplar commonly found on river banks, and so on. Wreaths of laurel were worn by Roman conquerors (and poets), while the flexible wood of the yew could be bent (for bows, among other things). Virgil records in the *Aeneid* (2.112) that the (hollow) Trojan horse was made of *acer* – maple.

They cannot finde that path, which first was showne,
But wander too and fro in wayes vnknowne,
Furthest from end then, when they neerest weene,
That makes them doubt, their wits be not their owne:
So many pathes, so many turnings seene,
That which of them to take, in diuerse doubt they been.

diuerse sundry, differing

11
At last resoluing forward still to fare,
  Till that some end they finde or in or out,
  That path they take, that beaten seemd most bare,
  And like to lead the labyrinth about;
  Which when by tract they hunted had throughout,
  At length it brought them to a hollow caue,
  Amid the thickest woods. The Champion stout
  Eftsoones dismounted from his courser braue,
And to the Dwarfe awhile his needlesse spere he gaue.

or . . . or either . . . or

like . . . about likely to lead them out of the labyrinth *by tract* path by path

eftsoones again, afterwards *courser* battle horse

12
Be well aware, quoth then that Ladie milde,
  Least suddaine mischiefe ye too rash prouoke:
  The danger hid, the place vnknowne and wilde,
  Breedes dreadfull doubts: Oft fire is without smoke,
  And perill without show: therefore your stroke
  Sir knight with-hold, till further triall made.
  Ah Ladie (said he) shame were to reuoke
  The forward footing for an hidden shade:
Vertue giues her selfe light, through darkenesse for to wade.

mischiefe harm, misfortune

reuoke retract
forward footing bold courage, advantage
wade step, go

13
Yea but (quoth she) the perill of this place
  I better wot then you, though now too late,
  To wish you backe returne with foule disgrace,
  Yet wisedome warnes, whilest foot is in the gate,
  To stay the steppe, ere forced to retrate.
  This is the wandring wood, this *Errours den*,
  A monster vile, whom God and man does hate:
  Therefore I read beware. Fly fly (quoth then
The fearefull Dwarfe:) this is no place for liuing men.

wot know

whilest . . . gate when walking in the road or way ('gate'); thus, *fig.* on the point of undertaking some action
stay hold back *retrate* retreat, turn back

14
But full of fire and greedy hardiment,
  The youthfull knight could not for ought be staide,
  But forth vnto the darksome hole he went,

greedy hardiment ambitious courage
for ought for aught (anything)

And looked in: his glistring armor made   *glistring* sparkling, glittering
    A litle glooming light, much like a shade,   *glooming* gloaming or dusky
    By which he saw the vgly monster plaine,
    Halfe like a serpent horribly displaide,   *displaide* revealed, unfolded (L
    But th'other halfe did womans shape retaine,   *displicare*, 'to unfold')
Most lothsom, filthie, foule, and full of vile disdaine.

15

And as she lay vpon the durtie ground,
    Her huge long taile her den all ouerspred,
    Yet was in knots and many boughtes vpwound,   *boughtes* coils, folds
    Pointed with mortall sting. Of her there bred
    A thousand yong ones, which she dayly fed,
    Sucking vpon her poisonous dugs, eachone   *dugs* breasts, teats
    Of sundry shapes, yet all ill fauored:
    Soone as that vncouth light vpon them shone,   *vncouth* unknown, unfamiliar
Into her mouth they crept, and suddain all were gone.

16

Their dam vpstart, out of her den effraide,   *effraide* frightened, startled
    And rushed forth, hurling her hideous taile
    About her cursed head, whose folds displaid
    Were stretcht now forth at length without entraile.   *entraile* coil, winding
    She lookt about, and seeing one in mayle
    Armed to point, sought backe to turne againe;
    For light she hated as the deadly bale,   *deadly bale* fatal evil, funeral pyre
    Ay wont in desert darknesse to remaine,   *ay* moreover, and (quasi-conj.)
Where plaine none might her see, nor she see any plaine.   *wont* tended, customed

17

Which when the valiant Elfe perceiu'd, he lept
    As Lyon fierce vpon the flying pray,
    And with his trenchand blade her boldly kept   *trenchand* cutting (Fr *trancher* 'to cut')
    From turning backe, and forced her to stay:
    Therewith enrag'd she loudly gan to bray,   *bray* cry out (in pain)

14.6–9 By which ... disdaine.] Errour's hybrid form echoes that of the monster Echidna – the original half-snake, half-woman whose womb bred the entire complement of monsters with which mythic Greek heroes contested. According to Hesiod (see *Theogony*, ll. 295–332), Echidna also lived in a cave and ate raw gobbets. Other poets had adapted Echidna's hybrid monstrosity before, most importantly Dante (*Inferno*, 17.10–12) and Langland (*Piers Plowman*, B-text, passus XVIII, 1.335). Spenser's Errour is, in turn, the basis of Milton's Sin; see *Paradise Lost*, 2.648–66.
    17.1 Elfe] Strictly speaking, Redcrosse is not a fairy knight, but (as he discovers later) a changeling, born of the royal Saxon line (cf. I.x.60, 64–5); he is nonetheless here, as elsewhere, 'accompted Elfins sonne' (I.x.60.2).

And turning fierce, her speckled taile aduaunst,
Threatning her angry sting, him to dismay:
Who nought aghast, his mightie hand enhaunst: *enhaunst* raised
The stroke down from her head vnto her shoulder glaunst.

18

Much daunted with that dint, her sence was dazd,
  Yet kindling rage, her selfe she gathered round,
  And all attonce her beastly body raizd *attonce* at once
  With doubled forces high aboue the ground:
  Tho wrapping vp her wrethed sterne arownd, *tho* then *wrethed sterne* coiled tail
  Lept fierce vpon his shield, and her huge traine
  All suddenly about his body wound,
  That hand or foot to stirre he stroue in vaine:
God helpe the man so wrapt in *Errours* endlesse traine.

19

His Lady sad to see his sore constraint, *constraint* confinement, distress
  Cride out, Now now Sir knight, shew what ye bee,
  Add faith vnto your force, and be not faint:
  Strangle her, else she sure will strangle thee.
  That when he heard, in great perplexitie, *perplexitie* trouble, complexity (L
  His gall did grate for griefe and high disdaine, *perplexus*, 'completely woven, tangled')
  And knitting all his force got one hand free, *gall* (lit.) gall-bladder, (fig.) pride
  Wherewith he grypt her gorge with so great paine, *grate* fret, chafe *knitting* combining
That soone to loose her wicked bands did her constraine. *gorge* neck

20

Therewith she spewd out of her filthy maw *maw* mouth
  A floud of poyson horrible and blacke,
  Full of great lumpes of flesh and gobbets raw,
  Which stunck so vildly, that it forst him slacke *vildly* vilely *slacke* release
  His grasping hold, and from her turne him backe:
  Her vomit full of bookes and papers was,
  With loathly frogs and toades, which eyes did lacke,
  And creeping sought way in the weedy gras:
Her filthy parbreake all the place defiled has. *parbreake* vomit

20.7 loathly frogs and toades,] See Revelation 16.13, in which frogs pour out of the mouth of Antichrist: frogs which, as the Calvinist gloss to the 1560 'Geneva' Bible explains, are to be read as the Pope's lying ambassadors.

21

As when old father *Nilus* gins to swell
    With timely pride aboue the *Aegyptian* vale,   *timely pride* seasonal increase
    His fattie waues do fertile slime outwell,   *fattie* rich, fertile
    And ouerflow each plaine and lowly dale:
    But when his later spring gins to auale,   *gins to auale* begins to abate
    Huge heapes of mudd he leaues, wherein there breed
    Ten thousand kindes of creatures, partly male
    And partly female of his fruitfull seed;
Such vgly monstrous shapes elswhere may no man reed.   *reed* discover

22

The same so sore annoyed has the knight,
    That welnigh choked with the deadly stinke,
    His forces faile, ne can no longer fight.
    Whose corage when the feend perceiu'd to shrinke,
    She poured forth out of her hellish sinke   *sinke* pit, pool (i.e. mouth)
    Her fruitfull cursed spawne of serpents small,
    Deformed monsters, fowle, and blacke as inke,
    Which swarming all about his legs did crall,
And him encombred sore, but could not hurt at all.   *encombred* hampered, burdened

23

As gentle Shepheard in sweete euen-tide,
    When ruddy *Phœbus* gins to welke in west,   *welke* shrink, fade, decline
    High on an hill, his flocke to vewen wide,
    Markes which do byte their hasty supper best;   *byte* nip at, eat
    A cloud of combrous gnattes do him molest,   *combrous* annoying
    All striuing to infixe their feeble stings,   *infixe* implant
    That from their noyance he no where can rest,   *noyance* annoyance
    But with his clownish hands their tender wings   *clownish* rustic, (hence) rough
He brusheth oft, and oft doth mar their murmurings.

24

Thus ill bestedd, and fearefull more of shame,   *bestedd* beset
    Then of the certaine perill he stood in,
    Halfe furious vnto his foe he came,
    Resolv'd in minde all suddenly to win,

    21.1 Nilus] Spontaneous generation in fertile Nile mud, deposited on Egyptian fields during the carefully controlled annual flood, was a commonplace of classical myth and poetry. See, for example, Ovid, *Metamorphoses*, 1.416–37.
    Stanza 23 combrous gnattes] This apparently unusual epic simile was adapted from Spenser's sources; see, for example, Homer, *Iliad*, 2.469–71, and Ariosto, *Orlando Furioso*, 14.109.

> Or soone to lose, before he once would lin;   *once* once and for all *lin* leave off, give up
> And strooke at her with more then manly force,
> That from her body full of filthie sin
> He raft her hatefull head without remorse;   *raft* cut off
> A streame of cole black bloud forth gushed from her corse.   *corse* body

25

> Her scattred brood, soone as their Parent deare
> They saw so rudely falling to the ground,
> Groning full deadly, all with troublous feare,
> Gathred themselues about her body round,
> Weening their wonted entrance to haue found   *wonted* usual, customary
> At her wide mouth: but being there withstood
> They flocked all about her bleeding wound,
> And sucked vp their dying mothers blood,
> Making her death their life, and eke her hurt their good.   *eke* also

26

> That detestable sight him much amazde,
> To see th'vnkindly Impes of heauen accurst,   *impes* offspring, children
> Deuoure their dam; on whom while so he gazd,
> Hauing all satisfide their bloudy thurst,
> Their bellies swolne he saw with fulnesse burst,
> And bowels gushing forth: well worthy end
> Of such as drunke her life, the which them nurst;
> Now needeth him no lenger labour spend,
> His foes haue slaine themselues, with whom he should contend.

27

> His Ladie seeing all, that chaunst, from farre
> Approcht in hast to greet his victorie,
> And said, Faire knight, borne vnder happy starre,
> Who see your vanquisht foes before you lye:
> Well worthy be you of that Armorie,
> Wherein ye haue great glory wonne this day,
> And proou'd your strength on a strong enimie,

24.4–5 Resolv'd ... lin;] Initial defeat followed by decisive resolution becomes a regular pattern in the poem's battle scenes; cf., for example, Redcrosse's battle against the dragon (I.xi.8–55), Prince Arthur's fight with Pyrochles and Cymochles (II.viii.30–52), or the tournament between Priamond, Diamond, Triamond and Cambel for the hand of Canacee (IV.iii.3–36).
25.7–9 They flocked ... good.] A parody of the Christian eucharist, possibly mediated by the well-known sixteenth-century emblem of Christ as a pelican, wounding its own breast to feed its young with its blood.

Your first aduenture: many such I pray,
And henceforth euer wish, that like succeed it may.

28
Then mounted he vpon his Steede againe,
   And with the Lady backward sought to wend;   *wend* go, travel
   That path he kept, which beaten was most plaine,
   Ne euer would to any by-way bend,
   But still did follow one vnto the end,
   The which at last out of the wood them brought.
   So forward on his way (with God to frend)
   He passeth forth, and new aduenture sought;
Long way he trauelled, before he heard of ought.

29
At length they chaunst to meet vpon the way
   An aged Sire, in long blacke weedes yclad,
   His feete all bare, his beard all hoarie gray,
   And by his belt his booke he hanging had;
   Sober he seemde, and very sagely sad,
   And to the ground his eyes were lowly bent,
   Simple in shew, and voyde of malice bad,
   And all the way he prayed, as he went,
And often knockt his brest, as one that did repent.

30
He faire the knight saluted, louting low,   *louting* bowing
   Who faire him quited, as that courteous was: *quited*, requited, answered
   And after asked him, if he did know
   Of straunge aduentures, which abroad did pas.
   Ah my deare Sonne (quoth he) how should, alas,
   Silly old man, that liues in hidden cell,
   Bidding his beades all day for his trespas,   *bidding his beades* praying
   Tydings of warre and worldly trouble tell?   *trespas* fault, sin
With holy father sits not with such things to mell.   *sits not* it does not befit
    mell with deal or meddle with

31
But if of daunger which hereby doth dwell,
   And homebred euill ye desire to heare,
   Of a straunge man I can you tidings tell,

29.2 *ff*. An aged Sire,] The description of the enchanter Archimago, called 'Hypocrisie' in the canto's argument, draws on the conventional dress of the friar or palmer. Spenser's most immediate debt is probably to Langland's *Piers Plowman*, A-text, passus XV, ll. 87–131, where Langland describes the hypocritical priest bearing 'a peyre bedes in her hande and a boke vnder her arme' (A XV, l. 119).

That wasteth all this countrey farre and neare.   *wasteth* destroys, spoils
Of such (said he) I chiefly do inquere,
And shall you well reward to shew the place,
In which that wicked wight his dayes doth weare: *weare* pass, spend
For to all knighthood it is foule disgrace,
That such a cursed creature liues so long a space.

32

Far hence (quoth he) in wastfull wildernesse   *wastfull* deserted, uncultivated
   His dwelling is, by which no liuing wight
   May euer passe, but thorough great distresse.
   Now (sayd the Lady) draweth toward night,
   And well I wote, that of your later fight   *wote* know *later* recent
   Ye all forwearied be: for what so strong,   *forwearied* exhausted
   But wanting rest will also want of might?
   The Sunne that measures heauen all day long,
At night doth baite his steedes the *Ocean* waues emong.   *baite* feed, repast

33

Then with the Sunne take Sir, your timely rest,
   And with new day new worke at once begin:
   Vntroubled night they say giues counsell best.
   Right well Sir knight ye haue aduised bin,
   (Quoth then that aged man;) the way to win   *win* succeed, prevail
   Is wisely to aduise: now day is spent;
   Therefore with me ye may take vp your In   *in* lodging
   For this same night. The knight was well content:
So with that godly father to his home they went.

34

A little lowly Hermitage it was,
   Downe in a dale, hard by a forests side,
   Far from resort of people, that did pas
   In trauell to and froe: a little wyde   *wyde* apart
   There was an holy Chappell edifyde,   *edifyde* built
   Wherein the Hermite dewly wont to say
   His holy things each morne and euentyde:
   Thereby a Christall streame did gently play,
Which from a sacred fountaine welled forth alway.

31.3–4 Of a straunge … and neare.] Archimago never fulfils his promise to inform Redcrosse of this 'straunge man' or the location of his dwelling, unless of course by 'straunge' he means 'hypocritical', and refers, with mischievous dissimulation, to himself. (Cf. *OED*, 'strange', *a*., 13.) Cf. also I.iii.29.

35

Arriued there, the little house they fill,
   Ne looke for entertainment, where none was:
   Rest is their feast, and all things at their will;
   The noblest mind the best contentment has.
   With faire discourse the euening so they pas:
   For that old man of pleasing wordes had store,   *store* a great deal
   And well could file his tongue as smooth as glas;
   He told of Saintes and Popes, and euermore
He strowd an *Aue-Mary* after and before.   *strowd* sprinkled, cast

36

The drouping Night thus creepeth on them fast,
   And the sad humour loading their eye liddes,   *sad humour* melancholy
   As messenger of *Morpheus* on them cast
   Sweet slombring deaw, the which to sleepe them biddes.
   Vnto their lodgings then his guestes he riddes: *riddes* dispatches, clears away
   Where when all drownd in deadly sleepe he findes,
   He to his study goes, and there amiddes
   His Magick bookes and artes of sundry kindes,
He seekes out mighty charmes, to trouble sleepy mindes.

37

Then choosing out few wordes most horrible,
   (Let none them read) thereof did verses frame,
   With which and other spelles like terrible,
   He bad awake blacke *Plutoes* griesly Dame,   *bad* commanded *griesly* horrifying
   And cursed heauen, and spake reprochfull shame
   Of highest God, the Lord of life and light;
   A bold bad man, that dar'd to call by name
   Great *Gorgon*, Prince of darknesse and dead night,
At which *Cocytus* quakes, and *Styx* is put to flight.

35.8–9 He told . . . and before.] The 'Ave Maria' ('Hail Mary') is a popular short Latin prayer, derived from the gospels, which during the sixteenth century acquired a second, petitionary clause.

36.3 Morpheus] Son of the god of sleep (Somnus); cf. Virgil, *Aeneid*, 5.854–6. In Ovid's *Metamorphoses* (11.410–748), Morpheus sends a dream and a vision to Alcyone to inform her of the death of her husband, Ceyx, an episode from which Spenser draws heavily in the following passage.

37.4 Plutoes griesly Dame,] The wife of Pluto, or Hades, lord of the underworld, was Proserpina, known to the Greeks as Persephone.

37.8 Gorgon . . . night,] 'Gorgon' is apparently a truncated form of 'Demogorgon', and not to be confused with Medusa, also known as Gorgon, who was killed by Perseus. Thomas Cooper, in the *Dictionarium Historicum & Poeticum* (London, 1565), calls Demogorgon 'an inchanter, whiche was supposed to be of suche excellencie, that he had authoritie ouer all spirites that made men afearde' (sig. G6ʳ).

37.9 Cocytus . . . and Styx] Two of the rivers of Hades; the others are Acheron, Phlegethon and Lethe.

38

And forth he cald out of deepe darknesse dred   *dread* fearful
  Legions of Sprights, the which like little flyes   *sprights* spirits
  Fluttring about his euer damned hed,
  A-waite whereto their seruice he applyes,
  To aide his friends, or fray his enimies: *fray* frighten, attack
  Of those he chose out two, the falsest twoo,
  And fittest for to forge true-seeming lyes;
  The one of them he gaue a message too,
The other by him selfe staide other worke to doo.

39

He making speedy way through spersed ayre,   *spersed* scattered
  And through the world of waters wide and deepe,
  To *Morpheus* house doth hastily repaire.   *repaire* go, proceed
  Amid the bowels of the earth full steepe,   *steepe* precipitous
  And low, where dawning day doth neuer peepe,
  His dwelling is; there *Tethys* his wet bed
  Doth euer wash, and *Cynthia* still doth steepe   *steepe* soak, bathe
  In siluer deaw his euer-drouping hed,
Whiles sad Night ouer him her mantle black doth spred.

40

Whose double gates he findeth locked fast,
  The one faire fram'd of burnisht Yuory,
  The other all with siluer ouercast;
  And wakefull dogges before them farre do lye,
  Watching to banish Care their enimy,
  Who oft is wont to trouble gentle sleepe.
  By them the Sprite doth passe in quietly,
  And vnto *Morpheus* comes, whom drowned deepe
In drowsie fit he findes: of nothing he takes keepe.

41

And more, to lulle him in his slumber soft,
  A trickling streame from high rocke tumbling downe
  And euer-drizling raine vpon the loft,
  Mixt with a murmuring winde, much like the sowne   *sowne* sound

39.6–9 there Tethys . . . doth spred] In other words, Morpheus is forever attended by the sea, by the moon and by darkness. Tethys, daughter of Uranus and the Earth, was wife of Oceanus and reputed mother of the world's great rivers and the ocean nymphs. Cynthia is another name for Artemis, or Diana, chaste goddess of the moon, derived from Mount Cynthus on the island of Delos, where she was said to have been born.

    40.1–3 Whose double gates . . . ouercast;] The double gates of the house of sleep are described in Virgil, *Aeneid*, 6.893–6.

Of swarming Bees, did cast him in a swowne: *swowne* swoon, fainting-fit
No other noyse, nor peoples troublous cryes,
As still are wont t'annoy the walled towne,
Might there be heard: but carelesse Quiet lyes,
Wrapt in eternall silence farre from enemyes.

42
The messenger approching to him spake,
But his wast wordes returnd to him in vaine:
So sound he slept, that nought mought him awake. *mought* might
Then rudely he him trust, and pusht with paine, *trust* seized
Whereat he gan to stretch: but he againe
Shooke him so hard, that forced him to speake.
As one then in a dreame, whose dryer braine
Is tost with troubled sights and fancies weake,
He mumbled soft, but would not all his silence breake.

43
The Sprite then gan more boldly him to wake,
And threatned vnto him the dreaded name
Of *Hecate*: whereat he gan to quake,
And lifting vp his lumpish head, with blame *lumpish* unwieldy, dull, lethargic
Halfe angry asked him, for what he came.
Hither (quoth he) me *Archimago* sent,
He that the stubborne Sprites can wisely tame,
He bids thee to him send for his intent *for his intent* to answer his design
A fit false dreame, that can delude the sleepers sent. *sent* senses, sensing

44
The God obayde, and calling forth straight way
A diuerse dreame out of his prison darke, *diuerse* multiform, changeable
Deliuered it to him, and downe did lay
His heauie head, deuoide of carefull carke, *carefull* troubling *carke* anxiety
Whose sences all were straight benumbd and starke. *starke* rigid, paralysed
He backe returning by the Yuorie dore,

42.7 dryer braine] Excess of either of the two dry humours, choler and melancholy, was thought to provoke visions. As Robert Burton writes in *The Anatomy of Melancholy*, choler is 'hot and dry, bitter', while melancholy is 'cold and dry, thick, black, and sour' (1.1.2.2), and 'it cannot be otherwise but that the *brain* must be affected ... in a cold dry distemperature of it in his substance, which is corrupt and becomes too cold, or too dry, or else too hot, as in mad-men.' When the humour is melancholic, 'sour and sharp', then 'from the sharpness of this humour proceed much waking, troublesome thoughts & dreams' (1.1.3.2–3).

43.2–3 the dreaded name of *Hecate*] Ovid's Medea calls Hecate (here, trisyllabic) *adiutrix ... cantusque artisque magorum* ('the helper of the spells and arts of magicians'; *Metamorphoses*, 7.195).

Remounted vp as light as chearefull Larke,
　　And on his litle winges the dreame he bore
In hast vnto his Lord, where he him left afore.   *afore* before

45

Who all this while with charmes and hidden artes,
　　Had made a Lady of that other Spright,
　　And fram'd of liquid ayre her tender partes   *fram'd* made
　　So liuely, and so like in all mens sight,   *like* fitting, beautiful
That weaker sence it could haue rauisht quight:
　　The maker selfe for all his wondrous witt,
　　Was nigh beguiled with so goodly sight:
　　Her all in white he clad, and ouer it
Cast a blacke stole, most like to seeme for *Vna* fit.

46

Now when that ydle dreame was to him brought,
　　Vnto that Elfin knight he bad him fly,
　　Where he slept soundly void of euill thought,
　　And with false shewes abuse his fantasy,   *abuse* deceive *fantasy* imagination
In sort as he him schooled priuily: *in sort as* in the way that *priuily* secretly
　　And that new creature borne without her dew,
　　Full of the makers guile, with vsage sly
　　He taught to imitate that Lady trew,
Whose semblance she did carrie vnder feigned hew.   *semblance* appearance

47

Thus well instructed, to their worke they hast,
　　And comming where the knight in slomber lay,
　　The one vpon his hardy head him plast,
　　And made him dreame of loues and lustfull play,
That nigh his manly hart did melt away,   *nigh* nearly
　　Bathed in wanton blis and wicked ioy:
　　Then seemed him his Lady by him lay,   *seemed him* it seemed to him
　　And to him playnd, how that false winged boy,
Her chast hart had subdewd, to learne Dame pleasures toy.

45.9 for Vna fit.] Una is only named for the first time here, when Archimago fashions a double to replace her.
46.6 borne without her dew,] A spirit born of the hand of a human maker will be endowed with 'guile', whereas a naturally born creature would by contrast receive its 'dew' – presumably the divine imprint consequent on natural generation.
47.8 that false winged boy,] Cupid, the blindfolded god of love and child of Venus.

48

And she her selfe of beautie soueraigne Queene,
   Faire *Venus* seemde vnto his bed to bring
   Her, whom he waking euermore did weene,   *waking* while awake, by day
   To be the chastest flowre, that ay did spring   *weene* conceive, believe *ay* ever
   On earthly braunch, the daughter of a king,
   Now a loose Leman to vile seruice bound:
   And eke the *Graces* seemed all to sing,
   Hymen iô Hymen, dauncing all around,
Whilst freshest *Flora* her with Yuie girlond crownd.

49

In this great passion of vnwonted lust,   *vnwonted* unusual
   Or wonted feare of doing ought amis,
   He started vp, as seeming to mistrust,
   Some secret ill, or hidden foe of his:
   Lo there before his face his Lady is,
   Vnder blake stole hyding her bayted hooke,
   And as halfe blushing offred him to kis,
   With gentle blandishment and louely looke,   *blandishment* flattering allurement
Most like that virgin true, which for her knight him took.

50

All cleane dismayd to see so vncouth sight,   *vncouth* unfamiliar
   And halfe enraged at her shamelesse guise,   *guise* manner
   He thought t'haue slaine her in his fierce despight:
   But hasty heat tempring with sufferance wise,   *sufferance* forbearance
   He stayde his hand, and gan himselfe aduise
   To proue his sense, and tempt her faigned truth.
   Wringing her hands in wemens pitteous wise,   *pitteous wise* pathetic, pitiful manner
   Tho can she weepe, to stirre vp gentle ruth,   *Tho can she* Then she began to *ruth* ruin
Both for her noble bloud, and for her tender youth.

48.2–6 Faire Venus . . . seruice bound] Some poets record that, when Paris awarded the golden apple to Helen of Sparta, Venus herself brought Helen to his bed – thereby setting in train the events that would lead to the Trojan War and, in turn, Homer's *Iliad*.

48.7 Graces] Daughters of Jove by Eurynome, and officiants at rites of beauty and love. Cf. VI.x.5–31, below.

48.8 Hymen iô Hymen,] The *Hymenaeon*, a marriage song invoking the blessing of Hymen, god of marriage, is a conventional element in the record of weddings in classical myth and history.

48.9 freshest Flora] Goddess of flowers, as in Ovid, *Fasti*, 5.195–274; or, according to another tradition, the name of a rich courtesan whose legacy, left to the city of Rome, was spent on games and festivities (cf. Cooper, *Dictionarium*, sig. H6ᵛ). E. K. mentions this latter tradition in the gloss to 'March' of Spenser's 1579 *The Shepheardes Calender*, ascribing it to Tacitus.

50.6 To proue . . . faigned truth.] Rather than rushing to condemnation, Redcrosse resolves to wait and test the accuracy of his perception of the false Una's harlotry.

51
And said, Ah Sir, my liege Lord and my loue,
  Shall I accuse the hidden cruell fate,
  And mightie causes wrought in heauen aboue,
  Or the blind God, that doth me thus amate,   *amate* dismay
  For hoped loue to winne me certaine hate?
  Yet thus perforce he bids me do, or die.   *perforce* by compulsion
  Die is my dew: yet rew my wretched state
  You, whom my hard auenging destinie
Hath made iudge of my life or death indifferently.

52
Your owne deare sake forst me at first to leaue
  My Fathers kingdome, There she stopt with teares;
  Her swollen hart her speach seemd to bereaue,   *bereaue* take away
  And then againe begun, My weaker yeares
  Captiu'd to fortune and frayle worldly feares,
  Fly to your faith for succour and sure ayde:
  Let me not dye in languor and long teares.
  Why Dame (quoth he) what hath ye thus dismayd?
What frayes ye, that were wont to comfort me affrayd?

53
Loue of your selfe, she said, and deare constraint
  Lets me not sleepe, but wast the wearie night
  In secret anguish and vnpittied plaint,   *plaint* complaint
  Whiles you in carelesse sleepe are drowned quight.
  Her doubtfull words made that redoubted knight
  Suspect her truth: yet since no' vntruth he knew,
  Her fawning loue with foule disdainefull spight
  He would not shend, but said, Deare dame I rew,   *shend* reprove, reproach
That for my sake vnknowne such griefe vnto you grew.

54
Assure your selfe, it fell not all to ground;
  For all so deare as life is to my hart,
  I deeme your loue, and hold me to you bound;   *deeme* judge, consider
  Ne let vaine feares procure your needlesse smart,   *smart* pain, vexation
  Where cause is none, but to your rest depart.

52.1–2 Your owne deare sake ... kingdome,] A lie, and one with religious significance: as we learn from 'A letter of the Authors ... to Sir Walter Raleigh', Una came to Gloriana's court seeking a champion to liberate her parents, and at first objected to the 'clownish' and untried Redcrosse. Christian love should be extended for God's sake, and not for the sake of the beloved; cf. e.g. Spenser's *Amoretti*, no. 68, ll. 9–13.

Not all content, yet seemd she to appease
Her mournefull plaintes, beguiled of her art,
And fed with words, that could not chuse but please,
So slyding softly forth, she turnd as to her ease.

55

Long after lay he musing at her mood,
  Much grieu'd to thinke that gentle Dame so light,
  For whose defence he was to shed his blood.
  At last dull wearinesse of former fight
  Hauing yrockt a sleepe his irkesome spright,   *irkesome* vexed, troubled *spright* spirit
  That troublous dreame gan freshly tosse his braine,   *tosse* disturb, agitate
  With bowres, and beds, and Ladies deare delight:
  But when he saw his labour all was vaine,
With that misformed spright he backe returnd againe.   *misformed* wrongly made

Canto II.

The guilefull great Enchaunter parts
The Redcrosse Knight from Truth:
Into whose stead faire falshood steps,   *stead* place
And workes him wofull ruth.   *workes* causes *ruth* ruin

1

By this the Northerne wagoner had set
  His seuenfold teme behind the stedfast starre,
  That was in Ocean waues yet neuer wet,
  But firme is fixt, and sendeth light from farre
  To all, that in the wide deepe wandring arre:
  And chearefull Chaunticlere with his note shrill
  Had warned once, that *Phœbus* fiery carre
  In hast was climbing vp the Easterne hill,
Full enuious that night so long his roome did fill.

1.1–5 the Northerne wagoner ... wandring arre:] The constellation of Boötes (Gr 'ox-driver', or ploughman) lies immediately adjacent to the seven-star asterism known in Great Britain and Ireland as the Plough, and in North America as the Big Dipper (part of the constellation called *Ursa major*, or the Great Bear). The ploughman driving the plough circles (like the rest of the night sky in the northern hemisphere) about the Pole Star, Polaris; in certain seasons and at certain times of the night, then, Boötes and the Plough will both 'set' behind Polaris, which itself never drops below the horizon. Spenser follows Ovid; cf., for example, *Metamorphoses*, 10.446–7.

1.6 chearefull Chaunticlere] Chaunticleer, the cock hero of Chaucer's 'Nun's Priest's Tale', begins his adventures with a terrifying dream; Spenser's choice of epithet, 'chearefull', may be a wry comment on Redcrosse's predicament.

1.7 Phœbus fiery carre] The sun; Phoebus is an epithet of Apollo, god of the sun.

2

When those accursed messengers of hell,
    That feigning dreame, and that faire-forged Spright
    Came to their wicked maister, and gan tell
    Their bootelesse paines, and ill succeeding night:
    Who all in rage to see his skilfull might
    Deluded so, gan threaten hellish paine
    And sad *Proserpines* wrath, them to affright.
    But when he saw his threatning was but vaine,
He cast about, and searcht his balefull bookes againe.

feigning dissembling
gan began
bootelesse fruitless, unprofitable

deluded frustrated

affright frighten

balefull pernicious, malignant

3

Eftsoones he tooke that miscreated faire,
    And that false other Spright, on whom he spred
    A seeming body of the subtile aire,
    Like a young Squire, in loues and lusty-hed
    His wanton dayes that euer loosely led,
    Without regard of armes and dreaded fight:
    Those two he tooke, and in a secret bed,
    Couered with darknesse and misdeeming night,
Them both together laid, to ioy in vaine delight.

lusty-hed vigour, lustfulness

misdeeming (that causes) misjudging

4

Forthwith he runnes with feigned faithfull hast
    Vnto his guest, who after troublous sights
    And dreames, gan now to take more sound repast,
    Whom suddenly he wakes with fearefull frights,
    As one aghast with feends or damned sprights,
    And to him cals, Rise rise vnhappy Swaine,
    That here wex old in sleepe, whiles wicked wights
    Haue knit themselues in *Venus* shamefull chaine;
Come see, where your false Lady doth her honour staine.

troublous full of trouble, troubling
repast rest, refection

swaine young man, lover
wex grows
knit joined, locked

5

All in amaze he suddenly vp start
    With sword in hand, and with the old man went;
    Who soone him brought into a secret part,
    Where that false couple were full closely ment
    In wanton lust and lewd embracement:
    Which when he saw, he burnt with gealous fire,
    The eye of reason was with rage yblent,
    And would haue slaine them in his furious ire,
But hardly was restreined of that aged sire.

ment mingled
embracement intercourse (*euph.*)

yblent blinded

hardly with difficulty

6

Returning to his bed in torment great,
   And bitter anguish of his guiltie sight,
   He could not rest, but did his stout heart eat,
   And wast his inward gall with deepe despight,   *wast* wear away, exhaust *gall* spirit, pride
   Yrkesome of life, and too long lingring night.   *yrkesome of* annoyed, disgusted with
   At last faire *Hesperus* in highest skie
   Had spent his lampe, & brought forth dawning light,   *spent his lampe* exhausted his light
   Then vp he rose, and clad him hastily;
The Dwarfe him brought his steed: so both away do fly.   *fly* depart in haste

7

Now when the rosy-fingred Morning faire,
   Weary of aged *Tithones* saffron bed,
   Had spred her purple robe through deawy aire,
   And the high hils *Titan* discouered,
   The royall virgin shooke off drowsy-hed,   *drowsy-hed* drowsiness
   And rising forth out of her baser bowre,   *baser bowre* lower room
   Lookt for her knight, who far away was fled,
   And for her Dwarfe, that wont to wait each houre;
Then gan she waile & weepe, to see that woefull stowre.   *stowre* unhappy, perilous circumstance

8

And after him she rode with so much speede
   As her slow beast could make; but all in vaine:
   For him so far had borne his light-foot steede,
   Pricked with wrath and fiery fierce disdaine,   *pricked* spurred, tormented
   That him to follow was but fruitlesse paine;
   Yet she her weary limbes would neuer rest,
   But euery hill and dale, each wood and plaine
   Did search, sore grieued in her gentle brest,
He so vngently left her, whom she louest best.   *vngently* discourteously

9

But subtill *Archimago*, when his guests
   He saw diuided into double parts,

   6.6–7 At last . . . his lampe,] The fading of Hesperus, or Vesper, the evening star, heralded the morning. The decline of Hesperus brings 'forth dawning light' because the same star – actually the planet Venus – is also called Eosphorus ('dawn bearer') and Phosphorus ('light bearer').
   7.1–3 the rosy-fingred Morning . . . deawy aire,] Eos, goddess of the dawn, fell in love with the Trojan prince Tithonus, and obtained Zeus's permission to grant him immortality. As one of the Homeric hymns records, though ('To Aphrodite', ll. 218–38), she neglected to secure him eternal youth, and so has spent much of eternity watching him babble in his bed of infirmity.
   7.4 Titan] Helios, the sun, called Titan because he was (by Hyperion) grandson to Earth and Titan. Cf. Virgil, *Aeneid*, 4.118–19 and Conti, *Mythologiae*, 5.17.

And *Vna* wandring in woods and forrests,
Th'end of his drift, he praisd his diuelish arts,
That had such might ouer true meaning harts;
Yet rests not so, but other meanes doth make,
How he may worke vnto her further smarts: *smarts* pains, torments
For her he hated as the hissing snake,
And in her many troubles did most pleasure take.

10
He then deuisde himselfe how to disguise;
For by his mightie science he could take
As many formes and shapes in seeming wise,   *in seeming wise* in appearance
As euer *Proteus* to himselfe could make:
Sometime a fowle, sometime a fish in lake,
Now like a foxe, now like a dragon fell,
That of himselfe he oft for feare would quake,
And oft would flie away. O who can tell
The hidden power of herbes, and might of Magicke spell?

11
But now seemde best, the person to put on   *person* disguise (L *persona*, 'mask')
Of that good knight, his late beguiled guest:
In mighty armes he was yclad anon: *anon* at once, immediately
And siluer shield, vpon his coward brest
A bloudy crosse, and on his crauen crest   *crest* the ridged top of a helmet; an
A bounch of haires discolourd diuersly: ornamental plume placed there
Full iolly knight he seemde, and well addrest,   *addrest* suited, prepared
And when he sate vpon his courser free,   *free* noble
Saint George himself ye would haue deemed him to be.

12
But he the knight, whose semblaunt he did beare,   *semblaunt* likeness
The true *Saint George* was wandred far away,
Still flying from his thoughts and gealous feare;
Will was his guide, and griefe led him astray.
At last him chaunst to meete vpon the way
A faithlesse Sarazin all arm'd to point,   *sarazin* pagan knight *to point* properly,
In whose great shield was writ with letters gay   exactly

10.3–4 As many formes ... could make:] Ovid records that Proteus, a sea-god, had *in plures ius ... transire figuras*, 'the power to assume many forms' (*Metamorphoses*, 8.730); the tradition stems originally from Homer, *Odyssey*, 4.414–18.
11.7–9 Full iolly ... seemde ...] This passage clearly echoes the description of Redcrosse at I.i.1.8–9. As with Una (see above, I.i.45.9), Redcrosse is only named (here and in the immediately following stanza) when he can be distinguished from his double; cf. also stanzas 14–15, below, where the name 'Redcrosse' first appears, in connection with Sans foy.

Sans foy: full large of limbe and euery ioint
He was, and cared not for God or man a point.   *a point* one bit, at all

13

He had a faire companion of his way,
   A goodly Lady clad in scarlot red,
   Purfled with gold and pearle of rich assay,   *purfled* edged, embroidered *assay*
   And like a *Persian* mitre on her hed   quality, proof
   She wore, with crownes and owches garnished,   *owches* brooches, precious ornaments
   The which her lauish louers to her gaue;
   Her wanton palfrey all was ouerspred
   With tinsell trappings, wouen like a waue,
Whose bridle rung with golden bels and bosses braue.   *bosses* ornamental studs *braue* fine

14

With faire disport and courting dalliaunce   *disport* amusement, merriment
   She intertainde her louer all the way: *dalliaunce* idle chat, flirtation
   But when she saw the knight his speare aduaunce,
   She soone left off her mirth and wanton play,
   And bad her knight addresse him to the fray:
   His foe was nigh at hand. He prickt with pride
   And hope to winne his Ladies heart that day,
   Forth spurred fast: adowne his coursers side
The red bloud trickling staind the way, as he did ride.

15

The knight of the *Redcrosse* when him he spide,
   Spurring so hote with rage dispiteous,   *dispiteous* merciless
   Gain fairely couch his speare, and towards ride: *couch* level, as for attack
   Soone meete they both, both fell and furious,
   That daunted with their forces hideous,
   Their steeds do stagger, and amazed stand,
   And eke themselues too rudely rigorous,
   Astonied with the stroke of their owne hand,   *astonied* astonished, made senseless
Do backe rebut, and each to other yeeldeth land.   *rebut* repel

---

12.6–8 A faithlesse ... Sans foy:] The use of the term 'Saracen' invokes the history of the Crusades, but in Spenser's allegory the knights Sans foy ('faithless') and his brothers Sans joy ('joyless') and Sans loy ('lawless') appear to be enemies to truth generally, and not just to Christian truth.

Stanza 13 A goodly Lady ...] This stanza may echo the language of the 1560 Geneva translation of Revelation, in its description of the Whore of Babylon (Rev. 17.4); as the gloss to that passage indicates, most English Protestants of this period considered the Whore of Babylon to be a prophetic representation of the Pope, and of Roman Christianity more generally. The word 'mitre' is equivocal, as it was used in this period to describe the headpiece of a Roman bishop, but was also used by travellers and antiquaries to describe various kinds of headgear (e.g. turbans, tiaras) worn by eastern, Turkish and Jewish people.

16
As when two rams stird with ambitious pride,
   Fight for the rule of the rich fleeced flocke,
   Their horned fronts so fierce on either side
   Do meete, that with the terrour of the shocke
   Astonied both, stand sencelesse as a blocke,
   Forgetfull of the hanging victory: *hanging* depending, unresolved
   So stood these twaine, vnmoued as a rocke,
   Both staring fierce, and holding idely,
The broken reliques of their former cruelty.   *reliques* remains

17
The *Sarazin* sore daunted with the buffe   *buffe* blow
   Snatcheth his sword, and fiercely to him flies;
   Who well it wards, and quyteth cuff with cuff: *quyteth* repays
   Each others equall puissaunce enuies,
   And through their iron sides with cruell spies
   Does seeke to perce: repining courage yields   *repining* grudging
   No foote to foe. The flashing fier flies
   As from a forge out of their burning shields,
And streames of purple bloud new dies the verdant fields.

18
Curse on that Crosse (quoth then the *Sarazin*)
   That keepes thy body from the bitter fit;   *bitter fit* death throes
   Dead long ygoe I wote thou haddest bin,
   Had not that charme from thee forwarned it: *forwarned* protected
   But yet I warne thee now assured sitt,   *assured sitt* brace yourself
   And hide thy head. Therewith vpon his crest
   With rigour so outrageous he smitt,   *smitt* smote, struck
   That a large share it hewd out of the rest,   *share* sheared piece
And glauncing downe his shield, from blame him fairely blest.
                                                          fairely blest soundly thrashed

19
Who thereat wondrous wroth, the sleeping spark
   Of natiue vertue gan eftsoones reuiue,
   And at his haughtie helmet making mark,
   So hugely stroke, that it the steele did riue,   *riue* cleave in two
   And cleft his head. He tumbling downe aliue,
   With bloudy mouth his mother earth did kis,

18.9 from blame ... blest] The construction 'from blame' is awkward, and probably indicates both that Sans foy strikes Redcrosse in censure for his fault (in leaving Una), and that the blow itself is a matter of shame and reproach for Redcrosse. See *OED*, 'from', *prep.*, 14. a, b.

Greeting his graue: his grudging ghost did striue
With the fraile flesh; at last it flitted is,
Whither the soules do fly of men, that liue amis.

20

The Lady when she saw her champion fall,
   Like the old ruines of a broken towre,
   Staid not to waile his woefull funerall,   *waile* mourn or complain for
   But from him fled away with all her powre;
   Who after her as hastily gan scowre,   *gan* began to *scowre* run, chase
   Bidding the Dwarfe with him to bring away
   The *Sarazins* shield, signe of the conqueroure.
   Her soone he ouertooke, and bad to stay,   *bad* commanded
For present cause was none of dread her to dismay.

21

She turning backe with ruefull countenaunce,
   Cride, Mercy mercy Sir vouchsafe to show
   On silly Dame, subiect to hard mischaunce,
   And to your mighty will. Her humblesse low
   In so ritch weedes and seeming glorious show,
   Did much enmoue his stout heroïcke heart,   *enmoue* stir within, affect
   And said, Deare dame, your suddein ouerthrow
   Much rueth me; but now put feare apart,   *rueth me* moves me with pity
And tell, both who ye be, and who that tooke your part.

22

Melting in teares, then gan she thus lament;
   The wretched woman, whom vnhappy howre
   Hath now made thrall to your commandement,   *commandement* (tetrasyllabic)
   Before that angry heauens list to lowre,   *list* pleased, chose *lowre* frown
   And fortune false betraide me to your powre,
   Was, (O what now auaileth that I was!)   *what . . . auaileth* what good is it
   Borne the sole daughter of an Emperour,
   He that the wide West vnder his rule has,
And high hath set his throne, where *Tiberis* doth pas.

20.6–7 Bidding the Dwarfe . . . conqueroure.] Spenser's verse elides the difference between the taking of the shield (the power to do which was the right, and thus the sign, of the conqueror), and the shield itself. Sans foy's shield – faithlessness – finally becomes Redcrosse's badge. On the confusion between intrinsic and extrinsic powers of signs, see also stanza 18, above.

22.7–9 Borne . . . doth pas.] Duessa's presentation of her own lineage and predicament is designed to parody that of Una. The reference to the River Tiber, which flows through Rome, obviously indicates St Peter's foundation and the Pope, here polemically imagined not as a spiritual but as a temporal ruler, and not as a chaste priest but an ambitious father.

23

He in the first flowre of my freshest age,
  Betrothed me vnto the onely haire
  Of a most mighty king, most rich and sage;
  Was neuer Prince so faithfull and so faire,
  Was neuer Prince so meeke and debonaire;
  But ere my hoped day of spousall shone,   *spousall* marriage, betrothal
  My dearest Lord fell from high honours staire,
  Into the hands of his accursed fone,   *fone* enemies (*arch.* plural)
And cruelly was slaine, that shall I euer mone.

24

His blessed body spoild of liuely breath,
  Was afterward, I know not how, conuaid
  And fro me hid: of whose most innocent death
  When tidings came to me vnhappy maid,
  O how great sorrow my sad soule assaid.
  Then forth I went his woefull corse to find,
  And many yeares throughout the world I straid,
  A virgin widow, whose deepe wounded mind
With loue, long time did languish as the striken hind.   *striken hind* wounded deer

25

At last it chaunced this proud *Sarazin*,
  To meete me wandring, who perforce me led
  With him away, but yet could neuer win
  The Fort, that Ladies hold in soueraigne dread.
  There lies he now with foule dishonour dead,
  Who whiles he liu'de, was called proud *Sans foy*,
  The eldest of three brethren, all three bred
  Of one bad sire, whose youngest is *Sans ioy*,
And twixt them both was borne the bloudy bold *Sans loy*.

26

In this sad plight, friendlesse, vnfortunate,
  Now miserable I *Fidessa* dwell,

24.1–3 His blessed body ... fro me hid:] The emphasis on the physical body of Christ, here, and the ensuing devotion with which Duessa claims to have sought it, continue to play on contemporary Protestant accounts of Roman religious practice as profanely material – mistaking the sign for its meaning. See also Plutarch's account of the Egyptian goddess Isis' search for the dismembered remains of her husband, Osiris, in 'On Isis and Osiris', *Moralia*, 5.
25.6–9 Sans foy ... Sans ioy ... Sans loy.] The three 'Sarazin' brothers appear in a sequence that emphasises their allegorical function. First to appear is the eldest, Sans foy (faithlessness), followed by Sans loy (lawlessness, at I.iii.33) and finally Sans ioy (joylessness, at I.iv.38), suggesting that while faith is best, even a faithless life by the law is better than the joylessness of reprobation.

Crauing of you in pitty of my state,
To do none ill, if please ye not do well.
He in great passion all this while did dwell,
More busying his quicke eyes, her face to view,
Then his dull eares, to heare what she did tell;
And said, faire Lady hart of flint would rew
The vndeserued woes and sorrowes, which ye shew.

27
Henceforth in safe assuraunce may ye rest,
Hauing both found a new friend you to aid,
And lost an old foe, that did you molest:
Better new friend then an old foe is said.
With chaunge of cheare the seeming simple maid
Let fall her eyen, as shamefast to the earth,   *shamefast* modest
And yeelding soft, in that she nought gain-said,
So forth they rode, he feining seemely merth,
And she coy lookes: so dainty they say maketh derth.

28
Long time they thus together traueiled,
Till weary of their way, they came at last,
Where grew two goodly trees, that faire did spred
Their armes abroad, with gray mosse ouercast,
And their greene leaues trembling with euery blast,
Made a calme shadow far in compasse round:
The fearefull Shepheard often there aghast   *aghast* terrified
Vnder them neuer sat, ne wont there sound   *sound* play
His mery oaten pipe, but shund th'vnlucky ground.

29
But this good knight soone as he them can spie,
For the coole shade thither hastly got:
For golden *Phœbus* now ymounted hie,
From fiery wheeles of his faire chariot
Hurled his beame so scorching cruell hot,
That liuing creature mote it not abide;
And his new Lady it endured not.
There they alight, in hope themselues to hide
From the fierce heat, and rest their weary limbs a tide.

Stanzas 28–45 Where grew two goodly trees . . .] The Fradubio episode loosely imitates the history of Polydorus in Virgil's *Aeneid*, 3.22–48, and the more recent precedent of the knight Astolfo in Ariosto's *Orlando Furioso*, 6.26–53.

30
Faire seemely pleasaunce each to other makes,
  With goodly purposes there as they sit:
  And in his falsed fancy he her takes   *falsed fancy* deceived imagination
  To be the fairest wight, that liued yit;   *that liued yit* that ever lived
  Which to expresse, he bends his gentle wit,
  And thinking of those braunches greene to frame   *thinking* intending
  A girlond for her dainty forehead fit,
  He pluckt a bough; out of whose rift there came
Small drops of gory bloud, that trickled downe the same.

31
Therewith a piteous yelling voyce was heard,
  Crying, O spare with guilty hands to teare
  My tender sides in this rough rynd embard,   *rynd* bark *embard* imprisoned
  But fly, ah fly far hence away, for feare
  Least to you hap, that happened to me heare,   *hap* chance, befall
  And to this wretched Lady, my deare loue,
  O too deare loue, loue bought with death too deare.
  Astond he stood, and vp his haire did houe,   *astond* astonished *houe* lift, rise
And with that suddein horror could no member moue.

32
At last whenas the dreadfull passion
  Was ouerpast, and manhood well awake,
  Yet musing at the straunge occasion,
  And doubting much his sence, he thus bespake;
  What voyce of damned Ghost from *Limbo* lake,
  Or guilefull spright wandring in empty aire,
  Both which fraile men do oftentimes mistake,   *mistake* cause to mistake, mislead
  Sends to my doubtfull eares these speaches rare,
And ruefull plaints, me bidding guiltlesse bloud to spare?

33
Then groning deepe, Nor damned Ghost, (quoth he,)
  Nor guilefull sprite to thee these wordes doth speake,
  But once a man *Fradubio*, now a tree,
  Wretched man, wretched tree; whose nature weake,
  A cruell witch her cursed will to wreake,
  Hath thus transformd, and plast in open plaines,

32.5 Limbo lake,] A hybrid representation – part-classical, part-Christian – of a holding place for lost souls. It was sometimes popularly reputed, in this period, that ghosts (like that of Old Hamlet) could return from purgatory, or limbo, to harass living humans.
  33.3 Fradubio,] Literally 'in doubt', from It *fra* ('between, among') and *dubbio* ('doubt').

Where *Boreas* doth blow full bitter bleake,
  And scorching Sunne does dry my secret vaines:
For though a tree I seeme, yet cold and heat me paines.

34
Say on *Fradubio* then, or man, or tree,
  Quoth then the knight, by whose mischieuous arts
  Art thou misshaped thus, as now I see?
  He oft finds med'cine, who his griefe imparts;
  But double griefs afflict concealing harts,
  As raging flames who striueth to suppresse.
  The author then (said he) of all my smarts,
  Is one *Duessa* a false sorceresse,
That many errant knights hath brought to wretchednesse.

35
In prime of youthly yeares, when corage hot
  The fire of loue and ioy of cheualree
  First kindled in my brest, it was my lot
  To loue this gentle Lady, whom ye see,
  Now not a Lady, but a seeming tree;
  With whom as once I rode accompanyde,
  Me chaunced of a knight encountred bee,
  That had a like faire Lady by his syde,
Like a faire Lady, but did fowle *Duessa* hyde.

36
Whose forged beauty he did take in hand,   *take in hand* (lit.) maintain, claim
  All other Dames to haue exceeded farre;
  I in defence of mine did likewise stand,
  Mine, that did then shine as the Morning starre:
  So both to battell fierce arraunged arre,   *arraunged* put in readiness
  In which his harder fortune was to fall
  Vnder my speare: such is the dye of warre:
  His Lady left as a prise martiall,   *martiall* (trisyllabic)
Did yield her comely person, to be at my call.   *at my call* in my power

37
So doubly lou'd of Ladies vnlike faire,
  Th'one seeming such, the other such indeede,

33.7 Boreas] The north wind.
34.8 Duessa a false sorceresse,] The feminising suffix –*ess* associates the witch Duessa's 'doubleness' (It *due*, 'two', or *duezza*, 'twoness') with her female form.

One day in doubt I cast for to compare,	*cast* contrived
Whether in beauties glorie did exceede;	*whether* which of the two
A Rosy girlond was the victors meede:	*meede* reward
Both seemde to win, and both seemde won to bee,	
So hard the discord was to be agreede.	
Frælissa was as faire, as faire mote bee,	
And euer false *Duessa* seemde as faire as shee.	

38

The wicked witch now seeing all this while	
The doubtfull ballaunce equally to sway,	
What not by right, she cast to win by guile,	
And by her hellish science raisd streight way	*science* knowledge or skill
A foggy mist, that ouercast the day,	
And a dull blast, that breathing on her face,	
Dimmed her former beauties shining ray,	
And with foule vgly forme did her disgrace:	
Then was she faire alone, when none was faire in place.	

39

Then cride she out, fye, fye, deformed wight,	
Whose borrowed beautie now appeareth plaine	
To haue before bewitched all mens sight;	
O leaue her soone, or let her soone be slaine.	
Her loathly visage viewing with disdaine,	
Eftsoones I thought her such, as she me told,	
And would haue kild her; but with faigned paine,	
The false witch did my wrathfull hand with-hold;	
So left her, where she now is turnd to treen mould.	*treen* tree-like (disyllabic) *mould* shape

40

Thens forth I tooke *Duessa* for my Dame,	
And in the witch vnweening ioyd long time,	*vnweening* ignorant, unsuspecting
Ne euer wist, but that she was the same,	*wist* knew
Till on a day (that day is euery Prime,	*prime* early morning (c. 6 a.m.)
When Witches wont do penance for their crime)	
I chaunst to see her in her proper hew,	
Bathing her selfe in origane and thyme:	

37.3 **One day in doubt ... compare,**] Fradubio's offence may in part stem from his determination to try a question that had already been decided by battle (see stanzas 35–6, above).

40.7 **origane and thyme:**] Oregano and thyme were reputed to have medicinal properties. According to John Gerard's *Herbal* (1633), thyme 'cleanseth the breast, lungs, reines, and matrix, and killeth wormes' (p. 574), while oregano 'healeth scabs, itches, and scuruinesse, being vsed in baths, and it taketh away the bad colour which commeth of the yellow jaundice' (p. 667).

A filthy foule old woman I did vew,
That euer to haue toucht her, I did deadly rew.   *deadly rew* exceedingly regret

41
Her neather partes misshapen, monstruous,
  Were hidd in water, that I could not see,
  But they did seeme more foule and hideous,
  Then womans shape man would beleeue to bee.
  Thens forth from her most beastly companie
  I gan refraine, in minde to slip away,
  Soone as appeard safe oportunitie:
  For danger great, if not assur'd decay   *decay* undoing
I saw before mine eyes, if I were knowne to stray.

42
The diuelish hag by chaunges of my cheare   *cheare* countenance, expression
  Perceiu'd my thought, and drownd in sleepie night,
  With wicked herbes and ointments did besmeare
  My bodie all, through charmes and magicke might,
  That all my senses were bereaued quight:
  Then brought she me into this desert waste,
  And by my wretched louers side me pight,   *pight* placed
  Where now enclosd in wooden wals full faste,
Banisht from liuing wights, our wearie dayes we waste.

43
But how long time, said then the Elfin knight,
  Are you in this misformed house to dwell?   *misformed* misshapen, evilly made
  We may not chaunge (quoth he) this euil plight,
  Till we be bathed in a liuing well;
  That is the terme prescribed by the spell.
  O how, said he, mote I that well out find,
  That may restore you to your wonted well?   *well* weal, happiness
  Time and suffised fates to former kynd
Shall vs restore, none else from hence may vs vnbynd.

44
The false *Duessa*, now *Fidessa* hight,   *hight* is called
  Heard how in vaine *Fradubio* did lament,
  And knew well all was true. But the good knight

43.3–5 We may not . . . spell.] The 'liuing well' of which Fradubio speaks is probably that symbolised by baptism; cf. John 4.14: 'whosoeuer drinketh of the water that I shal giue him, shal neuer be more athirst: but the water that I shal giue him, shalbe in him a wel of water, springing vp into euerlasting life.' Redcrosse is himself bathed in a living well during his fight with the dragon in canto xi (31.6), and thus by proxy redeems Fradubio's fault.

Full of sad feare and ghastly dreriment,   *ghastly dreriment* unease of the spirit
When all this speech the liuing tree had spent,
The bleeding bough did thrust into the ground,
That from the bloud he might be innocent,
And with fresh clay did close the wooden wound:
Then turning to his Lady, dead with feare her found.

45
Her seeming dead he found with feigned feare,
  As all vnweeting of that well she knew,   *vnweeting* ignorant *that* that which
  And paynd himselfe with busie care to reare
  Her out of carelesse swowne. Her eylids blew
  And dimmed sight with pale and deadly hew
  At last she vp gan lift: with trembling cheare
  Her vp he tooke, too simple and too trew,
  And oft her kist. At length all passed feare,
He set her on her steede, and forward forth did beare.

2. Book II, cantos xi–xii

In the first extract we saw Redcrosse at the beginning of his quest; here we see Guyon (knight of temperance) at the end of his. In 'A Letter of the Authors ... to Sir Walter Raleigh', Spenser writes of a 'Palmer bearing an Infant with bloody hands, whose Parents he complained to haue bene slayn by an Enchaunteresse called Acrasia'. The palmer seeks revenge, and the Queen of Faery, Gloriana, allots to Guyon the performance of the adventure – the subject of Book II – which shadows a moral instruction in temperance. We learn early in the book (in canto ii) that temperance consists in steering between extremes, shunning the vices of deficiency and excess. This is an idea that Spenser borrows from the second book of Aristotle's *Nicomachean Ethics*, though its emphasis on achieving a middle ground in all things harks back also to Elizabethan religious politics – and some critics have suggested that Guyon's adventures loosely recall major events in the life of Elizabeth's favourite and the champion of radical puritans, Robert Dudley, Earl of Leicester (d. 1588). Here Guyon finally reaches the Bower of Blisse, where Acrasia imprisons her captive knights in a Circean pleasure garden. Acrasia's temptations are subtle and dangerous because, being beautiful, they appeal directly to the soul; moreover, they increasingly appear to allegorise the pleasures of the poem itself. As Guyon's net begins to close around Acrasia and her arts of pleasure, Spenser seems to open up a dissociation between the beauty of his poem, to one side, and its philosophical purpose to the other. Can we accept Spenser's moral meaning, but reject the form by which it is achieved?

50 *The Faerie Queene*: A Reading Guide

Canto XII.

Guyon by Palmers gouernance,
passing through perils great,
Doth ouerthrow the Bowre of blisse,
and Acrasie defeat.

1
Now gins this goodly frame of Temperance   *gins* begins
   Fairely to rise, and her adorned hed
   To pricke of highest praise forth to aduance,   *pricke* mark, height
   Formerly grounded, and fast setteled
   On firme foundation of true bountihed;
   And that braue knight, that for this vertue fights,
   Now comes to point of that same perilous sted,   *sted* place, situation
   Where Pleasure dwelles in sensuall delights,
Mongst thousand dangers, & ten thousand magick mights.

2
Two dayes now in that sea he sayled has,
   Ne euer land beheld, ne liuing wight,
   Ne ought saue perill, still as he did pas:
   Tho when appeared the third *Morrow* bright,
   Vpon the waues to spred her trembling light,
   An hideous roaring farre away they heard,
   That all their senses filled with affright,
   And streight they saw the raging surges reard   *streight* straightaway
Vp to the skyes, that them of drowning made affeard.

3
Said then the Boteman, Palmer stere aright,
   And keepe an euen course; for yonder way

---

*Arg.4 **Acrasie**]* The enchantress at the centre of Guyon's quest is modelled on Homer's Circe, Ludovico Ariosto's Alcina, and Torquato Tasso's Armida; but Spenser's choice of name most clearly echoes Giangiorgio Trissino's Acratia, from the *Italia liberata dai Goti* (1547–8). The L *acrasia* derives from a near-pun in Gr: both ἀκρασία (fr. ἄκρατος, 'unmixed, intemperate') and ἀκρασία (fr. ἀκρατής, 'powerless, lacking self-control, incontinent'). Spenser exploits both strands.
   *2.1–4 **Two dayes ... third Morrow**]* Guyon's contest with Acrasia (like Redcrosse's encounter with the dragon in I.xii) is temporally structured by Christ's harrowing of hell.
   *3.1 **Said then the Boteman,**]* The ferryman, or boatman, who accompanies Guyon and the Palmer to Acrasia's bower plays an important, but slightly mysterious role. As an interpreter of the dangers they face on their passage, he takes on the part of Circe, who guides Odysseus through the perils of his *nostos*, or homecoming, in the middle books of the *Odyssey*. The implication for the allegory is that the soul requires some third element in its achievement of temperance – perhaps experience, or as some critics have argued, conscience.
   ***Stanzas 3–8**]* The boatman's 'euen course' between the Gulf of Greediness and the Rock of Reproach recalls Odysseus' navigation between Scylla and Charybdis, in *The Odyssey*, 12.55–110. It also points

We needes must passe (God do vs well acquight,)   *God ... acquight* God deliver us
   That is the *Gulfe of Greedinesse*, they say,
   That deepe engorgeth all this worldes pray: *worldes pray* worldly, transitory things
   Which hauing swallowd vp excessiuely,
   He soone in vomit vp againe doth lay,
   And belcheth forth his superfluity,
That all the seas for feare do seeme away to fly.

4

On th'other side an hideous Rocke is pight,
   Of mightie *Magnes* stone, whose craggie clift
   Depending from on high, dreadfull to sight,
   Ouer the waues his rugged armes doth lift,
   And threatneth downe to throw his ragged rift   *rift* chasm, mountain slope
   On who so commeth nigh; yet nigh it drawes
   All passengers, that none from it can shift:
   For whiles they fly that Gulfes deuouring iawes,
They on this rock are rent, and sunck in helplesse wawes.   *rent* torn apart *wawes* waves

5

Forward they passe, and strongly he them rowes,
   Vntill they nigh vnto that Gulfe arriue,
   Where streame more violent and greedy growes:
   Then he with all his puissance doth striue
   To strike his oares, and mightily doth driue
   The hollow vessell through the threatfull waue,
   Which gaping wide, to swallow them aliue,
   In th'huge abysse of his engulfing graue,
Doth rore at them in vaine, and with great terror raue.

6

They passing by, that griesly mouth doe see,
   Sucking the seas into his entralles deepe,   *entralles* bowels (but cf. 'enthrall')
   That seem'd more horrible then hell to bee,
   Or that darke dreadfull hole of *Tartare* steepe,
   Through which the damned ghosts doen often creepe
   Backe to the world, bad liuers to torment: *liuers* living people
   But nought that falles into this direfull deepe,
   Ne that approcheth nigh the wide descent,
May backe returne, but is condemned to be drent.   *drent* drowned

back to the book's earlier preoccupation with the Aristotelian account of all virtue as a mean course taken between two (vicious) extremes; see *FQ* II.ii.12–46, and the *Nicomachean Ethics*, 2.6–9.
   4.2 Magnes stone,] Spenser's figuration of the Rock of Reproach as a loadstone (L *magnes*) probably echoes a similar seacoast peril in Lord Berners's *Huon of Bourdeux* (c. 1530), ch. 108, where Huon speaks with Judas Iscariot before navigating between a 'perelous Goulfe' and 'the rock of the adamant'.

7

On th'other side, they saw that perilous Rocke,
   Threatning it selfe on them to ruinate,
   On whose sharpe clifts the ribs of vessels broke,
   And shiuered ships, which had bene wrecked late,
   Yet stuck, with carkasses exanimate   *exanimate* lifeless, inanimate
   Of such, as hauing all their substance spent
   In wanton ioyes, and lustes intemperate,
   Did afterwards make shipwracke violent,
Both of their life, and fame for euer fowly blent.   *blent* polluted

8

For thy, this hight *The Rocke of* vile *Reproch*,   *hight* is called
   A daungerous and detestable place,
   To which nor fish nor fowle did once approch,
   But yelling Meawes, with Seagulles hoarse and bace,   *meawes* common or herring gulls
   And Cormoyrants, with birds of rauenous race,
   Which still sate waiting on that wastfull clift,
   For spoyle of wretches, whose vnhappie cace,
   After lost credite and consumed thrift,
At last them driuen hath to this despairefull drift.

9

The Palmer seeing them in safetie past,
   Thus said; behold th'ensamples in our sights,
   Of lustfull luxurie and thriftlesse wast:
   What now is left of miserable wights,
   Which spent their looser daies in lewd delights,
   But shame and sad reproch, here to be red,
   By these rent reliques, speaking their ill plights?   *rent reliques* broken remains
   Let all that liue, hereby be counselled,
To shunne *Rocke of Reproch*, and it as death to dred.

10

So forth they rowed, and that *Ferryman*
   With his stiffe oares did brush the sea so strong,
   That the hoare waters from his frigot ran,
   And the light bubbles daunced all along,
   Whiles the salt brine out of the billowes sprong.
   At last farre off they many Islands spy,
   On euery side floting the floods emong:
   Then said the knight, Loe I the land descry,   *descry* see, catch sight of
Therefore old Syre thy course do thereunto apply.

11
That may not be, said then the *Ferryman*
  Least we vnweeting hap to be fordonne: *fordonne* undone, destroyed
  For those same Islands, seeming now and than,
  Are not firme lande, nor any certein wonne, *wonne* dwelling place
  But straggling plots, which to and fro do ronne
  In the wide waters: therefore are they hight
  The *wandring Islands*. Therefore doe them shonne;
  For they haue oft drawne many a wandring wight
Into most deadly daunger and distressed plight.

12
Yet well they seeme to him, that farre doth vew,
  Both faire and fruitfull, and the ground dispred
  With grassie greene of delectable hew,
  And the tall trees with leaues apparelled,
  Are deckt with blossomes dyde in white and red,
  That mote the passengers thereto allure; *mote* may, must
  But whosoeuer once hath fastened
  His foot thereon, may neuer it recure, *recure* recover
But wandreth euer more vncertein and vnsure.

13
As th'Isle of *Delos* whylome men report *whylome* sometimes
  Amid th'*Aegæan* sea long time did stray,
  Ne made for shipping any certaine port,
  Till that *Latona* traueiling that way,
  Flying from *Iunoes* wrath and hard assay,
  Of her faire twins was there deliuered,
  Which afterwards did rule the night and day;
  Thenceforth it firmely was established,
And for *Apolloes* honor highly herried. *herried* glorified, praised

14
They to him hearken, as beseemeth meete, *hearken to* obey
  And passe on forward: so their way does ly, *as beseemeth meete* as is proper

12.5 white and red,] The traditional, courtly heraldry of virtue and modesty; cf. Shakespeare, *The Rape of Lucrece*, ll. 50–71. The uncertainty of these islands (cf. line 9 of this stanza) may suggest the epistemological crisis consequent on making manners – the red and white of blushing courtly modesty – the basis of temperance. Because manners can be cultivated and feigned, they may not be a reliable sign of true virtue.
Stanza 13 th'Isle of *Delos*] Niobe, Queen of Thebes, recites the history of Latona (or Leto) in Ovid, *Metamorphoses*, 6.184 ff.. Harried by Juno across the earth, the Titan Latona was offered harbour on the wandering island of Delos, where she was subsequently delivered of the gods Apollo and Diana. Thereafter the island became fixed in its current position, among the Cyclades.

That one of those same Islands, which doe fleet *fleet* flit, dart about
   In the wide sea, they needes must passen by,
   Which seemd so sweet and pleasant to the eye,
   That it would tempt a man to touchen there:
   Vpon the banck they sitting did espy
   A daintie damzell, dressing of her heare,
By whom a litle skippet floting did appeare. *skippet* a little skiff or boat

15

She them espying, loud to them can call, *can* began to
   Bidding them nigher draw vnto the shore;
   For she had cause to busie them withall; *to . . . withall* with which to busy them
   And therewith loudly laught: But nathemore *therewith* on that account
   Would they once turne, but kept on as afore:
   Which when she saw, she left her lockes vndight, *vndight* undressed
   And running to her boat withouten ore,
   From the departing land it launched light,
And after them did driue with all her power and might.

16

Whom ouertaking, she in merry sort
   Them gan to bord, and purpose diuersly, *bord* address, engage in conversation
   Now faining dalliance and wanton sport, *purpose* converse, discourse
   Now throwing forth lewd words immodestly;
   Till that the Palmer gan full bitterly
   Her to rebuke, for being loose and light:
   Which not abiding, but more scornefully
   Scoffing at him, that did her iustly wite, *wite* blame, reproach
She turnd her bote about, and from them rowed quite.

17

That was the wanton *Phædria*, which late
   Did ferry him ouer the *Idle lake*:
   Whom nought regarding, they kept on their gate, *gate* way, path
   And all her vaine allurements did forsake,
   When them the wary Boateman thus bespake;
   Here now behoueth vs well to auyse,
   And of our safetie good heede to take; *safetie* (trisyllabic)
   For here before a perlous passage lyes,
Where many Mermayds haunt, making false melodies.

17.1–2 the wanton *Phædria* . . . *Idle lake*:] Phædria, also known as 'immodest Merth', appears on a skiff or ferry that gives Guyon passage over a 'perlous foord' (II.vi.19.9) in canto vi, here called the '*Idle lake*'. Along the way she lands him on a pleasant island, offers him 'dissolute delights', and then occasions his strife with the knight Cymochles.

Selections from the Poem 55

18
But by the way, there is a great Quicksand,
   And a whirlepoole of hidden ieopardy,
   Therefore, Sir Palmer, keepe an euen hand;
   For twixt them both the narrow way doth ly.
   Scarse had he said, when hard at hand they spy
   That quicksand nigh with water couered;
   But by the checked waue they did descry   *checked* impeded
   It plaine, and by the sea discoloured:
It called was the quicksand of *Vnthriftyhed*.

19
They passing by, a goodly Ship did see,
   Laden from far with precious merchandize,
   And brauely furnished, as ship might bee,
   Which through great disauenture, or mesprize,   *mesprize* mistake (cf. 'misprision')
   Her selfe had runne into that hazardize;   *hazardize* perilous situation
   Whose mariners and merchants with much toyle,
   Labour'd in vaine, to haue recur'd their prize,
   And the rich wares to saue from pitteous spoyle,
But neither toyle nor trauell might her backe recoyle.   *recoyle* drive, force back

20
On th'other side they see that perilous Poole,
   That called was the *Whirlepoole of decay*,
   In which full many had with haplesse doole   *haplesse* luckless *doole* grief, sorrow
   Beene suncke, of whom no memorie did stay:
   Whose circled waters rapt with whirling sway,   *rapt* swept along *sway* motion, force
   Like to a restlesse wheele, still running round,
   Did couet, as they passed by that way,   *couet* desire
   To draw the boate within the vtmost bound
Of his wide *Labyrinth*, and then to haue them dround.

21
But th'heedfull Boateman strongly forth did stretch
   His brawnie armes, and all his body straine,
   That th'vtmost sandy breach they shortly fetch,   *fetch* reach
   Whiles the dred daunger does behind remaine.

Stanzas 18–33] More loosely Odyssean perils beset the knight of temperance. The whirlpool and quicksand (stanzas 18–20) reprise the Gulf of Greediness and the Rock of Reproach, above (stanzas 3–9); the storm and sea monsters (stanzas 21–6) recall elements of Odysseus' Aeolian storm and visit to Circe's island; and both the 'dolefull Mayd' and mermaids (stanzas 27–9, 30–3) clearly imitate Odysseus' encounter with the Sirens (*Odyssey*, 12.165–200). The recapitulative pattern of these dangers suggests the need for close comparison, and differentiation, between paired elements – a distinctively Spenserian allegorical device.

Suddeine they see from midst of all the Maine, *maine* sea, open ocean
   The surging waters like a mountaine rise,
   And the great sea puft vp with proud disdaine,
   To swell aboue the measure of his guise, *guise* usual manner
As threatning to deuoure all, that his powre despise.

22

The waues come rolling, and the billowes rore
   Outragiously, as they enraged were,
   Or wrathfull *Neptune* did them driue before
   His whirling charet, for exceeding feare:
   For not one puffe of wind there did appeare,
   That all the three thereat woxe much afrayd, *woxe* grew
   Vnweeting, what such horrour straunge did reare. *vnweeting* not knowing
   Eftsoones they saw an hideous hoast arrayd,
Of huge Sea monsters, such as liuing sence dismayd.

23

Most vgly shapes, and horrible aspects,
   Such as Dame Nature selfe mote feare to see, *mote* must
   Or shame, that euer should so fowle defects
   From her most cunning hand escaped bee;
   All dreadfull pourtraicts of deformitee:
   Spring-headed *Hydraes*, and sea-shouldring Whales,
   Great whirlpooles, which all fishes make to flee,
   Bright Scolopendraes, arm'd with siluer scales,
Mighty *Monoceros*, with immeasured tayles.

24

The dreadfull Fish, that hath deseru'd the name
   Of Death, and like him lookes in dreadfull hew,
   The griesly Wasserman, that makes his game
   The flying ships with swiftnesse to pursew,
   The horrible Sea-satyre, that doth shew
   His fearefull face in time of greatest storme,
   Huge *Ziffius*, whom Mariners eschew

Stanzas 22–4 huge Sea monsters . . .] The 'spring-headed' hydra of Lerna was killed by Hercules (see Apollodorus, *The Library*, 2.5.2), but the name was conferred on a range of fish and serpents thought or supposed to live in the sea. The scolopendra was a mythical sea-beast supposedly capable of releasing itself from a hook, while the monoceros (Gr, 'single-horned') probably signified an outsize narwhal or swordfish. Mors marine, or 'death' (via L *mors*, 'death'), was another early name for the walrus; rosmarine was another alternative for the same creature, from L *rosmarus*. The ziffius (or xiphias) was a swordfish (from Gr ξίφος, 'sword'), while the wasserman and sea-satyr (or merman) are fantastic, borrowed from the descriptions in Konrad Gesner's *Historia animalium* (Zurich, 1551–8).

No lesse, then rockes, (as trauellers informe,)
And greedy *Rosmarines* with visages deforme.

25

All these, and thousand thousands many more,
   And more deformed Monsters thousand fold,
   With dreadfull noise, and hollow rombling rore,
   Came rushing in the fomy waues enrold,
   Which seem'd to fly for feare, them to behold:
   Ne wonder, if these did the knight appall;
   For all that here on earth we dreadfull hold,
   Be but as bugs to fearen babes withall,
Compared to the creatures in the seas entrall.

26

Feare nought, (then said the Palmer well auiz'd;)
   For these same Monsters are not these in deed,
   But are into these fearefull shapes disguiz'd
   By that same wicked witch, to worke vs dreed,   *worke ... dreed* cause us fear
   And draw from on this iourney to proceede.   *draw from ... proceede* prevent us from
   Tho lifting vp his vertuous staffe on hye,   proceeding *tho* then
   He smote the sea, which calmed was with speed,
   And all that dreadfull Armie fast gan flye
Into great *Tethys* bosome, where they hidden lye.

27

Quit from that daunger, forth their course they kept,   *quit* delivered
   And as they went, they heard a ruefull cry
   Of one, that wayld and pittifully wept,
   That through the sea resounding plaints did fly:
   At last they in an Island did espy
   A seemely Maiden, sitting by the shore,
   That with great sorrow and sad agony,
   Seemed some great misfortune to deplore,
And lowd to them for succour called euermore.

28

Which *Guyon* hearing, streight his Palmer bad,
   To stere the boate towards that dolefull Mayd,

26.9 Tethys bosome,] Tethys, daughter of Uranus and the Earth, wife of Oceanus, was often used by classical poets as a metonymy for the sea.
    Stanzas 27–33 a ruefull cry ...] Spenser's double account of the *Odyssey*'s sirens sees them not only as seductive and fatal singers, but also as damsels in distress – fitting for his romance context. These sirens thus represent an external as well as a psychological peril: to take pity on another's plight is to relent one's own rigour in and toward oneself.

That he might know, and ease her sorrow sad:
Who him auizing better, to him sayd;
Faire Sir, be not displeasd, if disobayd:
For ill it were to hearken to her cry;
For she is inly nothing ill apayd,   *inly . . . apayd* not at all distressed
But onely womanish fine forgery,   within (herself)
Your stubborne hart t'affect with fraile infirmity.

29

To which when she your courage hath inclind
  Through foolish pitty, then her guilefull bayt
  She will embosome deeper in your mind,
  And for your ruine at the last awayt.
  The knight was ruled, and the Boateman strayt
  Held on his course with stayed stedfastnesse,
  Ne euer shruncke, ne euer sought to bayt   *bayt* rest
  His tyred armes for toylesome wearinesse,
But with his oares did sweepe the watry wildernesse.

30

And now they nigh approched to the sted,
  Where as those Mermayds dwelt: it was a still
  And calmy bay, on th'one side sheltered
  With the brode shadow of an hoarie hill,
  On th'other side an high rocke toured still,
  That twixt them both a pleasaunt port they made,
  And did like an halfe Theatre fulfill:
  There those fiue sisters had continuall trade,
And vsd to bath themselues in that deceiptfull shade.

31

They were faire Ladies, till they fondly striu'd
  With th'*Heliconian* maides for maistery;
  Of whom they ouer-comen, were depriu'd
  Of their proud beautie, and th'one moyity   *moyity* half (of their bodies)
  Transform'd to fish, for their bold surquedry,   *surquedry* pride, arrogance
  But th'vpper halfe their hew retained still,
  And their sweet skill in wonted melody;

31.2 th'*Heliconian* maides] The nine muses. The mythic tradition gives many differing accounts of the origins of the Sirens. For the story of their singing contest with the muses, Spenser is indebted to Pausanias' *Description of Greece*, 9.34.3, and the Athenian comic poet Crobylus, cited by Conti, *Mythologiae*, 7.13. The Sirens are usually depicted as hybrids not of fish and women, but of birds and women; see e.g. Ovid, *Metamorphoses*, 5.552–62.

Which euer after they abusd to ill,   *to ill* for evil
T'allure weake trauellers, whom gotten they did kill.

32
So now to *Guyon*, as he passed by,
   Their pleasaunt tunes they sweetly thus applide;
   O thou faire sonne of gentle Faery,
   Thou art in mighty armes most magnifide
   Aboue all knights, that euer battell tride,
   O turne thy rudder hither-ward a while:
   Here may thy storme-bet vessell safely ride;
   This is the Port of rest from troublous toyle,
The worlds sweet In, from paine & wearisome turmoyle.

33
With that the rolling sea resounding soft,
   In his big base them fitly answered,   *base* ground; bass voice
   And on the rocke the waues breaking aloft,
   A solemne Meane vnto them measured,   *meane* the middle voice in a trio, alto
   The whiles sweet *Zephirus* lowd whisteled
   His treble, a straunge kinde of harmony;   *treble* orig. the third, top voice
   Which *Guyons* senses softly tickeled,
   That he the boateman bad row easily,
And let him heare some part of their rare melody.

34
But him the Palmer from that vanity,
   With temperate aduice discounselled,
   That they it past, and shortly gan descry
   The land, to which their course they leueled;
   When suddeinly a grosse fog ouer spred
   With his dull vapour all that desert has,
   And heauens chearefull face enueloped,
   That all things one, and one as nothing was,
And this great Vniuerse seemd one confused mas.

35
Thereat they greatly were dismayd, ne wist   *wist* knew
   How to direct their way in darkenesse wide,
   But feard to wander in that wastfull mist,
   For tombling into mischiefe vnespide.
   Worse is the daunger hidden, then descride.

33.5 Zephirus] The west wind, and harbinger of calm weather.

Suddeinly an innumerable flight
Of harmefull fowles about them fluttering, cride,
And with their wicked wings them oft did smight,
And sore annoyed, groping in that griesly night.

36
Euen all the nation of vnfortunate
 And fatall birds about them flocked were,
 Such as by nature men abhorre and hate,
 The ill-faste Owle, deaths dreadfull messengere,
 The hoars Night-rauen, trump of dolefull drere,   *dolefull drere* sad gloom
 The lether-winged Bat, dayes enimy,
 The ruefull Strich, still waiting on the bere,   *strich* screech-owl
 The Whistler shrill, that who so heares, doth dy,   *whistler* curlew
The hellish Harpies, prophets of sad destiny.

37
All those, and all that else does horrour breed,
 About them flew, and fild their sayles with feare:
 Yet stayd they not, but forward did proceed,
 Whiles th'one did row, and th'other stifly steare;
 Till that at last the weather gan to cleare,
 And the faire land it selfe did plainly show.
 Said then the Palmer, Lo where does appeare
 The sacred soile, where all our perils grow;
Therefore, Sir knight, your ready armes about you throw.

38
He hearkned, and his armes about him tooke,
 The whiles the nimble boate so well her sped,
 That with her crooked keele the land she strooke,
 Then forth the noble *Guyon* sallied,
 And his sage Palmer, that him gouerned;
 But th'other by his boate behind did stay.
 They marched fairly forth, of nought ydred,
 Both firmely armd for euery hard assay,
With constancy and care, gainst daunger and dismay.

Stanzas 35–6 an innumerable flight] The birds who attack Guyon and the Palmer here may owe something to Virgil's description of the Harpies (cf. 36.9, below), bird-women famous for molesting Phineus, King of Thrace; set hungry before a table spread lavishly with food, Phineus was repeatedly and forever interrupted by the Harpies, who continuously stole his meal and fouled his table. See Apollonius of Rhodes, *Argonautica*, ll. 178–499, and Virgil, *Aeneid*, 3.209–57.

 36.9 hellish Harpies ... destiny.] The Harpies attack Aeneas and his men on their entry into hell, where Celaeno, their leader, relates to Aeneas his ultimate 'sad destiny' in Italy; see *Aeneid*, 3.219–57.

39

Ere long they heard an hideous bellowing
  Of many beasts, that roard outrageously,
  As if that hungers point, or *Venus* sting
  Had them enraged with fell surquedry;
  Yet nought they feard, but past on hardily,
  Vntill they came in vew of those wild beasts:
  Who all attonce, gaping full greedily,
  And rearing fiercely their vpstarting crests,
Ran towards, to deuoure those vnexpected guests.

40

But soone as they approcht with deadly threat,
  The Palmer ouer them his staffe vpheld,
  His mighty staffe, that could all charmes defeat:
  Eftsoones their stubborne courages were queld,
  And high aduaunced crests downe meekely feld,
  In stead of fraying, they them selues did feare,   *fraying* frightening (others)
  And trembled, as them passing they beheld:
  Such wondrous powre did in that staffe appeare,
All monsters to subdew to him, that did it beare.

41

Of that same wood it fram'd was cunningly,
  Of which *Caduceus* whilome was made,
  Caduceus the rod of *Mercury*,
  With which he wonts the *Stygian* realmes inuade,
  Through ghastly horrour, and eternall shade;
  Th'infernall feends with it he can asswage,
  And *Orcus* tame, whom nothing can perswade,
  And rule the *Furyes*, when they most do rage:
Such vertue in his staffe had eke this Palmer sage.

Stanzas 39–41 many beasts ...] The last episode before arrival at the bower imitates elements of Odysseus' experience at Circe's island – a fitting conclusion, in Guyon's schematic reversal of Odyssean errancy. The transformation of the Circean Acrasia's beasts back into men, however, is left until the end of the canto (stanzas 85–7). The Palmer's quelling of Acrasia's beasts imitates a parallel scene in Tasso's *Gerusalemme Liberata* (15.49–52), where Ubaldo pacifies the enchantress Armida's hordes of Hircanian and African beasts.
  41.3 Caduceus] Hermes, or Mercury, sometimes known as *psychopompos* (Gr, 'soul-guider'), guided dying souls to Hades (the '*Stygian*' realmes', lying around the River Styx) with his rod, the caduceus. See Homer, *Odyssey*, 5.47–9; Virgil, *Aeneid*, 4.238–46; and Horace, *Odes*, 1.5.
  41.7 Orcus] An epithet of Hades (Pluto), god of hell, but sometimes also used of the ferryman of the Styx, Charon; sometimes (like the name Hades) it was also used of hell itself.
  41.8 the Furyes,] Or Eumenides, daughters of disputed parentage, by name Tisiphone, Megara and Alecto. As ministers of the gods, they visited vengeance on mortals, punishing them for their crimes with madness or misfortune on earth, or in hell with eternal torments.

42

Thence passing forth, they shortly do arriue,
   Whereas the Bowre of *Blisse* was situate;
   A place pickt out by choice of best aliue,
   That natures worke by art can imitate:
   In which what euer in this worldly state
   Is sweet, and pleasing vnto liuing sense,
   Or that may dayntiest fantasie aggrate,   *aggrate* please, satisfy
   Was poured forth with plentifull dispence,   *dispence* expenditure, purveyance
And made there to abound with lauish affluence.

43

Goodly it was enclosed round about,
   Aswell their entred guestes to keepe within,
   As those vnruly beasts to hold without;
   Yet was the sence thereof but weake and thin;
   Nought feard their force, that fortilage to win,   *fortilage* fortress
   But wisedomes powre, and temperaunces might,
   By which the mightiest things efforced bin: *efforced* won by force
   And eke the gate was wrought of substaunce light,
Rather for pleasure, then for battery or fight.

44

Yt framed was of precious yuory,
   That seemd a worke of admirable wit;
   And therein all the famous history
   Of *Iason* and *Medæa* was ywrit;
   Her mighty charmes, her furious louing fit,
   His goodly conquest of the golden fleece,
   His falsed faith, and loue too lightly flit,
   The wondred *Argo*, which in venturous peece
First through the *Euxine* seas bore all the flowr of *Greece*.

Stanzas 42–52 the Bowre of *Blisse*] Guyon's and the Palmer's initial entry into the bower evokes the tradition of the *locus amoenus* ('sweet' or 'blessed place'), as well as that of the *hortus conclusus* ('enclosed garden'). Spenser's models are legion; among the most important are Circe's island in Homer's *Odyssey* (7.112–32), Alcina's island in Ariosto's *Orlando Furioso* (6.19–25), and Armida's island in Tasso's *Gerusalemme Liberata* (15.53–16.16).

Stanzas 44–5 the famous history Of *Iason* and *Medæa*] The rightful heir of the kingdom of Iolchos, Jason was sent after the golden fleece of Colchis by his usurping uncle Pelias; with him he took a famous band of bold young men. During the expedition he atrracted the notice of, and fell in love with, the Colchian princess and enchantress Medea, and achieved the quest only through her help. They afterwards married. The story of Jason's infidelity and Medea's revenge is related most famously in Euripides' tragedy, *Medea*; but see also Apollonius of Rhodes, *Argonautica*, and Ovid, *Metamorphoses* 7.1–403. In Spenser's immediate source, Tasso's *Gerusalemme Liberata* (16.2–7), the gates depict the loves of Hercules and Iole, and Antony and Cleopatra.

Selections from the Poem 63

45
Ye might haue seene the frothy billowes fry   *fry* seethe, foam
  Vnder the ship, as thorough them she went,
  That seemd the waues were into yuory,
  Or yuory into the waues were sent;
  And other where the snowy substaunce sprent   *sprent* sprinkled
  With vermell, like the boyes bloud therein shed,   *vermell* vermilion or scarlet
  A piteous spectacle did represent,
  And otherwhiles with gold besprinkeled;
Yt seemd th'enchaunted flame, which did *Creusa* wed.

46
All this, and more might in that goodly gate
  Be red; that euer open stood to all,   *red* deciphered, discovered
  Which thither came: but in the Porch there sate
  A comely personage of stature tall,
  And semblaunce pleasing, more then naturall,
  That trauellers to him seemd to entize;
  His looser garment to the ground did fall,
  And flew about his heeles in wanton wize,
Not fit for speedy pace, or manly exercize.

47
They in that place him *Genius* did call:
  Not that celestiall powre, to whom the care
  Of life, and generation of all
  That liues, pertaines in charge particulare,   *in ... particulare* as a special duty
  Who wondrous things concerning our welfare,
  And straunge phantomes doth let vs oft forsee,
  And oft of secret ill bids vs beware:
  That is our Selfe, whom though we do not see,
Yet each doth in him selfe it well perceiue to bee.

45.9 Creusa] After being put aside by Jason, Medea – vengeful at her marginalisation – gave his new bride Creusa, daughter of Creon, King of Corinth, a poisoned garment. This wedding gift Creusa received as she was going to meet Jason, but instead she burst into flames the moment she put it on, and died in agony. The 'boyes bloud' sprinkled on the gates is that of Mermerus and Pheres, Medea's sons by Jason, whom she killed; see Euripides, *Medea*, ll. 1136 ff; and Apollodorus, *The Library*, 1.9.28.

47.2–9 Not that celestiall powre ... to bee.] The nature of the genius, *daemon*, or *Agdistes* is discussed at length in Plutarch's dialogue, *De genio Socratis* ('On the daemon of Socrates'), *Moralia*, 7, where Plutarch calls it a guiding spirit, sent to lead great souls toward truth and tranquillity. Other classical writers had suggested that (as for Marlowe) each soul was attended by two genii, one good and the other evil; it is this latter kind that guards the porch of the bower.

48

Therefore a God him sage Antiquity
   Did wisely make, and good *Agdistes* call:
   But this same was to that quite contrary,
   The foe of life, that good enuyes to all,
   That secretly doth vs procure to fall,
   Through guilefull semblaunts, which he makes vs see.
   He of this Gardin had the gouernall,   *gouernall* government, sovereignty
   And Pleasures porter was deuizd to bee,
Holding a staffe in hand for more formalitee.

49

With diuerse flowres he daintily was deckt,
   And strowed round about, and by his side
   A mighty Mazer bowle of wine was set,   *mazer* drinking bowl
   As if it had to him bene sacrifide;   *sacrifide* offered as a sacrifice
   Wherewith all new-come guests he gratifide:
   So did he eke Sir *Guyon* passing by:
   But he his idle curtesie defide,
   And ouerthrew his bowle disdainfully;
And broke his staffe, with which he charmed semblants sly.

50

Thus being entred, they behold around
   A large and spacious plaine, on euery side
   Strowed with pleasauns, whose faire grassy ground
   Mantled with greene, and goodly beautifide
   With all the ornaments of *Floraes* pride,
   Wherewith her mother Art, as halfe in scorne
   Of niggard Nature, like a pompous bride
   Did decke her, and too lauishly adorne,
When forth from virgin bowre she comes in th'early morne.

51

Thereto the Heauens alwayes Iouiall,   *Iouiall* marked by Jupiter's
   Lookt on them louely, still in stedfast state,   influence, joyful, merry
   Ne suffred storme nor frost on them to fall,
   Their tender buds or leaues to violate,
   Nor scorching heat, nor cold intemperate

    48.2 good Agdistes] Pausanias narrates the history of the *daemon* Agdistis, a powerful hermaphroditic spirit that sprang from the seed of Zeus, unwittingly spilled during sleep upon the earth. The gods, fearing his power, castrated him (*Description of Greece*, 7.17.10). Spenser almost certainly found the name, along with other details, in Conti's *Mythologiae*, 4.3.
    50.5 Floraes pride,] Flowers. On Flora, goddess of flowers, see I.i.48.9n, above.

T'afflict the creatures, which therein did dwell,
But the milde aire with season moderate
Gently attempred, and disposd so well,
That still it breathed forth sweet spirit & holesome smell.   *spirit* (monosyllabic)

52

More sweet and holesome, then the pleasaunt hill
  Of *Rhodope*, on which the Nimphe, that bore
  A gyaunt babe, her selfe for griefe did kill;
  Or the Thessalian *Tempe*, where of yore
  Faire *Daphne Phœbus* hart with loue did gore;
  Or *Ida*, where the Gods lou'd to repaire,
  When euer they their heauenly bowres forlore;
  Or sweet *Parnasse*, the haunt of Muses faire;   *haunt* favoured resort, retreat
Of *Eden* selfe, if ought with *Eden* mote compaire.

53

Much wondred *Guyon* at the faire aspect
  Of that sweet place, yet suffred no delight
  To sincke into his sence, nor mind affect,
  But passed forth, and lookt still forward right,
  Bridling his will, and maistering his might:
  Till that he came vnto another gate,
  No gate, but like one, being goodly dight   *dight* furnished, decked
  With boughes and braunches, which did broad dilate
Their clasping armes, in wanton wreathings intricate.

54

So fashioned a Porch with rare deuice,
  Archt ouer head with an embracing vine,
  Whose bounches hanging downe, seemd to entice
  All passers by, to tast their lushious wine,
  And did themselues into their hands incline,
  As freely offering to be gathered:
  Some deepe empurpled as the *Hyacint*,
  Some as the Rubine, laughing sweetly red,
Some like faire Emeraudes, not yet well ripened.

    52.1–3 Rhodope, on which the Nimphe,] A large mountain in Thrace. In the *Metamorphoses* (6.87–9), Ovid records how Rhodope and her husband, Haemus, King of Thrace, compared themselves to Zeus (Jove) and Hera (Juno), and were transformed into mountains for their pride.
    52.4–5 Thessalian Tempe,] A valley in Thessaly, south of Mount Olympus, and proverbial among poets for its idyllic beauty. Ovid narrates Apollo's love for Daphne in the *Metamorphoses*, 1.452 ff.
    52.6–7 Ida,] Ida, a mountain or ridge of mountains near Troy, was the scene of Paris' judgment between Hera (Juno), Athene (Minerva) and Aphrodite (Venus); see Ovid, *Heroides*, 16.53 ff.
    52.8 sweet Parnasse,] Mount Parnassus, a tall mountain north of the Gulf of Corinth, and sacred to the Muses.

55

And them amongst, some were of burnisht gold,
  So made by art, to beautifie the rest,
  Which did themselues emongst the leaues enfold,
  As lurking from the vew of couetous guest,
  That the weake bowes, with so rich load opprest,
  Did bow adowne, as ouer-burdened.
  Vnder that Porch a comely dame did rest,
  Clad in faire weeds, but fowle disordered,
And garments loose, that seemd vnmeet for womanhed.

56

In her left hand a Cup of gold she held,
  And with her right the riper fruit did reach,
  Whose sappy liquor, that with fulnesse sweld,
  Into her cup she scruzd, with daintie breach
  Of her fine fingers, without fowle empeach,
  That so faire wine-presse made the wine more sweet:
  Thereof she vsd to giue to drinke to each,
  Whom passing by she happened to meet:
It was her guise, all Straungers goodly so to greet.

57

So she to *Guyon* offred it to tast;
  Who taking it out of her tender hond,
  The cup to ground did violently cast,   *violently* (tetrasyllabic)
  That all in peeces it was broken fond,
  And with the liquor stained all the lond:
  Whereat *Excesse* exceedingly was wroth,
  Yet n'ote the same amend, ne yet withstond,   *n'ote* could not
  But suffered him to passe, all were she loth;
Who not regarding her displeasure forward goth.

58

There the most daintie Paradise on ground,
  It selfe doth offer to his sober eye,
  In which all pleasures plenteously abound,
  And none does others happinesse enuye:
  The painted flowres, the trees vpshooting hye,
  The dales for shade, the hilles for breathing space,
  The trembling groues, the Christall running by;
  And that, which all faire workes doth most aggrace,   *aggrace* favour, ornament
The art, which all that wrought, appeared in no place.

58.8–9 And that . . . no place.] Translating Tasso: 'E quel, che 'l bello o 'l caro accresce all' opre, | L' arte, che tutto fa, nulla si scopre' (*Gerusalemme Liberata*, 16.9).

59

One would haue thought, (so cunningly, the rude,
   And scorned parts were mingled with the fine,)
   That nature had for wantonesse ensude   *ensude* followed, imitated
   Art, and that Art at nature did repine;
   So striuing each th'other to vndermine,
   Each did the others worke more beautifie;
   So diff'ring both in willes, agreed in fine: *in fine* in their end, object
   So all agreed through sweete diuersitie,
This Gardin to adorne with all varietie.

60

And in the midst of all, a fountaine stood,
   Of richest substaunce, that on earth might bee,
   So pure and shiny, that the siluer flood
   Through euery channell running one might see;
   Most goodly it with curious imageree
   Was ouer-wrought, and shapes of naked boyes,
   Of which some seemd with liuely iollitee,
   To fly about, playing their wanton toyes,
Whilest others did them selues embay in liquid ioyes.   *embay* bathe, drench

61

And ouer all, of purest gold was spred,
   A trayle of yuie in his natiue hew:
   For the rich mettall was so coloured,
   That wight, who did not well auis'd it vew,
   Would surely deeme it to be yuie trew:
   Low his lasciuious armes adown did creepe,
   That themselues dipping in the siluer dew,
   Their fleecy flowres they tenderly did steepe,
Which drops of Christall seemd for wantones to weepe.

62

Infinit streames continually did well
   Out of this fountaine, sweet and faire to see,
   The which into an ample lauer fell,   *lauer* basin (of a fountain)
   And shortly grew to so great quantitie,
   That like a little lake it seemd to bee;
   Whose depth exceeded not three cubits hight,
   That through the waues one might the bottom see,

Stanzas 60–9 a fountaine stood ...] The fountain with its wanton maidens closely imitates the Tassonian original, with its '*due donzellette garrule e lascive*'; see *Gerusalemme Liberata*, 15.58–66.

All pau'd beneath with Iaspar shining bright,
That seemd the fountaine in that sea did sayle vpright.

63
And all the margent round about was set,   *margent* margin, perimeter
  With shady Laurell trees, thence to defend   *defend* deflect, keep out
  The sunny beames, which on the billowes bet,
  And those which therein bathed, mote offend.
  As *Guyon* hapned by the same to wend,   *wend* go, journey
  Two naked Damzelles he therein espyde,
  Which therein bathing, seemed to contend,
  And wrestle wantonly, ne car'd to hyde,
Their dainty parts from vew of any, which them eyde.

64
Sometimes the one would lift the other quight
  Aboue the waters, and then downe againe
  Her plong, as ouer maistered by might,
  Where both awhile would couered remaine,
  And each the other from to rise restraine;
  The whiles their snowy limbes, as through a vele,
  So through the Christall waues appeared plaine:
  Then suddeinly both would themselues vnhele,   *vnhele* uncover, display
And th'amarous sweet spoiles to greedy eyes reuele.

65
As that faire Starre, the messenger of morne,
  His deawy face out of the sea doth reare:
  Or as the *Cyprian* goddesse, newly borne
  Of th'Oceans fruitfull froth, did first appeare:
  Such seemed they, and so their yellow heare
  Christalline humour dropped downe apace.
  Whom such when *Guyon* saw, he drew him neare,
  And somewhat gan relent his earnest pace,
His stubborne brest gan secret pleasaunce to embrace.

66
The wanton Maidens him espying, stood
  Gazing a while at his vnwonted guise;
  Then th'one her selfe low ducked in the flood,

  65.1 that faire Starre ... of morne,] Phosphorus or Eosphorus: the planet Venus as the herald of morning. See I.ii.6.6–7n., above.
  65.3 the *Cyprian* goddesse,] Aphrodite, or Venus, born from the foam of the sea near the island of Cyprus (or, for other poets and mythographers, Cythera).

Abasht, that her a straunger did avise:
But th'other rather higher did arise,
And her two lilly paps aloft displayd,
And all, that might his melting hart entise
To her delights, she vnto him bewrayd:
The rest hid vnderneath, him more desirous made.

67

With that, the other likewise vp arose,
   And her faire lockes, which formerly were bownd
   Vp in one knot, she low adowne did lose:
   Which flowing long and thick, her cloth'd arownd,
   And th'yuorie in golden mantle gownd:
   So that faire spectacle from him was reft,
   Yet that, which reft it, no lesse faire was fownd:
   So hid in lockes and waues from lookers theft,
Nought but her louely face she for his looking left.

68

Withall she laughed, and she blusht withall,   *withall* moreover, in addition
   That blushing to her laughter gaue more grace,
   And laughter to her blushing, as did fall:
   Now when they spide the knight to slacke his pace,
   Them to behold, and in his sparkling face
   The secret signes of kindled lust appeare,
   Their wanton meriments they did encrease,
   And to him beckned, to approch more neare,
And shewd him many sights, that courage cold could reare.

69

On which when gazing him the Palmer saw,
   He much rebukt those wandring eyes of his,
   And counseld well, him forward thence did draw.
   Now are they come nigh to the *Bowre of blis*
   Of her fond fauorites so nam'd amis:
   When thus the Palmer; Now Sir, well auise;
   For here the end of all our trauell is: *trauell* travail, toil
   Here wonnes *Acrasia*, whom we must surprise,   *wonnes* dwells, lives
Else she will slip away, and all our drift despise.   *drift* intention, meaning; plot, design

70

Eftsoones they heard a most melodious sound,
   Of all that mote delight a daintie eare,
   Such as attonce might not on liuing ground,   *attonce* simultaneously, together

Saue in this Paradise, be heard elswhere:
Right hard it was, for wight, which did it heare,
To read, what manner musicke that mote bee:
For all that pleasing is to liuing eare,
Was there consorted in one harmonee,
Birdes, voyces, instruments, windes, waters, all agree.

71

The ioyous birdes shrouded in chearefull shade,
  Their notes vnto the voyce attempred sweet;
Th'Angelicall soft trembling voyces made
To th'instruments diuine respondence meet:
The siluer sounding instruments did meet
With the base murmure of the waters fall:
The waters fall with difference discreet,
  Now soft, now loud, vnto the wind did call:
The gentle warbling wind low answered to all.

72

There, whence that Musick seemed heard to bee,
  Was the faire Witch her selfe now solacing,
With a new Louer, whom through sorceree
And witchcraft, she from farre did thither bring:
There she had him now layd a slombering,
In secret shade, after long wanton ioyes:
Whilst round about them pleasauntly did sing
  Many faire Ladies, and lasciuious boyes,
That euer mixt their song with light licentious toyes.

73

And all that while, right ouer him she hong,
  With her false eyes fast fixed in his sight,
As seeking medicine, whence she was stong,
Or greedily depasturing delight: *depasturing* grazing on, eating up
And oft inclining downe with kisses light,
For feare of waking him, his lips bedewd,
And through his humid eyes did sucke his spright,
  Quite molten into lust and pleasure lewd;
Wherewith she sighed soft, as if his case she rewd.

74

The whiles someone did chaunt this louely lay;
  Ah see, who so faire thing doest faine to see,

Stanzas 74–5 this louely lay ...] A close imitation of the song sung in Armida's garden, in Tasso, *Gerusalemme Liberata*, 16.14–15.

In springing flowre the image of thy day;
Ah see the Virgin Rose, how sweetly shee
Doth first peepe forth with bashfull modestee,
That fairer seemes, the lesse ye see her may;
Lo see soone after, how more bold and free
Her bared bosome she doth broad display;
Loe see soone after, how she fades, and falles away.

75
So passeth, in the passing of a day,
   Of mortall life the leafe, the bud, the flowre,
   Ne more doth flourish after first decay,
   That earst was sought to decke both bed and bowre,   *earst* formerly, before, not long ago
   Of many a Ladie, and many a Paramowre:
   Gather therefore the Rose, whilest yet is prime,
   For soone comes age, that will her pride deflowre:
   Gather the Rose of loue, whilest yet is time,
Whilest louing thou mayst loued be with equall crime.   *crime* sin, offence

76
He ceast, and then gan all the quire of birdes
   Their diuerse notes t'attune vnto his lay,
   As in approuance of his pleasing words.   *approuance* approval, confirmation
   The constant paire heard all, that he did say,
   Yet swarued not, but kept their forward way,
   Through many couert groues, and thickets close,
   In which they creeping did at last display
   That wanton Ladie, with her louer lose,
Whose sleepie head she in her lap did soft dispose.

77
Vpon a bed of Roses she was layd,
   As faint through heat, or dight to pleasant sin,   *dight to* dressed, prepared for
   And was arayd, or rather disarayd,   *arayd . . . disarayd* dressed . . . undressed
   All in a vele of silke and siluer thin,
   That hid no whit her alablaster skin,   *no whit* not at all
   But rather shewd more white, if more might bee:
   More subtile web *Arachne* can not spin,
   Nor the fine nets, which oft we wouen see
Of scorched deaw, do not in th'aire more lightly flee.   *flee* blow, fly

---

77.7 Arachne] A Greek woman skilled at weaving, who challenged Athene (Minerva) to a contest, and lost; she hanged herself in despair, but was transformed to a spider. See Ovid, *Metamorphoses*, 6.1–145.

78

Her snowy brest was bare to readie spoyle
   Of hungry eies, which n'ote therewith be fild,
   And yet through languour of her late sweet toyle,
   Few drops, more cleare then Nectar, forth distild,
   That like pure Orient perles adowne it trild,   *trild* flowed, purled
   And her faire eyes sweet smyling in delight,
   Moystened their fierie beames, with which she thrild   *thrild* pierced; excited
   Fraile harts, yet quenched not; like starry light
Which sparckling on the silent waues, does seeme more bright.

79

The young man sleeping by her, seemd to bee
   Some goodly swayne of honorable place,
   That certes it great pittie was to see   *certes* certainly
   Him his nobilitie so foule deface;
   A sweet regard, and amiable grace,
   Mixed with manly sternnesse did appeare
   Yet sleeping, in his well proportiond face,
   And on his tender lips the downy heare
Did now but freshly spring, and silken blossomes beare.

80

His warlike armes, the idle instruments
   Of sleeping praise, were hong vpon a tree,
   And his braue shield, full of old moniments,   *moniments* heraldic signs; marks of battle
   Was fowly ra'st, that none the signes might see;   *ra'st* erased, scraped clear
   Ne for them, ne for honour cared hee,
   Ne ought, that did to his aduauncement tend,
   But in lewd loues, and wastfull luxuree,
   His dayes, his goods, his bodie he did spend:
O horrible enchantment, that him so did blend.   *blend* hinder, dishonour

81

The noble Elfe, and carefull Palmer drew
   So nigh them, minding nought, but lustfull game,
   That suddein forth they on them rusht, and threw
   A subtile net, which onely for the same
   The skilfull Palmer formally did frame.
   So held them vnder fast, the whiles the rest

    81.3–5 a subtile net,] The Palmer's net is fashioned on the model of that of Hephaistos (Vulcan), who similarly snared his wife Aphrodite (Venus) locked in the embrace of Ares (Mars). See Homer, *Odyssey*, 8.250–369.

Fled all away for feare of fowler shame.
The faire Enchauntresse, so vnwares opprest,
Tryde all her arts, & all her sleights, thence out to wrest.

82
And eke her louer stroue: but all in vaine;
   For that same net so cunningly was wound,
   That neither guile, nor force might it distraine.   *distraine* tear off, pull off
   They tooke them both, & both them strongly bound
   In captiue bandes, which there they readie found;
   But her in chaines of adamant he tyde;
   For nothing else might keepe her safe and sound;
   But *Verdant* (so he hight) he soone vntyde,
And counsell sage in steed thereof to him applyde.

83
But all those pleasant bowres and Pallace braue,
   Guyon broke downe, with rigour pittilesse;
   Ne ought their goodly workmanship might saue
   Them from the tempest of his wrathfulnesse,
   But that their blisse he turn'd to balefulnesse:
   Their groues he feld, their gardins did deface,
   Their arbers spoyld, their Cabinets suppresse,
   Their banket houses burne, their buildings race,
And of the fairest late, now made the fowlest place.

84
Then led they her away, and eke that knight
   They with them led, both sorrowfull and sad:
   The way they came, the same retourn'd they right,
   Till they arriued, where they lately had
   Charm'd those wild-beasts, that rag'd with furie mad.
   Which now awaking, fierce at them gan fly,
   As in their mistresse reskew, whom they lad;   *lad* led away
   But them the Palmer soone did pacify.
Then *Guyon* askt, what meant those beastes, which there did ly.

85
Said he, these seeming beasts are men indeed,
   Whom this Enchauntresse hath transformed thus,
   Whylome her louers, which her lusts did feed,
   Now turned into figures hideous,

Stanzas 84–7 those wild-beasts . . . which there did lye.] Cf. stanzas 39–41, above.

Acording to their mindes like monstruous.
Sad end (quoth he) of life intemperate,
And mournefull meed of ioyes delicious:
But Palmer, if it mote thee so aggrate,
Let them returned be vnto their former state.

86

Streight way he with his vertuous staffe them strooke,
   And streight of beasts they comely men became;
   Yet being men they did vnmanly looke,
   And stared ghastly, some for inward shame,
   And some for wrath, to see their captiue Dame:
   But one aboue the rest in speciall,
   That had an hog beene late, hight *Grille* by name,
   Repined greatly, and did him miscall,
That had from hoggish forme him brought to naturall.

87

Said *Guyon*, See the mind of beastly man,
   That hath so soone forgot the excellence
   Of his creation, when he life began,
   That now he chooseth, with vile difference,   *difference* disagreement, diversity
   To be a beast, and lacke intelligence.
   To whom the Palmer thus, The donghill kind
   Delights in filth and foule incontinence:
   Let *Grill* be *Grill*, and haue his hoggish mind,
But let vs hence depart, whilest wether serues and wind.   *serues* is favourable

3. Book III, cantos xi–xii

The third book of *The Faerie Queene* contains the legend of the lady Britomart, a mythical ancestor of the Tudor line and a champion of chastity. Spenser's vision of chastity is unexpectedly complex. Like his other virtues, it occupies a mean position between the two associated vices, those of abstinence and promiscuity, but its reach extends from sexual behaviour to all forms of love and friendship, and provokes meditations on interest and disinterest, magnanimity and jealousy. In the two cantos selected from this part of the poem, Spenser depicts the patron knight of chastity, Britomart, as she

    85.5 **Acording to their mindes . . .**] Spenser's version of the Circe myth explicitly moralises the transformation of her victims into beasts – a tradition of reading Homer that goes back to the early Greek commentators.
    86.6–87.8 **But one . . .**] In Plutarch's eponymous dialogue 'Gryllos' (fr. Gr *gryllos*, 'hog'), this Ithacan mariner debates with his king, Odysseus, the advantages of the bestial life over that of men. Plutarch's dialogue breaks off abruptly, perhaps by design; Spenser's Palmer imitates this abruption with his impatience.

leaves the house of the miserly, jealous and jilted husband Malbecco. Before long she happens upon Scudamour (the knight of love, after his name, *escu d'amour*, 'the shield of love'), and offers to help him in his attempt to redeem his own lady, Amoret, from the clutches of the evil magician Busirane. Her penetration of his enchanted castle draws heavily on Ovid's *Metamorphoses*, and on the English folktale known as 'Mr Fox', or the related legend of Bluebeard's castle. In this story, a maiden called Lady Mary is betrothed to the stranger, Fox, about whom she learns a terrible secret: in his castle, locked away in a back room, he keeps the bodies of all the women he has killed. She eventually exposes Fox and saves herself, while her brothers cut him to pieces – in psycho-sexual terms, a fantasy escape back into the chaste innocence of the family, in a world where all erotic lovers are rapists and murderers. Britomart's undoing of Busirane's mighty spells dissolves the apparently necessary association between erotic love and violation, creating the possibility of love without fear, and faith without jealousy. The play of different epic, mythographic and folk traditions in this part of *The Faerie Queene* is highly pointed; the key players in the smutty Malbecco fabliau of canto ix are named after Homeric originals (Paridell from Paris, and Hellenore from Helen), while Britomart uses an English folktale to break the power of an Ovidian erotic logic (cantos xi–xii). Her reformed chastity delivers Amoret from fear; it may also seek to deliver that upstart nation, England, from its contaminated genesis in the ruins of classical myth and literature.

Canto XI.

Britomart chaceth Ollyphant,
    findes Scudamour distrest:
Assayes the house of Busyrane,
    where Loues spoyles are exprest.   *spoyles* plunders, preys *exprest* shown

1
O Hatefull hellish Snake, what furie furst
    Brought thee from balefull house of *Proserpine*,

Arg.2 Scudamour] Scudamour's name, from Fr *escu d'amour* ('shield of love'), befits his position as the lover of Amoret, and the male counterpart to the chaste Britomart. Like the name of Britomart (who quests for the love of Artegall), Scudamour's name forms a neat hermaphroditic union with that of his lady: Scudamouret.
Arg.3 Busyrane,] The name of the enchanter draws on various accounts of the history of Busiris, an ancient and tyrannical king of Egypt.
1.2 balefull house of Proserpine,] Hades. Proserpina (or Persephone) presides over jealousy because, having been ravished into hell, she must spend eternity longing for the terrestrial and ethereal blisses now denied her.

Where in her bosome she thee long had nurst,
And fostred vp with bitter milke of tine, *fostred vp* nourished, raised
Fowle Gealosie, that turnest loue diuine *tine* sorrow, affliction
To ioylesse dread, and mak'st the louing hart
With hatefull thoughts to languish and to pine,
And feed it selfe with selfe-consuming smart?
Of all the passions in the mind thou vilest art.

2
O let him far be banished away,
And in his stead let Loue for euer dwell, *stead* place
Sweet Loue, that doth his golding wings embay *embay* bathe, steep
In blessed Nectar, and pure Pleasures well,
Vntroubled of vile feare, or bitter fell. *fell* gall, bile (L *fel*, 'gall')
And ye faire Ladies, that your kingdomes make
In th'harts of men, them gouerne wisely well,
And of faire *Britomart* ensample take,
That was as trew in loue, as Turtle to her make. *turtle* turtledove *make* mate

3
Who with Sir *Satyrane*, as earst ye red, *earst* before
Forth ryding from *Malbeccoes* hostlesse hous,
Far off aspyde a young man, the which fled *aspyde* perceived, saw
From an huge Geaunt, that with hideous
And hatefull outrage long him chaced thus;
It was that *Ollyphant*, the brother deare
Of that *Argante* vile and vitious,
From whom the *Squire of Dames* was reft whylere; *whylere* some time before
This all as bad as she, and worse, if worse ought were.

4
For as the sister did in feminine
And filthy lust exceede all woman kind,
So he surpassed his sex masculine,
In beastly vse that I did euer find;
Whom when as *Britomart* beheld behind
The fearefull boy so greedily pursew,
She was emmoued in her noble mind,
T'employ her puissaunce to his reskew, *puissance* (trisyllabic)
And pricked fiercely forward, where she him did vew.

3.1–2 Who with . . . hostlesse hous,] Cf. III.x.1.
3.6 that *Ollyphant*,] Satyrane had encountered Ollyphant's twin sister, the giant Argante, in III.vii (at 37–44), when he was saved by the lady knight Palladine. The Squire of Dames records the incestuous birth and childhood of Argante and Ollyphant at III.vii.47–9.

5
Ne was Sir *Satyrane* her far behinde,
  But with like fiercenesse did ensew the chace:
  Whom when the Gyaunt saw, he soone resinde
  His former suit, and from them fled apace;
  They after both, and boldly bad him bace,   *bad him bace* challenged him in flight
  And each did striue the other to out-goe,
  But he them both outran a wondrous space,
  For he was long, and swift as any Roe,   *roe* a kind of deer
And now made better speed, t'escape his feared foe.

6
It was not *Satyrane*, whom he did feare,
  But *Britomart* the flowre of chastity;
  For he the powre of chast hands might not beare,
  But always did their dread encounter fly:
  And now so fast his feet he did apply,
  That he has gotten to a forrest neare,
  Where he is shrowded in security.
  The wood they enter, and search euery where,
They searched diuersely, so both diuided were.

7
Faire *Britomart* so long him followed,
  That she at last came to a fountaine sheare, *sheare* clear and bright, unpolluted
  By which there lay a knight all wallowed
  Vpon the grassy ground, and by him neare
  His haberieon, his helmet, and his speare;   *haberieon* lightly mailed jacket
  A little off, his shield was rudely throwne,
  On which the winged boy in colours cleare
  Depeincted was, full easie to be knowne,   *depeincted* painted, depicted
And he thereby, where euer it in field was throwne.

8
His face vpon the ground did groueling ly,
  As if he had bene slombring in the shade,
  That the braue Mayd would not for courtesy,
  Out of his quiet slomber him abrade,
  Nor seeme too suddeinly him to inuade:

7.3 ff. **a knight all wallowed . . .**] Britomart's discovery and succouring of Scudamour is loosely based on originals by Ariosto and Tasso, themselves variations on a common romance motif; see *Orlando Furioso*, 2.34–43; *Gerusalemme Liberata*, 13.33–6; and Tasso's *Rinaldo*, 5.
7.7 **the winged boy**] Cupid. The painting of Cupid on his shield makes it 'full easie to be knowne' that this is Scudamour, 'the shield of Love'.

Still as she stood, she heard with grieuous throb
Him grone, as if his hart were peeces made,
And with most painefull pangs to sigh and sob,
That pitty did the Virgins hart of patience rob.

9
At last forth breaking into bitter plaintes
   He said; ô soueraigne Lord that sit'st on hye,
   And raignst in blis emongst thy blessed Saintes,
   How suffrest thou such shamefull cruelty,
   So long vnwreaked of thine enimy?
   Or hast, thou Lord, of good mens cause no heed?
   Or doth thy iustice sleepe, and silent ly?
   What booteth then the good and righteous deed,   *booteth* profits
If goodnesse find no grace, nor righteousnesse no meed?

10
If good find grace, and righteousnesse reward,
   Why then is *Amoret* in caytiue band,   *caytiue band* captivity
   Sith that more bounteous creature neuer far'd   *far'd* walked, went
   On foot, vpon the face of liuing land?
   Or if that heauenly iustice may withstand
   The wrongfull outrage of vnrighteous men,
   Why then is *Busirane* with wicked hand
   Suffred, these seuen monethes day in secret den
My Lady and my loue so cruelly to pen?

11
My Lady and my loue is cruelly pend
   In dolefull darkenesse from the vew of day,
   Whilest deadly torments do her chast brest rend,
   And the sharpe steele doth riue her hart in tway,   *riue* break, split *tway* two
   All for she *Scudamore* will not denay.
   Yet thou vile man, vile *Scudamore* art sound,   *sound* whole, uninjured
   Ne canst her ayde, ne canst her foe dismay;
   Vnworthy wretch to tread vpon the ground,
For whom so faire a Lady feeles so sore a wound.

12
There an huge heape of singulfes did oppresse   *singulfes* sighs
   His strugling soule, and swelling throbs empeach   *empeach* encumber, impede

---

10.8 these seuen monethes day] Seven months is also the term fixed for Florimell's imprisonment in the House of Proteus.

His foltring toung with pangs of drerinesse,   *foltring* stammering, stumbling
Choking the remnant of his plaintife speach,   *plaintife* lamenting; accusatory
As if his dayes were come to their last reach.
Which when she heard, and saw the ghastly fit,
Threatning into his life to make a breach,
Both with great ruth and terrour she was smit,
Fearing least from her cage the wearie soule would flit.

13
Tho stooping downe she him amoued light;   *amoued* nudged
  Who therewith somewhat starting, vp gan looke,
  And seeing him behind a straunger knight,
  Whereas no liuing creature he mistooke,
  With great indignaunce he that sight forsooke,
  And downe againe himselfe disdainefully
  Abiecting th'earth with his faire forhead strooke: *abiecting* throwing down
  Which the bold Virgin seeing, gan apply
Fit medcine to his griefe, and spake thus courtesly.

14
Ah gentle knight, whose deepe conceiued griefe
  Well seemes t'exceede the powre of patience,
  Yet if that heauenly grace some good reliefe
  You send, submit you to high prouidence,
  And euer in your noble hart prepense,   *prepense* consider (beforehand)
  That all the sorrow in the world is lesse,
  Then vertues might, and values confidence,
  For who nill bide the burden of distresse,   *nill* will not
Must not here thinke to liue: for life is wretchednesse.

15
Therefore, faire Sir, do comfort to you take,
  And freely read, what wicked felon so   *read* reveal, say
  Hath outrag'd you, and thrald your gentle make.   *thrald* captured, imprisoned
  Perhaps this hand may helpe to ease your woe,
  And wreake your sorrow on your cruell foe,
  At least it faire endeuour will apply.
  Those feeling wordes so neare the quicke did goe,
  That vp his head he reared easily,
And leaning on his elbow, these few wordes let fly.

12.9 **her cage**] Scudamour's soul – like every soul in the poem – is feminine.

16
What boots it plaine, that cannot be redrest,   *boots it* does it help *plaine* complain
  And sow vaine sorrow in a fruitlesse eare,
  Sith powre of hand, nor skill of learned brest,
  Ne worldly price cannot redeeme my deare,
  Out of her thraldome and continuall feare?
  For he the tyraunt, which her hath in ward   *in ward* under guard, in his power
  By strong enchauntments and blacke Magicke leare,   *leare* lore, learning
  Hath in a dungeon deepe her close embard,
And many dreadfull feends hath pointed to her gard.   *pointed* appointed

17
There he tormenteth her most terribly,
  And day and night afflicts with mortall paine,
  Because to yield him loue she doth deny,
  Once to me yold, not to be yold againe: *yold* yielded
  But yet by torture he would her constraine
  Loue to conceiue in her disdainfull brest,
  Till so she do, she must in doole remaine,   *doole* sorrow, grief
  Ne may by liuing meanes be thence relest:
What boots it then to plaine, that cannot be redrest?

18
With this sad hersall of his heauy stresse,   *hersall* rehearsal
  The warlike Damzell was empassiond sore,
  And said; Sir knight, your cause is nothing lesse,
  Then is your sorrow, certes if not more;   *certes* certainly
  For nothing so much pitty doth implore,   *implore* petition, demand
  As gentle Ladies helplesse misery.
  But yet, if please ye listen to my lore,
  I will with proofe of last extremity,
Deliuer her fro thence, or with her for you dy.

19
Ah gentlest knight aliue, (said *Scudamore*)
  What huge heroicke magnanimity
  Dwels in thy bounteous brest? what couldst thou more,
  If she were thine, and thou as now am I?
  O spare thy happy dayes, and them apply
  To better boot, but let me dye, that ought;   *boot* profit, end
  More is more losse: one is enough to dy.
  Life is not lost, (said she) for which is bought
Endlesse renowm, that more then death is to be sought.

20
Thus she at length perswaded him to rise,
   And with her wend, to see what new successe
   Mote him befall vpon new enterprise;
   His armes, which he had vow'd to disprofesse,   *disprofesse* renounce
   She gathered vp and did about him dresse,
   And his forwandred steed vnto him got: *forwandred* strayed
   So forth they both yfere make their progresse,   *yfere* together
   And march not past the mountenaunce of a shot,   *mountenance* extent, reach
Till they arriu'd, whereas their purpose they did plot.

21
There they dismounting, drew their weapons bold
   And stoutly came vnto the Castle gate;
   Whereas no gate they found, them to withhold,
   Nor ward to wait at morne and euening late,
   But in the Porch, that did them sore amate,   *amate* dismay
   A flaming fire, ymixt with smouldry smoke,   *smouldry* smothering
   And stinking Sulphure, that with griesly hate
   And dreadfull horrour did all entraunce choke,
Enforced them their forward footing to reuoke.

22
Greatly thereat was *Britomart* dismayd,
   Ne in that stownd wist, how her selfe to beare;   *stownd* situation, trial
   For daunger vaine it were, to haue assayd
   That cruell element, which all things feare,
   Ne none can suffer to approchen neare:
   And turning backe to *Scudamour*, thus sayd;
   What monstrous enmity prouoke we heare,
   Foolhardy as th'Earthes children, the which made
Battell against the Gods? so we a God inuade.

23
Daunger without discretion to attempt,
   Inglorious and beastlike is: therefore Sir knight,
   Aread what course of you is safest dempt,   *aread* tell *dempt* judged
   And how we with our foe may come to fight.
   This is (quoth he) the dolorous despight,
   Which earst to you I playnd: for neither may
   This fire be quencht by any wit or might,
   Ne yet by any meanes remou'd away,
So mighty be th'enchauntments, which the same do stay.   *stay* maintain

24
What is there else, but cease these fruitlesse paines,
    And leaue me to my former languishing;
    Faire *Amoret* must dwell in wicked chaines,
    And *Scudamore* here dye with sorrowing.
    Perdy not so; (said she) for shamefull thing
    It were t'abandon noble cheuisaunce,   *cheuisaunce* enterprise
    For shew of perill, without venturing:
    Rather let try extremities of chaunce,
Then enterprised prayse for dread to disauaunce.   *disauaunce* leave off pursuing

25
Therewith resolu'd to proue her vtmost might,
    Her ample shield she threw before her face,
    And her swords point directing forward right
    Assayld the flame, the which eftsoones gaue place,
    And did it selfe diuide with equall space,
    That through she passed; as a thunder bolt
    Perceth the yielding ayre, and doth displace
    The soring clouds into sad showres ymolt;   *ymolt* molten
So to her yold the flames, and did their force reuolt.   *reuolt* turn back

26
Whom whenas *Scudamour* saw past the fire,
    Safe and vntoucht, he likewise gan assay,
    With greedy will, and enuious desire,
    And bad the stubborne flames to yield him way:
    But cruell *Mulciber* would not obay
    His threatfull pride, but did the more augment
    His mighty rage, and with imperious sway
    Him forst (maulgre) his fiercenesse to relent,   *maulgre* notwithstanding
And backe retire, all scorcht and pitifully brent.   *brent* burned

27
With huge impatience he inly swelt,   *impatience* (tetrasyllabic) *swelt* burned
    More for great sorrow, that he could not pas,
    Then for the burning torment, which he felt,
    That with fell woodnesse he effierced was,   *woodnesse* frenzy *effierced* enraged
    And wilfully him throwing on the gras,
    Did beat and bounse his head and brest full sore;
    The whiles the Championesse now entred has
    The vtmost rowme, and past the formest dore,
The vtmost rowme, abounding with all precious store.

28

For round about, the wals yclothed were
   With goodly arras of great maiesty,   *arras* tapestry cloth
   Wouen with gold and silke so close and nere,
   That the rich metall lurked priuily,
   As faining to be hid from enuious eye;
   Yet here, and there, and euery where vnwares
   It shewd it selfe, and shone vnwillingly;
   Like a discolourd Snake, whose hidden snares   *discolourd* multi-coloured
Through the greene gras his long bright burnisht backe declares.

29

And in those Tapets weren fashioned
   Many faire pourtraicts, and many a faire feate,
   And all of loue, and all of lusty-hed,
   As seemed by their semblaunt did entreat;   *semblaunt* appearance
   And eke all *Cupids* warres they did repeate,
   And cruell battels, which he whilome fought   *whilome* once, in the past
   Gainst all the Gods, to make his empire great;
   Besides the huge massacres, which he wrought
On mighty kings and kesars, into thraldome brought.

30

Therein was writ, how often thundring *Ioue*
   Had felt the point of his hart-percing dart,
   And leauing heauens kingdome, here did roue
   In straunge disguize, to slake his scalding smart;
   Now like a Ram, faire *Helle* to peruart,
   Now like a Bull, *Europa* to withdraw:
   Ah, how the fearefull Ladies tender hart
   Did liuely seeme to tremble, when she saw
The huge seas vnder her t'obay her seruaunts law.

Stanzas 29–46 all *Cupids* warres . . .] The mythic catalogue that follows largely derives from Ovid's *Metamorphoses*, and particularly from Arachne's contest with Minerva at 6.103–28; Spenser's emphasis, like Arachne's, is on the humiliations to which the gods were subject by love.
   30.4 In straunge disguize . . .] As Conti writes (*Mythologiae*, 2.1), 'is there any shape which Jupiter did not assume, in order to possess the women he lusted after?'
   30.5 Now like a Ram . . .] The ram that delivered Helle from sacrifice was not, according to Ovid, Jove in disguise; see *Fasti*, 3.857–76.
   30.6 Now like a Bull . . .] See Ovid, *Metamorphoses*, 2.846–75.

31

Soone after that into a golden showre
   Him selfe he chaung'd faire *Danaë* to vew,
   And through the roofe of her strong brasen towre   *brasen* of brass
   Did raine into her lap an hony dew,
   The whiles her foolish garde, that little knew
   Of such deceipt, kept th'yron dore fast bard,
   And watcht, that none should enter nor issew;
   Vaine was the watch, and bootlesse all the ward,
Whenas the God to golden hew him selfe transfard.   *transfard* changed, metamorphosed

32

Then was he turnd into a snowy Swan,
   To win faire *Leda* to his louely trade: *trade* course, design
   O wondrous skill, and sweet wit of the man,
   That her in daffadillies sleeping made,
   From scorching heat her daintie limbes to shade:
   Whiles the proud Bird ruffing his fethers wyde,
   And brushing his faire brest, did her inuade;
   She slept, yet twixt her eyelids closely spyde,
How towards her he rusht, and smiled at his pryde.

33

Then shewd it, how the *Thebane Semelee*
   Deceiu'd of gealous *Iuno*, did require
   To see him in his soueraigne maiestee,
   Armd with his thunderbolts and lightning fire,
   Whence dearely she with death bought her desire.
   But faire *Alcmena* better match did make,
   Ioying his loue in likenesse more entire;
   Three nights in one, they say, that for her sake
He then did put, her pleasures lenger to partake.

34

Twise was he seene in soaring Eagles shape,
   And with wide wings to beat the buxome ayre,   *buxome* pliant, unresisting

---

   31.2 faire *Danae* to vew,] Ovid hardly touches the history of Danaë, which Spenser may have adapted from Conti, *Mythologiae* (7.18), or from Horace's ode on gold (*Odes*, 3.16), though the most likely source is Apollodorus, *The Library*, 2.4.1.
   32.2 To win faire *Leda*] Euripides introduces Helen with this story of her mother's rape in *Helen*, ll. 16–22; but neither Euripides nor Ovid appears to be the source of Spenser's detailed vision of the scene.
   33.1 *Thebane Semelee*] Jove's seduction of Semele is given in Hesiod, *Theogony*, ll. 940–2; and in Euripides, *Bacchae*, 1–42.
   33.6 But faire *Alcmena*] Apollodorus gives the history of Jove and Alcmena in *The Library*, 2.4.8.

Once, when he with *Asterie* did scape,
Againe, when as the *Troiane* boy so faire
He snatcht from *Ida* hill, and with him bare:
Wondrous delight it was, there to behould,
How the rude Shepheards after him did stare,
Trembling through feare, least down he fallen should
And often to him calling, to take surer hould.

35

In *Satyres* shape *Antiopa* he snatcht:
And like a fire, when he *Aegin*' assayd:
A shepheard, when *Mnemosyne* he catcht:
And like a Serpent to the *Thracian* mayd.
Whiles thus on earth great *Ioue* these pageaunts playd,
The winged boy did thrust into his throne,
And scoffing, thus vnto his mother sayd,
Lo now the heauens obey to me alone,
And take me for their *Ioue*, whiles *Ioue* to earth is gone.

36

And thou, faire *Phœbus*, in thy colours bright
Wast there enwouen, and the sad distresse,
In which that boy thee plonged, for despight,
That thou bewray'dst his mothers wantonnesse,   *bewray'dst* revealed
When she with *Mars* was meynt in ioyfulnesse: *meynt* mingled
For thy he thrild thee with a leaden dart,   *for thy* therefore
To loue faire *Daphne*, which thee loued lesse:
Lesse she thee lou'd, then was thy iust desart,
Yet was thy loue her death, & her death was thy smart.   *smart* pain, suffering

37

So louedst thou the lusty *Hyacinct*,
So louedst thou the faire *Coronis* deare:

    34.3 with *Asterie* did scape,] See Ovid, *Metamorphoses*, 6.108.
    34.4 the *Troiane* boy so faire] Ganymede; see Virgil, *Aeneid*, 5.249–57; and Ovid, *Metamorphoses*, 10.155–61.
    35.1 *Antiopa* he snatcht:] See Ovid, *Metamorphoses*, 6.110–11; and Homer, *Odyssey*, 11.260 ff.
    35.2–4 like a fire ... *Thracian* mayd.] Translating Ovid's 'Asopida luserit ignis, | Mnemosynen pastor, varius Deoida serpens' (6.113–14).
    36.5 When she with *Mars* was meynt] Leuconoe tells the story of Mars and Venus in *Metamorphoses*, 4.167–89.
    36.7 To loue faire *Daphne*,] See Ovid, *Metamorphoses*, 1.452–552.
    37.1 the lusty *Hyacinct*,] Orpheus tells the story of Apollo's love for Hyacinthus in *Metamorphoses*, 10.162–219.
    37.2 faire *Coronis*] Ovid narrates the history of Apollo's love for Coronis, her murder and the god's grief, in *Metamorphoses*, 2.542–632.

Yet both are of thy haplesse hand extinct,   *extinct* dead
Yet both in flowres do liue, and loue thee beare,
The one a Paunce, the other a sweet breare: *paunce* pansy *sweet breare* sweetbriar
For griefe whereof, ye mote haue liuely seene
The God himselfe rending his golden heare,
And breaking quite his gyrlond euer greene,
With other signes of sorrow and impatient teene.   *teene* suffering, pain

38
Both for those two, and for his owne deare sonne,
  The sonne of *Climene* he did repent,
  Who bold to guide the charet of the Sunne,
  Himselfe in thousand peeces fondly rent,
  And all the world with flashing fier brent,
  So like, that all the walles did seeme to flame.
  Yet cruell *Cupid*, not herewith content,
  Forst him eftsoones to follow other game,   *game* prey, quarry
And loue a Shepheards daughter for his dearest Dame.

39
He loued *Isse* for his dearest Dame,
  And for her sake her cattell fed a while,
  And for her sake a cowheard vile became,
  The seruant of *Admetus* cowheard vile,
  Whiles that from heauen he suffered exile.
  Long were to tell each other louely fit,   *fit* passion, ecstasy
  Now like a Lyon, hunting after spoile,
  Now like a Hag, now like a faulcon flit:
All which in that faire arras was most liuely writ.

40
Next vnto him was *Neptune* pictured,
  In his diuine resemblance wondrous lyke:
  His face was rugged, and his hoarie hed
  Dropped with brackish deaw; his three-forkt Pyke
  He stearnly shooke, and therewith fierce did stryke
  The raging billowes, that on euery syde
  They trembling stood, and made a long broad dyke,

    38.2 The sonne of *Climene*] Phaethon; Ovid relates the story of his ambition and death, and of Apollo's grief, in *Metamorphoses*, 1.750–2.400.
    39.1 *Isse*] Another part of Arachne's tapestry in Ovid, *Metamorphoses*, 6.122–4; this passage also includes Apollo's transformations into a lion, hawk and rustic. According to Euripides' *Alcestis*, Apollo suffered exile from heaven, and servitude under Admetus, because he killed the Cyclopes (*Alcestis*, ll. 1–9).

That his swift charet might haue passage wyde,
Which foure great *Hippodames* did draw in temewise tyde.   *in temewise tyde* yoked in pairs

41

His sea-horses did seeme to snort amayne,   *amayne* with full force
  And from their nosethrilles blow the brynie streame,
  That made the sparckling waues to smoke agayne,
  And flame with gold, but the white fomy creame,
  Did shine with siluer, and shoot forth his beame.
  The God himselfe did pensiue seeme and sad,
  And hong adowne his head, as he did dreame:
  For priuy loue his brest empierced had,
Ne ought but deare *Bisaltis* ay could make him glad.   *ay* ever

42

He loued eke *Iphimedia* deare,
  And *Aeolus* faire daughter *Arne* hight.
  For whom he turnd him selfe into a Steare,
  And fed on fodder, to beguile her sight.
  Also to win *Deucalions* daughter bright,
  He turnd him selfe into a Dolphin fayre;
  And like a winged horse he tooke his flight,
  To snaky-locke *Medusa* to repayre,
On whom he got faire *Pegasus*, that flitteth in the ayre.

43

Next *Saturne* was, (but who would euer weene,
  That sullein *Saturne* euer weend to loue?
  Yet loue is sullein, and *Saturnlike* seene,
  As he did for *Erigone* it proue.)
  That to a *Centaure* did him selfe transmoue.   *transmoue* transform
  So prou'd it eke that gracious God of wine,
  When for to compasse *Philliras* hard loue,   *compass* contrive, achieve

    40.9 Hippodames] Apparently Spenser's idiosyncratic version of *hippocampus*, a mythological sea-monster, part-horse, part-fish. Cf. 'sea-horses' in the first line of the following stanza.
    41.9 **ought but deare *Bisaltis*]** See Ovid, *Metamorphoses*, 6.117.
    42.1 **Iphimedia deare,**] See Homer, *Odyssey*, 11.305–14.
    42.2–5 **Aeolus faire daughter ... Deucalions daughter**] See Ovid, *Metamorphoses*, 6.115–20.
    42.8 **snaky-locke *Medusa*]** Perseus relates the story of Medusa's ravishment by Neptune at *Metamorphoses*, 4.790–803; she also features in Arachne's tapestry at 6.119–20.
    43.4–7 Erigone ... Philliras hard love,] In Ovid's account of the two maidens, it is Philyra whom Saturn rapes as a horse, begetting the centaur, Chiron; and Erigone who succumbs to Bacchus, 'God of wine' (*Metamorphoses*, 6.125–6). Spenser's transposition of the two maidens may have been occasioned by Apollodorus' account of Erigone, which recalls the fate of her father Icarius – torn to pieces after he offered wine to shepherds – before celebrating Erigone for the filial piety of her subsequent suicide (*The Library*, 3.14.7).

He turnd himselfe into a fruitfull vine,
And into her faire bosome made his grapes decline.

44

Long were to tell the amorous assayes,
   And gentle pangues, with which he maked meeke
   The mighty *Mars*, to learne his wanton playes:
   How oft for *Venus*, and how often eek
   For many other Nymphes he sore did shreek,
   With womanish teares, and with vnwarlike smarts,
   Priuily moystening his horrid cheek.
   There was he painted full of burning darts,
And many wide woundes launched through his inner parts.

45

Ne did he spare (so cruell was the Elfe)
   His owne deare mother, (ah, why should he so?)
   Ne did he spare sometime to pricke himselfe,   *pricke* wound; shoot at; arouse (with
   That he might tast the sweet consuming woe,   bawdy pun)
   Which he had wrought to many others moe.   *moe* more (in quantity)
   But to declare the mournfull Tragedyes,
   And spoiles, wherewith he all the ground did strow,
   More eath to number, with how many eyes   *eath* easy
High heauen beholds sad louers nightly theeueryes.   *theeueryes* furtive pleasures

46

Kings Queenes, Lords Ladies, Knights & Damzels gent
   Were heap'd together with the vulgar sort,
   And mingled with the raskall rablement,
   Without respect of person or of port,
   To shew Dan *Cupids* powre and great effort:
   And round about a border was entrayld,
   Of broken bowes and arrowes shiuered short,
   And a long bloudy riuer through them rayld,
So liuely and so like, that liuing sence it fayld.

47

And at the vpper end of that faire rowme,
   There was an Altar built of pretious stone,
   Of passing valew, and of great renowme,
   On which there stood an Image all alone,
   Of massy gold, which with his owne light shone;

Stanza 44 The mighty Mars . . . did shreek,] On Mars' love for Venus, see 36.5n., above.

    And wings it had with sundry colours dight,   *dight* dressed, adorned
      More sundry colours, then the proud *Pauone*
      Beares in his boasted fan, or *Iris* bright,
When her discolourd bow she spreds through heauen bright.

48

Blindfold he was, and in his cruell fist
    A mortall bow and arrowes keene did hold,
    With which he shot at randon, when him list,   *him list* it pleased him
    Some headed with sad lead, some with pure gold;
    (Ah man beware, how thou those darts behold)
    A wounded Dragon vnder him did ly,
    Whose hideous tayle his left foot did enfold,
    And with a shaft was shot through either eye,
That no man forth might draw, ne no man remedye.

49

And vnderneath his feet was written thus,
    Vnto the Victor of the Gods this bee:
    And all the people in that ample hous   *ample* capacious
    Did to that image bow their humble knee,
    And oft committed fowle Idolatree.
    That wondrous sight faire *Britomart* amazed,
    Ne seeing could her wonder satisfie,
    But euermore and more vpon it gazed,
The whiles the passing brightnes her fraile sences dazed.

50

Tho as she backward cast her busie eye,
    To search each secret of that goodly sted
    Ouer the dore thus written she did spye
    Be bold: she oft and oft it ouer-red,
    Yet could not find what sence it figured:
    But what so were therein or writ or ment,   *or ... or* either ... or
    She was no whit thereby discouraged
    From prosecuting of her first intent,
But forward with bold steps into the next roome went.

47.7 the proud *Pauone*] Peacock, fr. It *pavone*.
    47.8 *Iris* bright,] In the *Metamorphoses*, Iris, the goddess of the rainbow, has a *velamina mille colorum* ('a cloak of a thousand colours'; 11.589).
    50.1 Tho as she backward cast ...] Britomart probably looks back, here, to the door through which she passed at 27.8. At 54.1–5, she looks back at the next door, through which she passes, in turn, in this stanza.

51

Much fairer, then the former, was that roome,
   And richlier by many partes arayd:
   For not with arras made in painefull loome,
   But with pure gold it all was ouerlayd,
   Wrought with wilde Antickes, which their follies playd,   *antickes* fantastic or monstrous
   In the rich metall, as they liuing were: ornamentation
   A thousand monstrous formes therein were made,
   Such as false loue doth oft vpon him weare,
For loue in thousand monstrous formes doth oft appeare.

52

And all about, the glistring walles were hong
   With warlike spoiles, and with victorious prayes,
   Of mighty Conquerours and Captaines strong,
   Which were whilome captiued in their dayes
   To cruell loue, and wrought their owne decayes: *decayes* undoings
   Their swerds & speres were broke, & hauberques rent;   *hauberques* coats of mail
   And their proud girlonds of tryumphant bayes
   Troden in dust with fury insolent,
To shew the victors might and mercilesse intent.

53

The warlike Mayde beholding earnestly
   The goodly ordinance of this rich place,
   Did greatly wonder ne could satisfie
   Her greedy eyes with gazing a long space,
   But more she meruaild that no footings trace,
   Nor wight appear'd, but wastefull emptinesse,
   And solemne silence ouer all that place:
   Straunge thing it seem'd, that none was to possesse
So rich purueyance, ne them keepe with carefulnesse.   *purueyance* furnishing

54

And as she lookt about, she did behold,
   How ouer that same dore was likewise writ,
   Be bold, be bold, and euery where *Be bold,*
   That much she muz'd, yet could not construe it
   By any ridling skill, or commune wit.
   At last she spyde at that roomes vpper end,
   Another yron dore, on which was writ,
   Be not too bold; whereto though she did bend
Her earnest mind, yet wist not what it might intend.   *intend* mean, purport

54.6–8 At last ... bold;] Unlike the writing over the first two doors, which appeared *inside* the entrance, the admonitory inscription on the final door appears *outside* the entrance to the farther room.

55

Thus she there waited vntill euentyde,
   Yet liuing creature none she saw appeare:
   And now sad shadowes gan the world to hyde,
   From mortall vew, and wrap in darkenesse dreare;
   Yet nould she d'off her weary armes, for feare   *nould* would not *d'off* doff, take off
   Of secret daunger, ne let sleepe oppresse
   Her heauy eyes with natures burdein deare,
   But drew her selfe aside in sickernesse,
And her welpointed weapons did about her dresse.

Canto XII.

> *The maske of Cupid, and th'enchaunted*   *maske* pageant
>   *Chamber are displayd,*
> *Whence Britomart redeemes faire*
>   *Amoret, through charmes decayd.*

1

Tho when as chearelesse Night ycouered had
   Faire heauen with an vniuersall cloud,
   That euery wight dismayd with darknesse sad,
   In silence and in sleepe themselues did shroud,
   She heard a shrilling Trompet sound aloud,
   Signe of nigh battell, or got victory;
   Nought therewith daunted was her courage proud,
   But rather stird to cruell enmity,
Expecting euer, when some foe she might descry.   *descry* perceive, discover

2

With that, an hideous storme of winde arose,
   With dreadfull thunder and lightning atwixt,   *atwixt* between, at intervals
   And an earth-quake, as if it streight would lose
   The worlds foundations from his centre fixt;
   A direfull stench of smoke and sulphure mixt
   Ensewd, whose noyance fild the fearefull sted,   *noyance* disturbance, injurious effect
   From the fourth houre of night vntill the sixt;

This disposition loosely follows the temporal logic of Spenser's source in the Bluebeard legend, from which the portal inscriptions derive; Lady Mary, the heroine of the legend, avoids the fate of Mr Fox's other virgin victims because she anticipates the terrible fate that will await her on the other side of marriage. On the Bluebeard legend, see headnote.

   2.7 From the fourth houre . . .] The night consisted of four 'watches', each of three hours, running from 6 p.m. to 6 a.m. The storm here runs from 10 p.m. to midnight, when the masque commences.

Yet the bold *Britonesse* was nought ydred,   *ydred* frightened, cowed
Though much emmou'd, but stedfast still perseuered.

3
All suddenly a stormy whirlwind blew
   Throughout the house, that clapped euery dore,   *clapped* slammed shut
   With which that yron wicket open flew,   *wicket* gate, door
   As it with mightie leuers had bene tore:
   And forth issewd, as on the ready flore
   Of some Theatre, a graue personage,   *theatre* (trisyllabic)
   That in his hand a branch of laurell bore,
   With comely haueour and count'nance sage,   *haueour* deportment, manner
Yclad in costly garments, fit for tragicke Stage.

4
Proceeding to the midst, he still did stand,
   As if in mind he somewhat had to say,
   And to the vulgar beckning with his hand,
   In signe of silence, as to heare a play,
   By liuely actions he gan bewray   *actions* (trisyllabic) *bewray* represent
   Some argument of matter passioned;   *argument* summary, prologue
   Which doen, he backe retyred soft away,   *passioned* passionate, moving
   And passing by, his name discouered,
Ease, on his robe in golden letters cyphered.

5
The noble Mayd, still standing all this vewd,
   And merueild at his strange intendiment;   *intendiment* import, meaning
   With that a ioyous fellowship issewd
   Of Minstrals, making goodly meriment,
   With wanton Bardes, and Rymers impudent,
   All which together sung full chearefully
   A lay of loues delight, with sweet consent: *lay* song
   After whom marcht a iolly company,
In manner of a maske, enranged orderly.   *enranged* arranged, disposed

6
The whiles a most delitious harmony,
   In full straunge notes was sweetly heard to sound,
   That the rare sweetnesse of the melody
   The feeble senses wholly did confound,

3.5–9 And forth . . . tragicke Stage.] The first actor, Ease, comes dressed like the prologue to a theatrical tragedy. As the frame through which the rest of the masque is viewed, Ease's role is to establish an aesthetic distance between the masquers and 'the vulgar' (4.3).

And the fraile soule in deepe delight nigh dround:
And when it ceast, shrill trompets loud did bray,   *bray* sound shrilly
That their report did farre away rebound,
And when they ceast, it gan againe to play,
The whiles the maskers marched forth in trim aray.   *trim aray* neat, elegant order

7

The first was *Fancy*, like a louely boy,
  Of rare aspect, and beautie without peare;
  Matchable either to that ympe of *Troy*,   *ympe* child, scion, young man
  Whom *Ioue* did loue, and chose his cup to beare,
  Or that same daintie lad, which was so deare
  To great *Alcides*, that when as he dyde,
  He wailed womanlike with many a teare,
  And euery wood, and euery valley wyde
He fild with *Hylas* name; the Nymphes eke *Hylas* cryde.

8

His garment neither was of silke nor say,   *say* a fine woollen cloth
  But painted plumes, in goodly order dight,   *dight* arranged
  Like as the sunburnt *Indians* do aray
  Their tawney bodies, in their proudest plight: *plight* condition, dress
  As those same plumes, so seemd he vaine and light,
  That by his gate might easily appeare;
  For still he far'd as dauncing in delight,
  And in his hand a windy fan did beare,
That in the idle aire he mou'd still here and there.

9

And him beside marcht amorous *Desyre*,
  Who seemd of riper yeares, then th'other Swaine,
  Yet was that other swayne this elders syre,
  And gaue him being, commune to them twaine:
  His garment was disguised very vaine,
  And his embrodered Bonet sat awry;

    7.3–4 **that ympe . . . to beare,**] Ganymede; see xi.34.4n., above.
    7.5–9 **Or that . . . Hylas cryde.**] For the love of Hercules (sometimes known, as here, by the patronymic Alcides) for Hylas, and his grief at Hylas' death, see Apollonius Rhodius, *Argonautica*, 1.1207–362. Apollodorus records in *The Library* (1.9.19) that Hercules returned to Argos after the death of Hylas, and became a slave at the court of the Queen Omphale; this may be the source of Spenser's emphasis, in this stanza, on Hercules' 'womanlike' wailing.
    8.1–4 **His garment . . . plight:**] Contemporary accounts of Native Americans described and showed them adorned with feathers during ceremonial occasions; see, for example, Theodore de Bry's engravings (based on John White's original watercolours) in Thomas Hariot's *A briefe and true report of the new found land of Virginia* (Frankfurt: John Wechel, 1590).

Twixt both his hands few sparkes he close did straine,
   Which still he blew, and kindled busily,
That soone they life conceiu'd, & forth in flames did fly.

10

Next after him went *Doubt*, who was yclad
   In a discolour'd cote, of straunge disguyse,   *discolour'd* of many colours
   That at his backe a brode Capuccio had,   *capuccio* hood (of a cloak)
   And sleeues dependant *Albanese*-wyse: *dependant* hanging
   He lookt askew with his mistrustfull eyes,
   And nicely trode, as thornes lay in his way,
   Or that the flore to shrinke he did auyse,
   And on a broken reed he still did stay
His feeble steps, which shrunke, when hard theron he lay.

11

With him went *Daunger*, cloth'd in ragged weed,
   Made of Beares skin, that him more dreadfull made,
   Yet his owne face was dreadfull, ne did need
   Straunge horrour, to deforme his griesly shade;
   A net in th'one hand, and a rustie blade
   In th'other was, this Mischiefe, that Mishap;
   With th'one his foes he threatned to inuade,
   With th'other he his friends ment to enwrap:
For whom he could not kill, he practizd to entrap.

12

Next him was *Feare*, all arm'd from top to toe,
   Yet thought himselfe not safe enough thereby,
   But feard each shadow mouing to and fro,
   And his owne armes when glittering he did spy,
   Or clashing heard, he fast away did fly,
   As ashes pale of hew, and wingyheeld;   *wingyheeld* with wings on his feet
   And euermore on daunger fixt his eye,
   Gainst whom he alwaies bent a brasen shield,
Which his right hand vnarmed fearefully did wield.

13

With him went *Hope* in rancke, a handsome Mayd,   *in rancke* in line, abreast
   Of chearefull looke and louely to behold;
   In silken samite she was light arayd,   *samite* a rich cloth of silk, often gilt

10.4 Albanese-wyse:] In the Scottish fashion. Long-sleeved gowns were typical of Scottish dress in this period.

And her faire lockes were wouen vp in gold;
She alway smyld, and in her hand did hold
An holy water Sprinckle, dipt in deowe,
With which she sprinckled fauours manifold,
On whom she list, and did great liking sheowe,
Great liking vnto many, but true loue to feowe.

14

And after them *Dissemblance*, and *Suspect*
Marcht in one rancke, yet an vnequall paire:
For she was gentle, and of milde aspect,
Courteous to all, and seeming debonaire,
Goodly adorned, and exceeding faire:
Yet was that all but painted, and purloynd,
And her bright browes were deckt with borrowed haire:
Her deedes were forged, and her words false coynd,
And alwaies in her hand two clewes of silke she twynd.   *clewes* wound balls of thread

15

But he was foule, ill fauoured, and grim,
Vnder his eyebrowes looking still askaunce;
And euer as *Dissemblance* laught on him,
He lowrd on her with daungerous eyeglaunce;
Shewing his nature in his countenance;
His rolling eyes did neuer rest in place,
But walkt each where, for feare of hid mischaunce,
Holding a lattice still before his face,
Through which he still did peepe, as forward he did pace.

16

Next him went *Griefe*, and *Fury* matcht yfere;
Griefe all in sable sorrowfully clad,
Downe hanging his dull head, with heauy chere,
Yet inly being more, then seeming sad:
A paire of Pincers in his hand he had,
With which he pinched people to the hart,
That from thenceforth a wretched life they lad,
In wilfull languor and consuming smart,
Dying each day with inward wounds of dolours dart.

13.6 **An holy water Sprinckle,**] An asperge, or aspergillum – a rod topped with a perforated reservoir, used ceremonially in Catholic liturgy to sprinkle (L *aspergere*) holy water.
 15.8 **Holding a lattice ... face,**] A lattice or blind, sometimes called a jalousie or jealousy, enabled someone inside (typically a woman) to see out, without herself being visible.

17

But *Fury* was full ill appareiled
  In rags, that naked nigh she did appeare,
  With ghastly lookes and dreadfull drerihed;
  For from her backe her garments she did teare,
  And from her head oft rent her snarled heare:
  In her right hand a firebrand she did tosse
  About her head, still roming here and there;
  As a dismayed Deare in chace embost,   *embost* exhausted, foaming with exhaustion
Forgetfull of his safety, hath his right way lost.

18

After them went *Displeasure* and *Pleasance*,
  He looking lompish and full sullein sad,
  And hanging downe his heauy countenance;
  She chearefull fresh and full of ioyance glad,
  As if no sorrow she ne felt ne drad;   *ne ... ne* neither ... nor
  That euill matched paire they seemd to bee:
  An angry Waspe th'one in a viall had
  Th'other in hers an hony-lady Bee;
Thus marched these sixe couples forth in faire degree.

19

After all these there marcht a most faire Dame,
  Led of two grysie villeins, th'one *Despight*,
  The other cleped *Cruelty* by name:
  She dolefull Lady, like a dreary Spright,
  Cald by strong charmes out of eternall night,
  Had deathes owne image figurd in her face,
  Full of sad signes, fearefull to liuing sight;
  Yet in that horror shewd a seemely grace,
And with her feeble feet did moue a comely pace.

20

Her brest all naked, as net iuory,
  Without adorne of gold or siluer bright,   *adorne* adornment
  Wherewith the Craftesman wonts it beautify,
  Of her dew honour was despoyled quight,
  And a wide wound therein (O ruefull sight)
  Entrenched deepe with knife accursed keene,
  Yet freshly bleeding forth her fainting spright,
  (The worke of cruell hand) was to be seene,
That dyde in sanguine red her skin all snowy cleene.

21

At that wide orifice her trembling hart
  Was drawne forth, and in siluer basin layd,
  Quite through transfixed with a deadly dart,
  And in her bloud yet steeming fresh embayd:
  And those two villeins, which her steps vpstayd,
  When her weake feete could scarcely her sustaine,
  And fading vitall powers gan to fade,
  Her forward still with torture did constraine,
And euermore encreased her consuming paine.

22

Next after her the winged God himselfe
  Came riding on a Lion rauenous,
  Taught to obay the menage of that Elfe,   *menage* handling, direction
  That man and beast with powre imperious
  Subdeweth to his kingdome tyrannous:
  His blindfold eyes he bad a while vnbind,
  That his proud spoyle of that same dolorous
  Faire Dame he might behold in perfect kind;
Which seene, he much reioyced in his cruell mind.

23

Of which full proud, himselfe vp rearing hye,
  He looked round about with sterne disdaine;
  And did suruay his goodly company:
  And marshalling the euill ordered traine,
  With that the darts which his right did straine,
  Full dreadfully he shooke that all did quake,
  And clapt on hie his coulourd winges twaine,   *winges* (disyllabic)
  That all his many it affraide did make:
Tho blinding him againe, his way he forth did take.

24

Behinde him was *Reproch, Repentance, Shame*;
  Reproch the first, *Shame* next, *Repent* behind:
  Repentance feeble, sorrowfull, and lame:
  Reproch despightfull, carelesse, and vnkind;
  Shame most ill fauourd, bestiall, and blind:

22.1 the winged God himselfe] Cupid. The association of Cupid, god of love, with the power and 'rauenous' appetite of the lion was a commonplace of the emblem tradition; see e.g. *Potentissimus affectus, amor* ('Love, the most powerful passion') in Geoffrey Whitney's *Choice of Emblemes* (Leiden: Christopher Plantin, 1586), the text of which begins: 'The Lions grimme, behoulde, doe not resiste, | But yealde them selues, and Cupiddes chariot drawe' (p. 63).

Shame lowrd, *Repentance* sigh'd, *Reproch* did scould;
Reproch sharpe stings, *Repentance* whips entwind,
Shame burning brond-yrons in her hand did hold:
All three to each vnlike, yet all made in one mould.

25

And after them a rude confused rout
   Of persons flockt, whose names is hard to read: *is* it is *read* know, tell
   Emongst them was sterne *Strife*, and *Anger* stout,
   Vnquiet *Care*, and fond *Vnthriftihead*,
   Lewd *Losse of Time*, and *Sorrow* seeming dead,
   Inconstant *Chaunge*, and false *Disloyaltie*,
   Consuming *Riotise*, and guilty *Dread*,
   Of heauenly vengeance, faint *Infirmitie*,
Vile *Pouertie*, and lastly *Death* with infamie.

26

There were full many moe like maladies,   *moe* more (in quantity)
   Whose names and natures I n'ote readen well;   *n'ote* may not
   So many moe, as there be phantasies
   In wauering wemens wit, that none can tell,
   Or paines in loue, or punishments in hell;
   And which disguized marcht in masking wise,
   About the chamber by the Damozell,
   And then returned, hauing marched thrise,
Into the inner roome, from whence they first did rise.

27

So soone as they were in, the dore streight way
   Fast locked, driuen with that stormy blast,
   Which first it opened; and bore all away.
   Then the braue Maid, which all this while was plast,
   In secret shade, and saw both first and last,
   Issewed forth, and went vnto the dore,
   To enter in, but found it locked fast:
   It vaine she thought with rigorous vprore
For to efforce, when charmes had closed it afore.

28

Where force might not auaile, there sleights and art   *auaile* be of use
   She cast to vse, both fit for hard emprize;   *emprize* enterprise, undertaking
   For thy from that same roome not to depart
   Till morrow next, she did her selfe auize,   *auize* counsel
   When that same Maske againe should forth arize.

The morrow next appeard with ioyous cheare,
Calling men to their daily exercize,
Then she, as morrow fresh, her selfe did reare
Out of her secret stand, that day for to outweare.

29

All that day she outwore in wandering,
    And gazing on that Chambers ornament,
    Till that againe the second euening
    Her couered with her sable vestiment,
    Wherewith the worlds faire beautie she hath blent: *blent* blinded
    Then when the second watch was almost past,
    That brasen dore flew open, and in went
    Bold *Britomart*, as she had late forecast,
Neither of idle shewes, nor of false charmes aghast.

30

So soone as she was entred, round about
    She cast her eies, to see what was become
    Of all those persons, which she saw without:
    But lo, they streight were vanisht all and some,
    Ne liuing wight she saw in all that roome,
    Saue that same woefull Ladie, both whose hands
    Were bounden fast, that did her ill become,
    And her small wast girt round with yron bands,
Vnto a brasen pillour, by the which she stands.

31

And her before the vile Enchaunter sate,
    Figuring straunge characters of his art,   *figuring* giving figure to, notating
    With liuing bloud he those characters wrate,
    Dreadfully dropping from her dying hart,
    Seeming transfixed with a cruell dart,
    And all perforce to make her him to loue.   *perforce* by force, compulsion
    Ah who can loue the worker of her smart?
    A thousand charmes he formerly did proue;   *proue* try
Yet thousand charmes could not her stedfast heart remoue.   *remoue* alter

32

Soone as that virgin knight he saw in place,
    His wicked bookes in hast he ouerthrew,
    Not caring his long labours to deface,   *deface* spoil, ruin
    And fiercely ronning to that Lady trew,
    A murdrous knife out of his pocket drew,

The which he thought, for villeinous despight,
      In her tormented bodie to embrew: *embrew* stain, dye, soak
      But the stout Damzell to him leaping light,
   His cursed hand withheld, and maistered his might.

33

From her, to whom his fury first he ment,
   The wicked weapon rashly he did wrest,
   And turning to her selfe his fell intent,
   Vnwares it strooke into her snowie chest,
   That little drops empurpled her faire brest.
   Exceeding wroth therewith the virgin grew,
   Albe the wound were nothing deepe imprest,   *albe* although *imprest* stamped in
   And fiercely forth her mortall blade she drew,
To giue him the reward for such vile outrage dew.

34

So mightily she smote him, that to ground
   He fell halfe dead; next stroke him should haue slaine,
   Had not the Lady, which by him stood bound,
   Dernely vnto him called to abstaine,   *dernely* dismally
   From doing him to dy. For else her paine
   Should be remedilesse, sith none but hee,
   Which wrought it, could the same recure againe.
   Therewith she stayd her hand, loth stayd to bee;
For life she him enuyde, and long'd reuenge to see.   *enuyde* begrudged

35

And to him said, Thou wicked man, whose meed
   For so huge mischiefe, and vile villany
   Is death, or if that ought do death exceed,
   Be sure, that nought may saue thee from to dy,
   But if that thou this Dame doe presently   *but if* unless
   Restore vnto her health, and former state;
   This doe and liue, else die vndoubtedly.
   He glad of life, that lookt for death but late,
Did yield himselfe right willing to prolong his date.

34.4 vnto him called] Both the 1590 and the 1596 texts read 'him' here, where Spenser presumably means 'her' (for Amoret is calling to Britomart). However, for all that Amoret knows, the helmeted Britomart *is* a male knight – and, indeed, the sexual comedy of IV.i, in which Amoret finally discovers Britomart's sex, depends on her initial misprision.

36
And rising vp, gan streight to ouerlooke   *streight* immediately
  Those cursed leaues, his charmes backe to reuerse;
  Full dreadfull things out of that balefull booke
  He red, and measur'd many a sad verse,
  That horror gan the virgins hart to perse,
  And her faire lockes vp stared stiffe on end,
  Hearing him those same bloudy lines reherse;
  And all the while he red, she did extend
Her sword high ouer him, if ought he did offend.   *ought* in any way

37
Anon she gan perceiue the house to quake,   *anon* soon, instantly
  And all the dores to rattle round about;
  Yet all that did not her dismaied make,
  Nor slacke her threatfull hand for daungers dout,   *threatfull* threatening
  But still with stedfast eye and courage stout   *daungers dout* suspicion of some danger
  Abode, to weet what end would come of all.   *abode* persisted
  At last that mightie chaine, which round about
  Her tender waste was wound, adowne gan fall,
And that great brasen pillour broke in peeces small.

38
The cruell steele, which thrild her dying hart,
  Fell softly forth, as of his owne accord,
  And the wyde wound, which lately did dispart   *dispart* divide, cleave
  Her bleeding brest, and riuen bowels gor'd,   *gor'd* stabbed, pierced
  Was closed vp, as it had not bene bor'd,   *bor'd* drilled, pierced
  And euery part to safety full sound,   *safety* (trisyllabic)
  As she were neuer hurt, was soone restor'd:
  Tho when she felt her selfe to be vnbound,
And perfect hole, prostrate she fell vnto the ground.

39
Before faire *Britomart*, she fell prostrate,
  Saying, Ah noble knight, what worthy meed
  Can wretched Lady, quit from wofull state,
  Yield you in liew of this your gratious deed?
  Your vertue selfe her owne reward shall breed,
  Euen immortall praise, and glory wyde,
  Which I your vassall, by your prowesse freed,   *vassall* bondwoman, servant
  Shall through the world make to be notifyde,   *make* cause *notifyde* advertised
And goodly well aduance, that goodly well was tryde.

40

But *Britomart* vprearing her from ground,
   Said, Gentle Dame, reward enough I weene
   For many labours more, then I haue found,
   This, that in safety now I haue you seene,
   And meane of your deliuerance haue beene:
   Henceforth faire Lady comfort to you take,
   And put away remembrance of late teene;
   In stead thereof know, that your louing Make,
Hath no lesse griefe endured for your gentle sake.

41

She much was cheard to heare him mentiond,   *mentiond* (trisyllabic)
   Whom of all liuing wights she loued best.
   Then laid the noble Championesse strong hond
   Vpon th'enchaunter, which had her distrest
   So sore, and with foule outrages opprest:
   With that great chaine, wherewith not long ygo
   He bound that pitteous Lady prisoner, now relest,
   Himselfe she bound, more worthy to be so,
And captiue with her led to wretchednesse and wo.

42

Returning backe, those goodly roomes, which erst
   She saw so rich and royally arayd,   *arayd* appointed, furnished
   Now vanisht vtterly, and cleane subuerst   *subuerst* undermined, undone
   She found, and all their glory quite decayd,
   That sight of such a chaunge her much dismayd.
   Thence forth descending to that perlous Porch,   *perlous* dangerous
   Those dreadfull flames she also found delayd,   *delayd* weakened, abated
   And quenched quite, like a consumed torch,
That erst all entrers wont so cruelly to scorch.   *wont* was accustomed

43

More easie issew now, then entrance late
   She found: for now that fained dreadfull flame,
   Which chokt the porch of that enchaunted gate,
   And passage bard to all, that thither came,
   Was vanisht quite, as it were not the same,
   And gaue her leaue at pleasure forth to passe.
   Th'Enchaunter selfe, which all that fraud did frame,   *frame* design, create
   To haue efforst the loue of that faire lasse,
Seeing his worke now wasted deepe engrieued was.

44

But when the victoresse arriued there,
   Where late she left the pensiue *Scudamore*,
   With her owne trusty Squire, both full of feare,
   Neither of them she found where she them lore: *lore* left
   Thereat her noble hart was stonisht sore;
   But most faire *Amoret*, whose gentle spright
   Now gan to feede on hope, which she before
   Conceiued had, to see her owne deare knight,
Being thereof beguyld was fild with new affright.

45

But he sad man, when he had long in drede
   Awayted there for *Britomarts* returne,
   Yet saw her not nor signe of her good speed,   *speed* success
   His expectation to despaire did turne,
   Misdeeming sure that her those flames did burne;   *misdeeming* suspecting, dreading;
   And therefore gan aduize with her old Squire,   mistakenly supposing
   Who her deare nourslings losse no lesse did mourne,
   Thence to depart for further aide t'enquire:
Whence let them wend at will, whilest here I doe respire.

[*The final five stanzas of the canto in the 1590 edition of the poem, omitted and revised in 1596, follow.*]

*43

At last she came vnto the place, where late
   She left Sir *Scudamour* in great distresse,
   Twixt dolour and despight halfe desperate,
   Of his loues succour, of his owne redresse,
   And of the hardie *Britomarts* successe:
   There on the cold earth him now thrown she found,
   In wilfull anguish, and dead heauinesse,
   And to him cald; whose voices knowen sound
Soone as he heard, himself he reared light from ground.

*44

There did he see, that most on earth him ioyd,
   His dearest loue, the comfort of his dayes,
   Whose too long absence him had sore annoyd,

45.6 her old Squire,] Glauce, Britomart's aged nurse, had originally accompanied her on her quest, dressed as her squire. Despite disappearing from the poem in III.iii, Spenser revives her – perhaps clumsily – here, in 1596, in preparation for her role in Book IV.

And wearied his life with dull delayes:
Straight he vpstarted from the loathed layes,
And to her ran with hasty egernesse,
Like as a Deare, that greedily embayes   *embayes* bathes, wets (itself)
In the coole soile, after long thirstinesse,   *soile* pool, watering hole
Which he in chace endured hath, now nigh breathlesse.

*45
Lightly he clipt her twixt his armes twaine,   *clipt* clasped, clutched
And streightly did embrace her body bright,
Her body, late the prison of sad paine,
Now the sweet lodge of loue and deare delight:
But she faire Lady ouercommen quight
Of huge affection, did in pleasure melt,
And in sweete rauishment pourd out her spright:
No word they spake, nor earthly thing they felt,
But like two senceles stocks in long embracement dwelt.   *stocks* trunks, blocks

*46
Had ye them seene, ye would haue surely thought,
That they had beene that faire *Hermaphrodite*,
Which that rich *Romane* of white marble wrought,
And in his costly Bath causd to bee site:
So seemd those two, as growne together quite,
That *Britomart* halfe enuying their blesse,
Was much empassiond in her gentle sprite,
And to her selfe oft wisht like happinesse,
In vaine she wisht, that fate n'ould let her yet possesse.   *n'ould* would not

*47
Thus doe those louers with sweet counteruayle,   *counteruayle* reciprocation
Each other of loues bitter fruit despoile.
But now my teme begins to faint and fayle,
All woxen weary of their iournall toyle: *iournall* daytime
Therefore I will their sweatie yokes assoyle   *assoyle* unloose, discharge
At this same furrowes end, till a new day:

***44.7–9 Like as a Deare ... breathlesse.**] Cf. Psalm 42.1–2: 'As the harte brayeth for the riuers of water, so panteth my soule after thee, O God. My soule thirsteth for God, euen for the liuing God: when shall I come and appeare before the presence of God?'

***Stanza 46 that faire *Hermaphrodite*,**] Spenser appears to be referring here to a specific statue. Unfortunately, the only recorded hermaphrodite statue that seems to fit Spenser's description was installed in a Roman bath decades after the publication of this part of *The Faerie Queene*. The first recorded find of a hermaphrodite statue was in 1608, outside the church of Santa Maria della Vittoria, and was quickly acquired by Cardinal Scipione Borghese; he commissioned the sculptor Bernini, several years later, to make a quilted couch on which the hermaphrodite could rest.

And ye faire Swayns, after your long turmoyle,
  Now cease your worke, and at your pleasure play;
Now cease your worke; to morrow is an holy day.

4. Book V, proem and cantos i–ii

After the narrative vagrancy of the middle books of the poem, the straight quest structure of Book V seems at first a great relief. Artegall, the knight of justice, has been trained by the goddess Astræa in the deep lore of justice, both distributive and corrective. On his quest to deliver the princess Irena from the tyrant Grantorto, Artegall is accompanied by her iron servant, Talus, whose resistless force gives Artegall the power he needs to impose his judgments. In these two opening cantos, we see some of the accidents that befall them as they begin to map out the distinctions between common justice, equity and mercy. From the outset, Artegall's interventions are judicial, as he decides between the competing claims of opposed parties, reforms civil abuses and puts down illegitimate authorities. In these judgments he is guided by precedents. For example, the judgment of Solomon from 1 Kings, Chapter 3 structures his response to the bloody knight Sanglier, and Langland's *Piers Plowman* informs his presentation of Pollente and Munera in canto ii. Artegall's journey, even in these opening cantos, appears to reflect the native English legal and political tradition, as understood by most Elizabethan common lawyers: a people ruled by a hereditary monarch, but a monarch in turn limited by a set of customs and positive laws, and bound by the authority of precedent. Thus even Artegall, Astræa's deputy and the judge of equity – that is, the judge of justice in the widest sense of 'what is fair' – finds he cannot stay Talus's heavy execution of the law. The result is that a new, sustained violence seems to pervade the book. Gone are the joyous, often magical reconciliations and friendships of the previous book, and in their wake Artegall and Talus leave a landscape littered with the fragments of bodies.

THE FIFT
BOOKE OF THE
FAERIE QVEENE.

Contayning,

THE LEGEND OF ARTEGALL

OR

OF IUSTICE.

1

So oft as I with state of present time,
   The image of the antique world compare,
   When as mans age was in his freshest prime,
   And the first blossome of faire vertue bare,   *bare* bore, carried
   Such oddes I finde twixt those, and these which are,   *oddes* inequalities, disparities
   As that, through long continuance of his course,
   Me seemes the world is runne quite out of square,   *out of square* out of order, alignment
   From the first point of his appointed sourse,
And being once amisse growes daily wourse and wourse.

2

For from the golden age, that first was named,
   It's now at earst become a stonie one;   *at earst* at once
   And men themselues, the which at first were framed   *framed* made, created
   Of earthly mould, and form'd of flesh and bone,   *mould* soil
   Are now transformed into hardest stone:
   Such as behind their backs (so backward bred)
   Were throwne by *Pyrrha* and *Deucalione*:

Title THE LEGEND OF ARTEGALL] Although first mentioned in Book II (at ix.6.9), Artegall, the knight of justice, is not properly introduced until III.ii.10 ff., when Britomart first sees him in Merlin's magic mirror; his lineage and future are set out at III.iii.25–9. He bears Achilles' arms, and is known (before his quest) for his upright dealing. His name derives from that of a Briton king mentioned in Geoffrey of Monmouth's *Historia regum Britanniae* (3.15–17): Arthgallo, one of the sons of the cruel tyrant Morvidus, himself slain by a monster from the Irish Sea. Spenser employs different spellings of the name at different points of the poem, so that while 'Arthegall' in Book III may suggest that he is Arthur's match, 'Artegall' in Book V points toward his skill as a judge.

Stanza 2 the golden age ...] This stanza plays with Ovid's conceit (in *Metamorphoses*, 1.89 ff.) of a degenerating succession of ages, culminating in the present: golden, silver, brazen and finally iron. But so wicked had the iron world become that, in Ovid's account, it was destroyed in a great flood, of which the only two survivors were Pyrrha and her husband Deucalion (*Metamorphoses*, 1.262 ff.). The goddess Themis counsels them to throw the bones of their mother behind them as they walk; realising that she means stones, the bones of the earth, they repopulate the world with humans sprung from stones – whence, Ovid, claims, we derive our hardness and stamina for toil (1.414–15).

    And if then those may any worse be red,   *red* discovered, found out
    They into that ere long will be degendered.

3
Let none then blame me, if in discipline
    Of vertue and of ciuill vses lore,   *vses* customs *lore* teaching, discipline
    I doe not forme them to the common line   *line* shape, practice
    Of present dayes, which are corrupted sore,
    But to the antique vse, which was of yore,
    When good was onely for it selfe desyred,
    And all men sought their owne, and none no more;
    When Iustice was not for most meed outhyred,   *meed* reward *outhyred* set to sale
But simple Truth did rayne, and was of all admyred.

4
For that which all men then did vertue call,
    Is now cald vice; and that which vice was hight,   *hight* called
    Is now hight vertue, and so vs'd of all:
    Right now is wrong, and wrong that was is right,
    As all things else in time are chaunged quight.
    Ne wonder; for the heauens reuolution
    Is wandred farre from, where it first was pight,   *pight* placed, fixed
    And so doe make contrarie constitution
Of all this lower world, toward his dissolution.

5
For who so list into the heauens looke,   *list* desires, pleases
    And search the courses of the rowling spheares,
    Shall find that from the point, where they first tooke
    Their setting forth, in these few thousand yeares
    They all are wandred much; that plaine appeares.
    For that same golden fleecy Ram, which bore
    Phrixus and *Helle* from their stepdames feares,
    Hath now forgot, where he was plast of yore,
And shouldred hath the Bull, which fayre *Europa* bore.

    3.1–2 discipline . . . lore,] Moral and political philosophy.
    4.6 ff. **the heauens reuolution**] In addition to rotating on its axis, the earth also wobbles – very slowly, like a top as it spins – in a motion that causes the precession of the equinoxes. The effect of precession on the 'reuolution' of fixed stars in the night sky is slight, but discernible over millennia of documented observations.
    5.6–9 **For that . . . *Europa* bore.**] The ram is the house of Aries, and the bull Taurus; for the story of Phrixus and Helle, see Apollodorus, *The Library*, 1.9.1, and for Europa Ovid, *Metamorphoses*, 2.832 ff. The position of the sun at the vernal equinox (when the length of the day is exactly equal to the length of the night – around 21 March) was, at the time the Babylonians invented the zodiac, in the constellation of Aries. It has since drifted eastward and now lies in Pisces. Looked at in other way, it seems (as Spenser suggests) that the constellation Aries has moved westward, displacing Taurus.

6

And eke the Bull hath with his bow-bent horne
   So hardly butted those two twinnes of *Ioue*,
   That they haue crusht the Crab, and quite him borne
   Into the great *Nemæan* lions groue.
   So now all range, and doe at randon roue
   Out of their proper places farre away,
   And all this world with them amisse doe moue,
   And all his creatures from their course astray,
Till they arriue at their last ruinous decay.

7

Ne is that same great glorious lampe of light,   *ne* nor
   That doth enlumine all these lesser fyres,   *enlumine* illuminate
   In better case, ne keepes his course more right,
   But is miscaried with the other Spheres.
   For since the terme of fourteene hundred yeres,
   That learned *Ptolomæe* his hight did take,
   He is declyned from that marke of theirs,
   Nigh thirtie minutes to the Southerne lake;
That makes me feare in time he will vs quite forsake.

8

And if to those Ægyptian wisards old,
   Which in Star-read were wont haue best insight,   *star-read* astronomy
   Faith may be giuen, it is by them told,
   That since the time they first tooke the Sunnes hight,
   Foure times his place he shifted hath in sight,
   And twice hath risen, where he now doth West,   *west* set (in the west)
   And wested twice, where he ought rise aright.
   But most is *Mars* amisse of all the rest,
And next to him old *Saturne*, that was wont be best.   *was wont* used to be

---

   6.1–4 And eke ... lions groue.] As above, as a result of the precession of equinoxes, it appears that Taurus has displaced Gemini (the twins of Jove, Castor and Pollux), that Gemini has displaced Cancer, and Cancer Leo.
   Stanza 7 that ... lampe of light ...] The axis of the Earth's rotation is not orthogonal to the plane described by its revolution around the sun (the ecliptic). The difference between the equatorial plane and the ecliptic also changes as a result of the precession of the equinoxes. Over the 1400 years between Ptolemy's observations and Spenser's composition of *The Faerie Queene* in the 1590s, the ecliptic dropped about a third of a degree (or twenty minutes) to the south.
   8.1–7 And if ... aright.] Spenser's source for these claims is the *The Famous Hystory of Herodotus* (London: Thomas Marshe, 1584), f. 109^v.
   8.8–9 Mars ... Saturne] Before Kepler and Brahe established the elliptical orbits of the planets about the sun, astronomical observation struggled to understand the apparently irregular courses taken by Mars and Saturn.

9

For during *Saturnes* ancient raigne it's sayd,
   That all the world with goodnesse did abound:
   All loued vertue, no man was affrayd
   Of force, ne fraud in wight was to be found: *wight* man, person
   No warre was knowne, no dreadfull trompets sound,
   Peace vniuersall rayn'd mongst men and beasts,
   And all things freely grew out of the ground:
   Iustice sate high ador'd with solemne feasts,
And to all people did diuide her dred beheasts.   *diuide* distribute *beheasts* commands

10

Most sacred vertue she of all the rest,
   Resembling God in his imperiall might;
   Whose soueraine powre is herein most exprest,
   That both to good and bad he dealeth right,
   And all his workes with Iustice hath bedight.   *bedight* decked, dressed around
   That powre he also doth to Princes lend,
   And makes them like himselfe in glorious sight,
   To sit in his owne seate, his cause to end,   *end* determine
And rule his people right, as he doth recommend.

11

Dread Souerayne Goddesse, that doest highest sit
   In seate of iudgement, in th' Almighties place,
   And with magnificke might and wondrous wit
   Doest to thy people righteous doome aread,   *doome* judgment *aread* declare, interpret
   That furthest Nations filles with awfull dread,   *awfull* reverential, awed
   Pardon the boldnesse of thy basest thrall,   *thrall* subject, slave
   That dare discourse of so diuine a read,   *read* matter of consideration, counsel
   As thy great iustice praysed ouer all:
The instrument whereof loe here thy *Artegall*.

Canto I.

Artegall trayn'd in Iustice lore
Irenaes quest pursewed,
He doeth auenge on Sanglier
his Ladies bloud embrewed.   *embrewed* stained, defiled

Stanza 9 during *Saturnes* ancient raigne] Saturn's reign was the golden age of which Ovid writes in *Metamorphoses*, 1.89–112; its end coincided with the advent of Jove.
   Stanza 11 Dread Souerayne Goddesse,] The appeal equivocates between Astræa, goddess of justice (see V.i.5, below), and Elizabeth – the effect of which is to equate the two.

1

Though vertue then were held in highest price,
    In those old times, of which I doe intreat,   *intreat of* handle, deal with
    Yet then likewise the wicked seede of vice
    Began to spring which shortly grew full great,
    And with their boughes the gentle plants did beat.
    But euermore some of the vertuous race
    Rose vp, inspired with heroicke heate,
    That cropt the branches of the sient base,   *sient* scion, new-growing shoot
And with strong hand their fruitfull rancknes did deface.   *deface* cut down, spoil

2

Such first was *Bacchus*, that with furious might
    All th' East before vntam'd did ouerronne,
    And wrong repressed, and establisht right,
    Which lawlesse men had formerly fordonne.   *fordonne* destroyed
    There Iustice first her princely rule begonne.
    Next *Hercules* his like ensample shewed,
    Who all the West with equall conquest wonne,
    And monstrous tyrants with his club subdewed;
The club of Iustice dread, with kingly powre endewed.

3

And such was he, of whom I haue to tell,
    The Champion of true Iustice *Artegall*.
    Whom (as ye lately mote remember well)   *mote* may
    An hard aduenture, which did then befall,
    Into redoubted perill forth did call;   *redoubted* fearful, formidable
    That was to succour a distressed Dame,
    Whom a strong tyrant did vniustly thrall,
    And from the heritage, which she did clame,   *heritage* inheritance, estate
Did with strong hand withhold: *Grantorto* was his name.

4

Wherefore the Lady, which *Eirena* hight,
    Did to the Faery Queene her way addresse,

Stanza 2 Such first was Bacchus ... Next Hercules] The fullest source for the various mythical histories of Dionysus (Bacchus) is Diodorus Siculus' *Library of History*, Books 3 and 4. While Conti summarises some of these traditions in *Mythologiae*, 5.13, Spenser's version here suggests knowledge of the original. Diodorus' account of the Greek myths of Hercules follows immediately after his treatment of Bacchus, in the *Library of History*, 4.8–39, and similarly stresses the hero's civilising influence in Iberia, France and Italy.

    3.9 Grantorto **was his name.**] Fr. It *gran*, 'great', and *torto*, 'wrong'. 'Tort' was the technical legal term for the violation of a duty imposed by law, or a civil wrong (L *injuria*), as opposed to a crime committed against an individual.

    4.1 Eirena **hight,**] Fr. Gr εἰρήνη, 'peace', or from the Gaelic name for Ireland, Éire. The connection with Ireland reflects the political allegory of this section of the poem, which shadows social, political and military means of reform (or, from another perspective, oppression) in Ireland.

To whom complayning her afflicted plight,   *plight* condition, situation
  She her besought of gratious redresse.
  That soueraine Queene, that mightie Emperesse,
  Whose glorie is to aide all suppliants pore,
  And of weake Princes to be Patronesse,
  Chose *Artegall* to right her to restore;
For that to her he seem'd best skild in righteous lore.

5

For *Artegall* in iustice was vpbrought
  Euen from the cradle of his infancie,
  And all the depth of rightfull doome was taught
  By faire *Astræa*, with great industrie,
  Whilest here on earth she liued mortallie.
  For till the world from his perfection fell
  Into all filth and foule iniquitie,
  Astræa here mongst earthly men did dwell,
And in the rules of iustice them instructed well.

6

Whiles through the world she walked in this sort,
  Vpon a day she found this gentle childe,
  Amongst his peres playing his childish sport:
  Whom seeing fit, and with no crime defilde,
  She did allure with gifts and speaches milde,
  To wend with her. So thence him farre she brought   *wend* go, travel
  Into a caue from companie exilde,
  In which she noursled him, till yeares he raught,   *noursled* raised, fostered *raught* reached
And all the discipline of iustice there him taught.

7

There she him taught to weigh both right and wrong
  In equall ballance with due recompence,
  And equitie to measure out along,
  According to the line of conscience,
  When so it needs with rigour to dispence.

5.4 faire *Astræa*,] The Daughter of Zeus and Themis, Astræa, goddess of justice, was the last of the gods to abandon the Earth at the end of Saturn's golden age (cf. Ovid, *Metamorphoses*, 1.149–50, and the discussion of Astræa's departure in Conti, *Mythologiae*, 2.2). She was immediately given a place in the night sky as the constellation Virgo (the virgin), adjacent to Libra (the scales).
    7.1–5 There she him taught ... to dispence.] An Aristotelian distinction between legal justice and conscientious justice – between what is lawful, and what is fair or right – informed early modern English theory. Following Aristotle, sixteenth-century English lawyers called conscientious justice *epieikeia*, or used the Latin term, *aequitas* – in English, equity. Equitable judgment referred the circumstances of a given case to the intention of the law (or lawgiver), correcting the conventional or written law in order to

Of all the which, for want there of mankind,
She caused him to make experience   *experience* practice, trial
Vpon wyld beasts, which she in woods did find,
With wrongfull powre oppressing others of their kind.

8

Thus she him trayned, and thus she him taught,
   In all the skill of deeming wrong and right,   *deeming* judging
   Vntill the ripenesse of mans yeares he raught;
   That euen wilde beasts did feare his awfull sight,
   And men admyr'd his ouerruling might;
   Ne any liu'd on ground, that durst withstand
   His dreadfull heast, much lesse him match in fight,   *heast* command, judgment
   Or bide the horror of his wreakfull hand,   *bide* endure *wreakfull* retributive
When so he list in wrath lift vp his steely brand.   *brand* sword

9

Which steely brand, to make him dreaded more,
   She gaue vnto him, gotten by her slight   *slight* skill, prudence
   And earnest search, where it was kept in store
   In *Ioues* eternall house, vnwist of wight,   *vnwist* unknown
   Since he himselfe it vs'd in that great fight
   Against the *Titans*, that whylome rebelled   *whylome* once, long ago
   Gainst highest heauen; *Chrysaor* it was hight;
   Chrysaor that all other swords excelled,
Well prou'd in that same day, when *Ioue* those Gyants quelled.

10

For of most perfect metall it was made,
   Tempred with Adamant amongst the same,
   And garnisht all with gold vpon the blade
   In goodly wise, whereof it tooke his name,   *wise* manner
   And was of no lesse vertue, then of fame.   *vertue* force, quality
   For there no substance was so firme and hard,
   But it would pierce or cleaue, where so it came;
   Ne any armour could his dint out ward,   *dint* blow *out ward* deflect, parry
But wheresoeuer it did light, it throughly shard.   *light* land, make contact *shard* sheared

avoid an unjust outcome. Equity must be distinguished from mercy, which is the remission of a just (even equitable) penalty on grounds of compassion or pity. See Aristotle, *Nicomachean Ethics*, 5 (1137a-1138a).

Stanza 9 Which steely brand ...] The name Chrysaor comes from the Gr χρυσός and ἄορ, 'golden sword'. It was the name of one of the sons of Neptune, got on the gorgon Medusa (see Hesiod, *Theogony*, ll. 280-99), who fathered the three-headed monster Geryon. Spenser's association of the sword with Jove's battle against the Titans suggests that Artegall's justice owes as much to imperial authority as it does to Astræan justice, or right.

11
Now when the world with sinne gan to abound, *gan* began
   Astræa loathing lenger here to space *space* walk, pace
   Mongst wicked men, in whom no truth she found,
   Return'd to heauen, whence she deriu'd her race; *heauen* (monsyllabic)
   Where she hath now an euerlasting place,
   Mongst those twelue signes, which nightly we doe see
   The heauens bright-shining baudricke to enchace; *baudricke* belt (the zodiac)
   And is the *Virgin*, sixt in her degree, *enchace* set or inlaid with jewels
And next her selfe her righteous ballance hanging bee.

12
But when she parted hence, she left her groome
   An yron man, which did on her attend
   Alwayes, to execute her stedfast doome,
   And willed him with *Artegall* to wend,
   And doe what euer thing he did intend.
   His name was *Talus*, made of yron mould, *mould* material, nature; matrix
   Immoueable, resistlesse, without end.
   Who in his hand an yron flale did hould,
With which he thresht out falshood, and did truth vnfould. *vnfould* reveal

13
He now went with him in this new inquest,
   Him for to aide, if aide he chaunst to neede,
   Against that cruell Tyrant, which opprest
   The faire *Irena* with his foule misdeede,
   And kept the crowne in which she should succeed.
   And now together on their way they bin,
   When as they saw a Squire in squallid weed, *squallid weed* fouled or dirty garments
   Lamenting sore his sorowfull sad tyne, *tyne* grief, trouble
With many bitter teares shed from his blubbred eyne.

14
To whom as they approched, they espide
   A sorie sight, as euer seene with eye;

11.5–6 Where . . . mongst those twelue signes,] The zodiac, in which Virgo and Libra occupy the sixth and seventh places, respectively.
   *Stanza 12 **His name was Talus . . .***] Apollonius Rhodius records in the *Argonautica* (4.1638–72) that a bronze giant called Talos warded the cliffs of Crete; his name apparently derived from Gr τλάω, 'to endure, abide'. In the *Minos*, a Socratic dialogue in the style of Plato, Rhadamanthos and Talos feature as Minos' deputies, who dispensed legal justice in Cretan cities and rural villages, respectively. Talos' reliance on written laws (engraved in metal) led him to be called (in an apparently euhemeristic account of the mythic tradition) a brazen man. His name also connects him, through L *talio* ('such, the like') and *lex talionis* ('law of retaliation'), to a fundamentally arithmetical and retaliative theory of justice.

An headlesse Ladie lying him beside,
In her owne blood all wallow'd wofully,
That her gay clothes did in discolour die.   *discolour* stain, discoloration
Much was he moued at that ruefull sight;
And flam'd with zeale of vengeance inwardly,
He askt, who had that Dame so fouly dight;   *dight* treated, abused
Or whether his owne hand, or whether other wight?

15

Ah woe is me, and well away (quoth hee)   *well away* a sorrowful exclamation
   Bursting forth teares, like springs out of a banke,   *banke* ridge, shelf
   That euer I this dismall day did see:
   Full farre was I from thinking such a pranke;   *pranke* wicked act, crime (L *scelus*)
   Yet litle losse it were, and mickle thanke,   *mickle thanke* great gain, advantage
   If I should graunt that I haue doen the same,
   That I mote drinke the cup, whereof she dranke: *mote* might
   But that I should die guiltie of the blame,
The which another did, who now is fled with shame.

16

Who was it then (sayd *Artegall*) that wrought?
   And why, doe it declare vnto me trew.
   A knight (said he) if knight he may be thought,
   That did his hand in Ladies bloud embrew,   *embrew* stain, dye
   And for no cause, but as I shall you shew.
   This day as I in solace sate hereby   *solace* pleasure, recreation
   With a fayre loue, whose losse I now do rew,
   There came this knight, hauing in companie
This lucklesse Ladie, which now here doth headlesse lie.

17

He, whether mine seem'd fayrer in his eye,
   Or that he wexed weary of his owne,   *wexed* grew
   Would change with me; but I did it denye;
   So did the Ladies both, as may be knowne,
   But he, whose spirit was with pride vpblowne,
   Would not so rest contented with his right,
   But hauing from his courser her downe throwne,
   Fro me reft mine away by lawlesse might,   *reft* stole
And on his steed her set, to beare her out of sight.

18

Which when his Ladie saw, she follow'd fast,
   And on him catching hold, gan loud to crie

Not so to leaue her, nor away to cast,
But rather of his hand besought to die.
With that his sword he drew all wrathfully,
And at one stroke cropt off her head with scorne,
In that same place, whereas it now doth lie.
So he my loue away with him hath borne,
And left me here, both his & mine owne loue to morne.

19

Aread (sayd he) which way then did he make?   *aread* declare, tell
 And by what markes may he be knowne againe?
 To hope (quoth he) him soone to ouertake,
 That hence so long departed, is but vaine:
 But yet he pricked ouer yonder plaine,
 And as I marked, bore vpon his shield,
 By which it's easie him to know againe,
 A broken sword within a bloodie field;
Expressing well his nature, which the same did wield.

20

No sooner sayd, but streight he after sent
 His yron page, who him pursew'd so light,
 As that it seem'd aboue the ground he went:
 For he was swift as swallow in her flight,
 And strong as Lyon in his Lordly might.
 It was not long, before he ouertooke
 Sir *Sanglier*; (so cleeped was that Knight)   *cleeped* named, called
 Whom at the first he ghessed by his looke,
And by the other markes, which of his shield he tooke.

21

He bad him stay, and backe with him retire;
 Who full of scorne to be commaunded so,
 The Lady to alight did eft require,   *eft* then, after
 Whilest he reformed that vnciuill fo:
 And streight at him with all his force did go.   *streight* straightaway
 Who mou'd no more therewith, then when a rocke
 Is lightly stricken with some stones throw;

19.8–9 A broken sword ...] In early modern political iconography, the sword symbolised (as for Artegall's Chrysaor) the power of the prince to defend the people and to enforce the law. Sanglier's emblem thus suggests criminal impunity: the broken state of society in which justice is powerless. Cf. George Wither, *A Collection of Emblemes, Ancient and Moderne* (London: Henry Taunton, 1635), no 3: 'The *Law* is given to *direct*; The *Sword*, to *punish* and *protect*.'

20.7–9 Sir Sanglier ... he tooke.] Artegall has encountered this knight before, at IV.iv.40.1–7, where he defeated him in a tournament. The name comes from Fr *sanglier*, 'wild boar'.

But to him leaping, lent him such a knocke,
That on the ground he layd him like a sencelesse blocke.

22

But ere he could him selfe recure againe,   *ere* before *recure* recover
  Him in his iron paw he seized had;
  That when he wak't out of his warelesse paine,   *wareless* unconscious, senseless
  He found him selfe vnwist, so ill bestad,   *vnwist* unknown *bestad* beset
  That lim he could not wag. Thence he him lad,   *wag* move, stir
  Bound like a beast appointed to the stall:
  The sight whereof the Lady sore adrad,   *adrad* frightened
  And fain'd to fly for feare of being thrall;
But he her quickly stayd, and forst to wend withall.

23

When to the place they came, where *Artegall*
  By that same carefull Squire did then abide,
  He gently gan him to demaund of all,   *gently* courteously
  That did betwixt him and that Squire betide.   *betide* befall, occur
  Who with sterne countenance and indignant pride
  Did aunswere, that of all he guiltlesse stood,
  And his accuser thereuppon defide:
  For neither he did shed that Ladies bloud,
Nor tooke away his loue, but his owne proper good.   *proper* personal, particular

24

Well did the Squire perceiue him selfe too weake,
  To aunswere his defiaunce in the field,
  And rather chose his challenge off to breake,
  Then to approue his right with speare and shield.
  And rather guilty chose him selfe to yield.
  But *Artegall* by signes perceiuing plaine,
  That he it was not, which that Lady kild,
  But that strange Knight, the fairer loue to gaine,
Did cast about by sleight the truth thereout to straine.   *cast about* contrive, devise

25

And sayd, now sure this doubtfull causes right
  Can hardly but by Sacrament be tride,
  Or else by ordele, or by blooddy fight;
  That ill perhaps mote fall to either side.

25.1–4 Sacrament ... ordele ... blooddy fight;] The traditional medieval methods for determining judgment in a trial of right were sacrament (oath-swearing), ordeal (e.g. by fire or water) or combat. In all three cases it was presumed that the 'trial' would issue in God's will.

But if ye please, that I your cause decide,	*decide* judge
Perhaps I may all further quarrell end,	
So ye will sweare my iudgement to abide.	*so* as long as, if
Thereto they both did franckly condiscend,	*franckly* freely *condiscend* yield, consent
And to his doome with listfull eares did both attend.	*listfull* attentive

26

Sith then (sayd he) ye both the dead deny,	*sith* since
And both the liuing Lady claime your right,	
Let both the dead and liuing equally	
Deuided be betwixt you here in sight,	
And each of either take his share aright.	
But looke who does dissent from this my read,	*read* counsel, judgment
He for a twelue moneths day shall in despight	*in despight* as a mark of his contempt
Beare for his penaunce that same Ladies head;	
To witnesse to the world, that she by him is dead.	

27

Well pleased with that doome was *Sangliere*,
   And offred streight the Lady to be slaine.
   But that same Squire, to whom she was more dere,
   When as he saw she should be cut in twaine,
   Did yield, she rather should with him remaine
   Aliue, then to him selfe be shared dead;
   And rather then his loue should suffer paine,
   He chose with shame to beare that Ladies head.
True loue despiseth shame, when life is cald in dread.

28

Whom when so willing *Artegall* perceaued;	
Not so thou Squire, (he sayd) but thine I deeme	
The liuing Lady, which from thee he reaued:	*reaued* stole
For worthy thou of her doest rightly seeme.	
And you, Sir Knight, that loue so light esteeme,	
As that ye would for little leaue the same,	
Take here your owne, that doth you best beseeme,	*beseeme* suit, fit
And with it beare the burden of defame;	
Your owne dead Ladies head, to tell abrode your shame.	

    26.3–5] Artegall's 'sleight' alludes to Solomon's famous judgment at I Kings 3.16–27, in which he settles a dispute between two women over an infant by offering to divide the infant between them. As in this case, the claimant moved by genuine love immediately capitulates, and is rewarded.

29

But *Sangliere* disdained much his doome,
   And sternly gan repine at his beheast; *repine at* grudge at, complain of
   Ne would for ought obay, as did become,
   To beare that Ladies head before his breast.
   Vntill that *Talus* had his pride represt,
   And forced him, maulgre, it vp to reare. *maulgre* notwithstanding, regardless
   Who when he saw it bootelesse to resist, *booteless* pointless, fruitless
   He tooke it vp, and thence with him did beare,
As rated Spaniell takes his burden vp for feare. *rated* scolded, chid

30

Much did that Squire Sir *Artegall* adore,
   For his great iustice, held in high regard;
   And as his Squire him offred euermore
   To serue, for want of other meete reward, *meete* suitable, fitting
   And wend with him on his aduenture hard.
   But he thereto would by no meanes consent;
   But leauing him forth on his iourney far'd:
   Ne wight with him but onely *Talus* went.
They two enough t' encounter an whole Regiment.

            Canto II.

    Artegall heares of Florimell,
      Does with the Pagan fight:
    Him slaies, drownes Lady Munera,
      Does race her castle quight. *race* raze, destroy *quight* completely

1

Nought is more honorable to a knight,
   Ne better doth beseeme braue cheualry,
   Then to defend the feeble in their right,
   And wrong redresse in such as wend awry.
   Whilome those great Heroes got thereby
   Their greatest glory, for their rightfull deedes,
   And place deserued with the Gods on hy.
   Herein the noblesse of this knight exceedes,
Who now to perils great for iustice sake proceedes.

1.5–7 Whilome ... Gods on hy.] Spenser mentions the civil reformations wrought by Bacchus and Hercules above, at V.i.2–3; but most of the heroes of Greek myth would fit this general description, especially Perseus and Theseus. The smooth combination of the romance ('cheualry') and mythic ('great Heroes') traditions is characteristic of Spenser's approach to his heterogeneous material.

2
To which as he now was vppon the way,
   He chaunst to meet a Dwarfe in hasty course;
   Whom he requir'd his forward hast to stay,
   Till he of tidings mote with him discourse.
   Loth was the Dwarfe, yet did he stay perforse,   *perforse* (compelled) by force
   And gan of sundry newes his store to tell,
   And to his memory they had recourse:
   But chiefely of the fairest *Florimell*,
How she was found againe, and spousde to *Marinell*.   *spousde* betrothed

3
For this was *Dony*, *Florimels* owne Dwarfe,
   Whom hauing lost (as ye haue heard whyleare)   *whyleare* some time ago
   And finding in the way the scattred scarfe,
   The fortune of her life long time did feare.
   But of her health when *Artegall* did heare,
   And safe returne, he was full inly glad,   *inly* within (i.e. sincerely)
   And askt him where, and when her bridale cheare
   Should be solemniz'd: for if time he had,   *solemniz'd* celebrated
He would be there, and honor to her spousall ad.   *spousall* wedding

4
Within three daies (quoth hee) as I do here,
   It will be at the Castle of the strond;
   What time if naught me let, I will be there   *what time* at which time *me let*
   To doe her seruice, so as I am bond.   prevents me
   But in my way a little here beyond
   A cursed cruell Sarazin doth wonne,   *wonne* dwell
   That keepes a Bridges passage by strong hond,
   And many errant Knights hath there fordonne;
That makes all men for feare that passage for to shonne.

5
What mister wight (quoth he) and how far hence   *mister* manner (of)
   Is he, that doth to trauellers such harmes?

   3.1 Dony, Florimels **owne Dwarfe,**] Prince Arthur first encounters Florimell's dwarf at III.v.3.
   4.2 Castle of the strond;] Marinell's ward of the '*Rich strond*' at III.iv.20–3, where he enjoys a monopoly on sea-borne riches, granted by Neptune, is allegorically associated with his misogynist chastity. The site of the marriage indicates his thorough reform.
   4.7 keepes . . . by strong hond,] While the toll-bridge is a reasonably common romance topos, legal control over a bridge or river crossing is also one example of a class of lucrative rights – some extended by the crown, others based on local 'custom of . . . law' (11.7) – enjoyed by privileged subjects in sixteenth-century England. Artegall's reformation of this 'custom' thus has clear contemporary economic and political overtones.

He is (said he) a man of great defence;
Expert in battell and in deedes of armes;
And more emboldned by the wicked charmes,
With which his daughter doth him still support;
Hauing great Lordships got and goodly farmes,
Through strong oppression of his powre extort;
By which he stil them holds, & keepes with strong effort.

6

And dayly he his wrong encreaseth more,
   For neuer wight he lets to passe that way;
   Ouer his Bridge, albee he rich or poore,   *albee he* whether he be
   But he him makes his passage-penny pay: *passage-penny* toll
   Else he doth hold him backe or beat away.
   Thereto he hath a groome of euill guize,   *guize* manner, appearance
   Whose scalp is bare, that bondage doth bewray,
   Which pols and pils the poore in piteous wize;   *pols and pils* robs, plunders
But he him selfe vppon the rich doth tyrannize.

7

His name is hight *Pollente*, rightly so
   For that he is so puissant and strong,   *puissant* powerful
   That with his powre he all doth ouergo,
   And makes them subiect to his mighty wrong;
   And some by sleight he eke doth vnderfong.   *eke* also *vnderfong* entrap, deceive
   For on a Bridge he custometh to fight,   *custometh* is accustomed
   Which is but narrow, but exceeding long;
   And in the same are many trap fals pight,   *pight* fixed, situated
Through which the rider downe doth fall through ouersight.

8

And vnderneath the same a riuer flowes,
   That is both swift and dangerous deepe withall;
   Into the which whom so he ouerthrowes,
   All destitute of helpe doth headlong fall,
   But he him selfe, through practise vsuall,
   Leapes forth into the floud, and there assaies
   His foe confused through his sodaine fall,
   That horse and man he equally dismaies,
And either both them drownes, or trayterously slaies.

7.1–2 Pollente . . . puissant and strong,] The name is derived fr. L *pollentia*, 'power, force'.

9

Then doth he take the spoile of them at will,   *take the spoile of* plunder
  And to his daughter brings, that dwels thereby:
  Who all that comes doth take, and therewith fill
  The coffers of her wicked threasury;
  Which she with wrongs hath heaped vp so hy,
  That many Princes she in wealth exceedes,
  And purchast all the countrey lying ny
  With the reuenue of her plenteous meedes,   *meedes* rewards, spoils; bribes
Her name is *Munera*, agreeing with her deedes.

10

Thereto she is full faire, and rich attired,
  With golden hands and siluer feete beside,
  That many Lords haue her to wife desired:
  But she them all despiseth for great pride.
  Now by my life (sayd he) and God to guide,   *God to guide* by God (an
  None other way will I this day betake,   asseveration)
  But by that Bridge, whereas he doth abide:
  Therefore me thither lead. No more he spake,
But thitherward forthright his ready way did make.

11

Vnto the place he came within a while,
  Where on the Bridge he ready armed saw
  The Sarazin, awayting for some spoile.
  Who as they to the passage gan to draw,
  A villaine to them came with scull all raw,
  That passage money did of them require,
  According to the custome of their law.
  To whom he aunswerd wroth, loe there thy hire;   *hire* reward
And with that word him strooke, that streight he did expire.

12

Which when the Pagan saw, he wexed wroth,
  And streight him selfe vnto the fight addrest,
  Ne was Sir Artegall behinde: so both
  Together ran with ready speares in rest.
  Right in the midst, whereas they brest to brest
  Should meete, a trap was letten downe to fall
  Into the floud: streight leapt the Carle vnblest,   *Carle* churl, villain

---

9.9 Munera .. her deedes.] The name derives from L *munus* (genitive *muneris*), 'gift, bribe'. Spenser's Munera in many respects imitates Langland's Lady Meed, in *Piers Plowman*, 2.8–17.

Well weening that his foe was falne withall: *weening* supposing, believing
But he was well aware, and leapt before his fall.

13

There being both together in the floud,
   They each at other tyrannously flew;   *tyrannously* felly, cruelly
   Ne ought the water cooled their whot bloud,   *ought* aught, at all *whot* hot
   But rather in them kindled choler new.
   But there the Paynim, who that vse well knew   *Paynim* pagan *vse* practice
   To fight in water, great aduantage had,
   That oftentimes him nigh he ouerthrew: *nigh* nearly
   And eke the courser, whereuppon he rad,
Could swim like to a fish, whiles he his backe bestrad.   *bestrad* straddled, sat astride

14

Which oddes when as Sir *Artegall* espide,   *oddes* difference, advantage
   He saw no way, but close with him in hast;   *close with* encounter hand to hand
   And to him driuing strongly downe the tide,
   Vppon his iron coller griped fast,
   That with the straint his wesand nigh he brast.   *wesand* throat, windpipe *brast* burst
   There they together stroue and struggled long,
   Either the other from his steede to cast;
   Ne euer *Artegall* his griple strong   *griple* grip, grasp
For anything wold slacke, but still vppon him hong.

15

As when a Dolphin and a Sele are met,
   In the wide champian of the Ocean plaine: *champian* level, open ground
   With cruell chaufe their courages they whet,   *chaufe* passion, fury
   The maysterdome of each by force to gaine,
   And dreadfull battaile twixt them do darraine: *darraine* arrange, prosecute
   They snuf, they snort, they bounce, they rage, they rore,
   That all the sea disturbed with their traine,   *traine* thrashing, watery wake
   Doth frie with fome aboue the surges hore.   *frie* boil, seethe *hore* greyish-white
Such was betwixt these two the troublesome vprore.

16

So *Artegall* at length him forst forsake
   His horses backe, for dread of being drownd,
   And to his handy swimming him betake.   *handy swimming* dog-paddle
   Eftsoones him selfe he from his hold vnbownd,   *eftsoones* again, afterwards
   And then no ods at all in him he fownd:
   For *Artegall* in swimming skilfull was,
   And durst the depth of any water sownd.   *durst* dared *sownd* plumb

So ought each Knight, that vse of perill has,　　　　*vse* experience, practice
In swimming be expert through waters force to pas.

17
Then very doubtfull was the warres euent,　　　　*euent* outcome
　Vncertaine whether had the better side:　　　　*whether* which of the two
　For both were skild in that experiment,
　And both in armes well traind and throughly tride.
　But *Artegall* was better breath'd beside,　　　　*better breath'd* of greater stamina
　And towards th' end, grew greater in his might,
　That his faint foe no longer could abide
　His puissance, ne beare him selfe vpright,
But from the water to the land betooke his flight.

18
But *Artegall* pursewd him still so neare,
　With bright Chrysaor in his cruell hand,
　That as his head he gan a litle reare
　Aboue the brincke, to tread vpon the land,
　He smote it off, that tumbling on the strand
　It bit the earth for very fell despight,　　　　*despight* scorn, contempt
　And gnashed with his teeth, as if he band　　　　*band* cursed
　High God, whose goodnesse he despaired quight,　　*quight* completely
Or curst the hand, which did that vengeance on him dight.　　*dight* perform

19
His corps was carried downe along the Lee,　　　　*Lee* meadow, open ground *or*
　Whose waters with his filthy bloud it stayned:　　the River Lee, near London *or* the River
　But his blasphemous head, that all might see,　　Lee, Munster, Ireland
　He pitcht vpon a pole on high ordayned;
　Where many years it afterwards remayned,
　To be a mirrour to all mighty men,
　In whose right hands great power is contayned,
　That none of them the feeble ouerren,
But alwaies doe their powre within iust compasse pen.　　*compasse* extent, limit

20
That done, vnto the Castle he did wend,
　In which the Paynims daughter did abide,
　Guarded of many which did her defend:
　Of whom he entrance sought, but was denide,
　And with reprochfull blasphemy defide,
　Beaten with stones downe from the battilment,
　That he was forced to withdraw aside;

And bad his seruant *Talus* to inuent *bad* commanded, instructed
Which way he enter might, without endangerment. *inuent* discover, find out

21
Eftsoones his Page drew to the Castle gate,
　And with his iron flale at it let flie,
　That all the warders it did sore amate, *amate* dismay
　The which erewhile spake so reprochfully, *erewhile* (not long) before
　And made them stoupe, that looked earst so hie. *earst* at first, formerly
　Yet still he bet, and bounst vppon the dore,
　And thundred strokes thereon so hideouslie,
　That all the peece he shaked from the flore,
And filled all the house with feare and great vprore.

22
With noise whereof the Lady forth appeared
　Vppon the Castle wall, and when she saw
　The daungerous state, in which she stood, she feared
　The sad effect of her neare ouerthrow;
　And gan entreat that iron man below,
　To cease his outrage, and him faire besought,
　Sith neither force of stones which they did throw,
　Nor powr of charms, which she against him wrought,
Might otherwise preuaile, or make him cease for ought.

23
But when as yet she saw him to proceede,
　Vnmou'd with praiers, or with piteous thought, *piteous* pitying
　She ment him to corrupt with goodly meede;
　And causde great sackes with endlesse riches fraught, *fraught* burdened, laden
　Vnto the battilment to be vpbrought,
　And powred forth ouer the Castle wall,
　That she might win some time, though dearly bought
　Whilest he to gathering of the gold did fall.
But he was nothing mou'd, nor tempted therewithall.

24
But still continu'd his assault the more,
　And layd on load with his huge yron flaile,
　That at the length he has yrent the dore, *yrent* torn away
　And made way for his maister to assaile.
　Who being entred, nought did then auaile
　For wight, against his powre them selues to reare:
　Each one did flie; their hearts began to faile,

And hid them selues in corners here and there;
And eke their dame halfe dead did hide her self for feare.

25
Long they her sought, yet no where could they finde her,
   That sure they ween'd she was escapt away:
   But *Talus*, that could like a limehound winde her,   *winde* scent, *thus* trace or follow
   And all things secrete wisely could bewray,
   At length found out, whereas she hidden lay
   Vnder an heape of gold. Thence he her drew
   By the faire lockes, and fowly did array,
   Withouten pitty of her goodly hew,
That *Artegall* him selfe her seemelesse plight did rew.   *seemelesse* unseemly

26
Yet for no pitty would he change the course
   Of Iustice, which in *Talus* hand did lye,
   Who rudely hayld her forth without remorse,   *hayld* drew, dragged
   Still holding vp her suppliant hands on hye,
   And kneeling at his feete submissiuely.
   But he her suppliant hands, those hands of gold,
   And eke her feete, those feete of siluer trye,   *trye* select, excellent
   Which sought vnrighteousnesse, and iustice sold,
Chopt off, and nayld on high, that all might them behold.

27
Her selfe then tooke he by the sclender wast,
   In vaine loud crying, and into the flood
   Ouer the Castle wall adowne her cast,
   And there her drowned in the durty mud:
   But the streame washt away her guilty blood.
   Thereafter all that mucky pelfe he tooke,   *mucky pelfe* dirty money
   The spoile of peoples euill gotten good,
   The which her sire had scrap't by hooke and crooke,   *by hooke and crooke* by any means necessary
And burning all to ashes, powr'd it downe the brooke.

28
And lastly all that Castle quite he raced,   *raced* razed, demolished
   Euen from the sole of his foundation,   *sole* floor of a building's foundation
   And all the hewen stones thereof defaced,   *defaced* ruined, broke up
   That there mote be no hope of reparation,
   Nor memory thereof to any nation.
   All which when *Talus* throughly had perfourmd,
   Sir *Artegall* vndid the euill fashion,   *fashion* custom

And wicked customes of that Bridge refourmed.　　　*customes* tolls, exactions
Which done, vnto his former iourney he retourned.

29
In which they measur'd mickle weary way,　　　　　*mickle* great, very
　Till that at length nigh to the sea they drew;
　By which as they did trauell on a day,
　They saw before them, far as they could vew,
　Full many people gathered in a crew;
　Whose great assembly they did much admire.
　For neuer there the like resort they knew.
　So towardes them they coasted, to enquire
What thing so many nations met, did there desire.

30
There they beheld a mighty Gyant stand
　Vpon a rocke, and holding forth on hie
　An huge great paire of ballance in his hand,　　　*ballance* scales
　With which he boasted in his surquedrie,　　　　 *surquedrie* arrogance, pride
　That all the world he would weigh equallie,
　If ought he had the same to counterpoys.　　　　 *counterpoys* counterbalance
　For want whereof he weighed vanity,
　And fild his ballaunce full of idle toys:
Yet was admired much of fooles, women, and boys.

31
He sayd that he would all the earth vptake,
　And all the sea, deuided each from either:
　So would he of the fire one ballaunce make,
　And one of th' ayre, without or wind, or wether:　　*or . . . or* either . . . or
　Then would he ballaunce heauen and hell together,
　And all that did within them all containe;
　Of all whose weight, he would not misse a fether.
　And looke what surplus did of each remaine,
He would to his owne part restore the same againe.

32
For why, he sayd they all vnequall were,　　　　　*for why* because
　And had encroched vppon others share,
　Like as the sea (which plaine he shewed there)
　Had worne the earth, so did the fire the aire,

30.1–3 a mighty Gyant . . . paire of ballance] The appearance of the giant with the scales refigures the earlier image of Astræa with her balance (V.i.11).

So all the rest did others parts empaire.   *empaire* damage, diminish
    And so were realmes and nations run awry.
    All which he vndertooke for to repaire,
    In sort as they were formed aunciently;
And all things would reduce vnto equality.

33

Therefore the vulgar did about him flocke,
    And cluster thicke vnto his leasings vaine,   *leasings* lies
    Like foolish flies about an hony crocke,   *crocke* earthen jar
    In hope by him great benefite to gaine,
    And vncontrolled freedome to obtaine.
All which when *Artegall* did see, and heare,
    How he mis-led the simple peoples traine,   *simple ... traine* mob of simple people
    In sdeignfull wize he drew vnto him neare,   *sdeignfull* disdainful
And thus vnto him spake, without regard or feare.

34

Thou that presum'st to weigh the world anew,
    And all things to an equall to restore,
    In stead of right me seemes great wrong dost shew,
    And far aboue thy forces pitch to sore.
    For ere thou limit what is lesse or more
    In euery thing, thou oughtest first to know,
    What was the poyse of euery part of yore: *poyse* weight, significance
    And looke then how much it doth ouerflow,
Or faile thereof, so much is more then iust to trow.   *to trow* to be believed, thought

35

For at the first they all created were
    In goodly measure, by their Makers might,
    And weighed out in ballaunces so nere,   *so nere* so carefully, meticulously
    That not a dram was missing of their right,   *dram* an eighth of an ounce
    The earth was in the middle centre pight,   *pight* placed
    In which it doth immoueable abide,
    Hemd in with waters like a wall in sight;
    And they with aire, that not a drop can slide:
Al which the heauens containe, & in their courses guide.

32.9 equality] The princely and aristocratic regimes of early modern Europe favoured Aristotle's claim, in the *Nicomachean Ethics*, that a just distribution of rights and resources would follow proportional rather than arithmetical equality; that is, to the better sort, more should be given, and to the worse, less (cf. *Nicomachean Ethics*, 5.3). The giant's argument here promotes an arithmetical distribution similar to that proposed by sixteenth-century Anabaptists, or – later – to that of the Levellers during the English Civil War. Indeed, stanzas 29–54 of this canto were adapted and republished as an anti-Leveller pamphlet, entitled *The Faerie Leveller*, in 1648.

36

Such heauenly iustice doth among them raine,
    That euery one doe know their certaine bound,
    In which they doe these many yeares remaine,
    And mongst them al no change hath yet beene found.
    But if thou now shouldst weigh them new in pound,   *in pound* by the pound
    We are not sure they would so long remaine:
    All change is perillous, and all chaunce vnsound.
    Therefore leaue off to weigh them all againe,
Till we may be assur'd they shall their course retaine.

37

Thou foolish Elfe (said then the Gyant wroth)
    Seest not, how badly all things present bee,
    And each estate quite out of order goth?
    The sea it selfe doest thou not plainely see
    Encroch vppon the land there vnder thee;
    And th' earth it selfe how daily its increast,
    By all that dying to it turned be.
    Were it not good that wrong were then surceast,   *surceast* brought to an end, stopped
And from the most, that some were giuen to the least?

38

Therefore I will throw downe these mountaines hie,
    And make them leuell with the lowly plaine:
    These towring rocks, which reach vnto the skie,
    I will thrust downe into the deepest maine,   *maine* sea, open ocean
    And as they were, them equalize againe.
    Tyrants that make men subiect to their law,
    I will suppresse, that they no more may raine;
    And Lordings curbe, that commons ouer-aw;   *commons* commoners, the 'third estate'
And all the wealth of rich men to the poore will draw.

39

Of things vnseene how canst thou deeme aright,
    Then answered the righteous *Artegall*,
    Sith thou misdeem'st so much of things in sight?
    What though the sea with waues continuall
    Doe eate the earth, it is no more at all:
    Ne is the earth the lesse, or loseth ought,
    For whatsoeuer from one place doth fall,

38.1–5 Therefore ... equalize againe.] Echoes of Isaiah 40.4 intensify Spenser's presentation of the giant's hubris: 'Euery valley shalbe exalted, and euery mountaine and hill shalbe made lowe: and the crooked shalbe streight, and the rough places plaine.'

Is with the tide vnto an other brought:
For there is nothing lost, that may be found, if sought.

40
Likewise the earth is not augmented more,
   By all that dying into it doe fade.
   For of the earth they formed were of yore,   *of yore* anciently, long time since
   How euer gay their blossome or their blade
   Doe flourish now, they into dust shall vade.   *vade* vanish, decay (cf. L *vadere*)
   What wrong then is it, if that when they die,
   They turne to that, whereof they first were made?
   All in the powre of their great Maker lie:
All creatures must obey the voice of the most hie.

41
They liue, they die, like as he doth ordaine,
   Ne euer any asketh reason why.
   The hils doe not the lowly dales disdaine;
   The dales doe not the lofty hils enuy.
   He maketh Kings to sit in souerainty;
   He maketh subiects to their powre obay;
   He pulleth downe, he setteth vp on hy;
   He giues to this, from that he takes away.
For all we haue is his: what he list doe, he may.

42
What euer thing is done, by him is donne,
   Ne any may his mighty will withstand;
   Ne any may his soueraine power shonne,
   Ne loose that he hath bound with stedfast band.
   In vaine therefore doest thou now take in hand,
   To call to count, or weigh his workes anew,
   Whose counsels depth thou canst not vnderstand,
   Sith of things subiect to thy daily vew
Thou doest not know the causes, nor their courses dew.

43
For take thy ballaunce, if thou be so wise,
   And weigh the winde, that vnder heauen doth blow;
   Or weigh the light, that in the East doth rise;
   Or weigh the thought, that from mans mind doth flow.
   But if the weight of these thou canst not show,
   Weigh but one word which from thy lips doth fall.
   For how canst thou those greater secrets know,

That doest not know the least thing of them all?
Ill can he rule the great, that cannot reach the small.

44
Therewith the Gyant much abashed sayd;
   That he of little things made reckoning light,
   Yet the least word that euer could be layd
   Within his ballaunce, he could way aright.
   Which is (sayd he) more heauy then in weight,
   The right or wrong, the false or else the trew?
   He answered, that he would try it streight,
   So he the words into his ballaunce threw,
But streight the winged words out of his ballaunce flew.

45
Wroth wext he then, and sayd, that words were light,   *wroth* angry *wext* grew, became
   Ne would within his ballaunce well abide.
   But he could iustly weigh the wrong or right.
   Well then, sayd *Artegall*, let it be tride.
   First in one ballance set the true aside.
   He did so first; and then the false he layd
   In th' other scale; but still it downe did slide,
   And by no meane could in the weight be stayd.
For by no meanes the false will with the true be wayd.

46
Now take the right likewise, said *Artegale*,
   And counterpeise the same with so much wrong.
   So first the right he put into one scale;
   And then the Gyant stroue with puissance strong
   To fill the other scale with so much wrong.
   But all the wrongs that he therein could lay,
   Might not it peise; yet did he labour long,   *peise* equal in weight, balance
   And swat, and chauf'd, and proued euery way: *proued* tried
Yet all the wrongs could not a litle right downe way.

47
Which when he saw, he greatly grew in rage,
   And almost would his balances haue broken:
   But *Artegall* him fairely gan asswage,   *asswage* mollify, appease, soothe
   And said; be not vpon thy balance wroken: *wroken* revenged
   For they doe nought but right or wrong betoken;
   But in the mind the doome of right must bee;
   And so likewise of words, the which be spoken,

The eare must be the ballance, to decree
And iudge, whether with truth or falshood they agree.

48
But set the truth and set the right aside,
    For they with wrong or falshood will not fare;   *fare* go, consort
    And put two wrongs together to be tride,
    Or else two falses, of each equall share;
    And then together doe them both compare.
    For truth is one, and right is euer one.
    So did he, and then plaine it did appeare,
    Whether of them the greater were attone.   *attone* together; or, for 'attonce',
But right sate in the middest of the beame alone.   immediately

49
But he the right from thence did thrust away,
    For it was not the right, which he did seeke;
    But rather stroue extremities to way,
    Th' one to diminish, th' other for to eeke.   *eeke* increase
    For of the meane he greatly did misleeke.
    Whom when so lewdly minded *Talus* found,
    Approching nigh vnto him cheeke by cheeke,
    He shouldered him from off the higher ground,
And down the rock him throwing, in the sea him dround.

50
Like as a ship, whom cruell tempest driues
    Vpon a rocke with horrible dismay,
    Her shattered ribs in thousand peeces riues,
    And spoyling all her geares and goodly ray,   *geares and . . . ray* stuff and tackle
    Does make her selfe misfortunes piteous pray.   *pray* victim
    So downe the cliffe the wretched Gyant tumbled;
    His battred ballances in peeces lay,
    His timbered bones all broken rudely rumbled,
So was the high aspyring with huge ruine humbled.

51
That when the people, which had there about
    Long wayted, saw his sudden desolation,   *desolation* catastrophe, ruin; grief
    They gan to gather in tumultuous rout,
    And mutining, to stirre vp ciuill faction,   *mutining* rebelling
    For certaine losse of so great expectation.   *ciuill faction* political dissension
    For well they hoped to haue got great good;
    And wondrous riches by his innouation.

Therefore resoluing to reuenge his blood,
They rose in armes, and all in battell order stood.

52
Which lawlesse multitude him comming to
  In warlike wise, when *Artegall* did vew,
  He much was troubled, ne wist what to doo.
  For loth he was his noble hands t' embrew
  In the base blood of such a rascall crew;
  And otherwise, if that he should retire,
  He fear'd least they with shame would him pursew.
  Therefore he *Talus* to them sent, t' inquire
The cause of their array, and truce for to desire.   *array* 'battell order' (cf. 51.9, above)

53
But soone as they him nigh approching spide,
  They gan with all their weapons him assay,
  And rudely stroke at him on euery side:
  Yet nought they could him hurt, ne ought dismay.
  But when at them he with his flaile gan lay,
  He like a swarme of flyes them ouerthrew;
  Ne any of them durst come in his way,
  But here and there before his presence flew,
And hid themselues in holes and bushes from his vew.

54
As when a Faulcon hath with nimble flight
  Flowne at a flush of Ducks, foreby the brooke,   *foreby* near to
  The trembling foule dismayd with dreadfull sight
  Of death, the which them almost ouertooke,
  Doe hide themselues from her astonying looke,   *astonying* paralysing, petrifying
  Amongst the flags and couert round about.   *flags* marsh-reeds, rushes
  When *Talus* saw they all the field forsooke   *couert* hiding places
  And none appear'd of all that raskall rout,
To *Artegall* he turn'd, and went with him throughout.

5. Book VI, cantos x–xi

Calidore, the knight of courtesy, is charged with the capture of the Blatant Beast – a monster with a thousand barking and poisonous tongues, first seen at the end of Book V in the company of Detraction and Envy. But like most of Spenser's knights before him, Calidore does not seem to have a firm grasp of the virtue he is meant to patronise. After some arbitrary, dishonest and occasionally clumsy judgments in the opening few cantos of the book, he disappears from narrative view until canto ix – and then he returns not to pursue his adventure, but to put aside his weapons and take up the simple life of a shepherd. Though Calidore's truancy is motivated by love – for a country lass called Pastorella – it is nonetheless among the simple hinds and herds that he discovers the true nature of grace and courtesy. In these cantos, Calidore goes back to Spenser's roots in pastoral poetry, and even meets Spenser's own persona, the poet of *The Shepheardes Calender*, Colin Clout, for a lesson in decorous civility. It is this weird, meta-poetic encounter, in which Spenser intrudes into his own poem to chastise his hero, that prepares Calidore for his final challenge. When the shepherds are massacred and Pastorella is captured by brigands, Calidore reluctantly resumes his epic quest, making the best of a fallen world. Courtesy in these cantos emerges neither as a trivial science of social graces, nor as the simple native practice of an ideal, lost world, but as a hard-edged and sometimes cynical instinct for politic outcomes. Calidore's courtesy perfects Artegall's tough justice, but even at the end of Book VI it is brute force that must subdue the Blatant Beast, and there are still occasions when good knights must wade in gore.

Canto X.

Calidore sees the Graces daunce,
 To Colins melody:
The whiles his Pastorell is led,
 Into captiuity.

1
Who now does follow the foule *Blatant Beast*,
 Whilest *Calidore* does follow that faire Mayd,
 Vnmyndfull of his vow and high beheast,   *beheast* promise
 Which by the Faery Queene was on him layd,
 That he should neuer leaue, nor be delayd
 From chacing him, till he had it attchieued?
 But now entrapt of loue, which him betrayd,
 He mindeth more, how he may be relieued
With grace from her, whose loue his heart hath sore engrieued.

1.1–6 Who now ... attchieued?] Calidore's quest to subdue the Blatant Beast is outlined at VI.i.1–10: it is 'a Monster bred of hellishe race' that 'doth wound, and bite, and cruelly torment' both knights and ladies. The beast first appears in the company of the hags Envy and Detraction at the end of Book V (xii.28–43), when it attacks Artegall on his return from the salvage island, and its discourteous, barking mouth remains the symbol of its slanderous evil. Calidore was following the beast in VI.ix when he stumbled upon a community of shepherds, and fell into distracted love with Pastorella (VI.ix.5–12).

2
That from henceforth he meanes no more to sew   *sew* pursue
  His former quest, so full of toile and paine;
  Another quest, another game in vew   *game* quarry
  He hath, the guerdon of his loue to gaine: *guerdon* reward
  With whom he myndes for euer to remaine,
  And set his rest amongst the rusticke sort,
  Rather then hunt still after shadowes vaine
  Of courtly fauour, fed with light report,
Of euery blaste, and sayling alwaies on the port.

3
Ne certes mote he greatly blamed be,   *certes* certainly *mote* may
  From so high step to stoupe vnto so low.
  For who had tasted once (as oft did he)
  The happy peace, which there doth ouerflow,
  And prou'd the perfect pleasures, which doe grow
  Amongst poore hyndes, in hils, in woods, in dales,   *hyndes* rustics, country people
  Would neuer more delight in painted show
  Of such false blisse, as there is set for stales,   *set for stales* laid out as a decoy
T'entrap vnwary fooles in their eternall bales.   *bales* miseries, sufferings

4
For what hath all that goodly glorious gaze
  Like to one sight, which *Calidore* did vew?
  The glaunce whereof their dimmed eies would daze,
  That neuer more they should endure the shew
  Of that sunne-shine, that makes them looke askew.
  Ne ought in all that world of beauties rare,
  (Saue onely *Glorianaes* heauenly hew
  To which what can compare?) can it compare;
The which as commeth now, by course I will declare.

5
One day as he did raunge the fields abroad,
  Whilest his faire *Pastorella* was elsewhere,
  He chaunst to come, far from all peoples troad,   *troad* tread, path
  Vnto a place, whose pleasaunce did appere
  To passe all others, on the earth which were:
  For all that euer was by natures skill
  Deuiz'd to worke delight, was gathered there,
  And there by her were poured forth at fill,
As if this to adorne, she all the rest did pill.   *pill* strip, spoil, exhaust

    5.4–9 ff. vnto a place ... did pill.] This place is both like and unlike the Bowre of Blisse (cf. II.xii, above): like the bower, it is a *locus amoenus*, seemingly made for pleasant play; but unlike the bower,

6

It was an hill plaste in an open plaine,
  That round about was bordered with a wood
  Of matchlesse hight, that seem'd th'earth to disdaine,
  In which all trees of honour stately stood,
  And did all winter as in sommer bud,
  Spredding pauilions for the birds to bowre,
  Which in their lower braunches sung aloud;
  And in their tops the soring hauke did towre, *tower* rise, mount up
Sitting like King of fowles in maiesty and powre.

7

And at the foote thereof, a gentle flud
  His siluer waues did softly tumble downe,
  Vnmard with ragged mosse or filthy mud,
  Ne mote wylde beastes, ne mote the ruder clowne *clowne* rustic, peasant
  Thereto approch, ne filth mote therein drowne:
  But Nymphes and Faeries by the bancks did sit,
  In the woods shade, which did the waters crowne,
  Keeping all noysome things away from it, *noysome* injurious, noxious
And to the waters fall tuning their accents fit.

8

And on the top thereof a spacious plaine
  Did spred it selfe, to serue to all delight,
  Either to daunce, when they to daunce would faine, *faine* delight, be glad
  Or else to course about their bases light; *bases* stations or marks for running
  Ne ought there wanted, which for pleasure might
  Desired be, or thence to banish bale: *bale* evil, grief, sorrow
  So pleasauntly the hill with equall hight,
  Did seeme to ouerlooke the lowly vale;
Therefore it rightly cleeped was mount *Acidale*. *cleeped* called

9

They say that *Venus*, when she did dispose
  Her selfe to pleasaunce, vsed to resort *vsed* was accustomed
  Vnto this place, and therein to repose

its pleasures have all arisen through 'natures skill', and not through art. Its presiding spirit is a god, and not an enchantress – though this is a distinction that might not have carried much weight for Spenser's early Protestant readers.
  8.9 Acidale.] On Acidale as a surname for Venus, see Virgil, *Aeneid*, 1.729–34. Servius claims in his commentary on these lines of Virgil that 'Acidale' may derive from Gr ἀκιδας, 'free from care', or (more plausibly) from the name of a spring called Acidalio, in Boeotia, *in quo se Gratiae lavant, quas Veneri esse constat sacratas* ('in which the Graces bathe themselves, sacred to Venus, as is fitting'). Martial uses the epithet in the *Epigrams*, at 6.13.5.

And rest her selfe, as in a gladsome port,
   Or with the Graces there to play and sport;
   That euen her owne Cytheron, though in it
   She vsed most to keepe her royall court,
   And in her soueraine Maiesty to sit,
She in regard hereof refusde and thought vnfit.

10
Vnto this place when as the Elfin Knight
   Approcht, him seemed that the merry sound
   Of a shrill pipe he playing heard on hight,
   And many feete fast thumping th'hollow ground,
   That through the woods their Eccho did rebound.
   He nigher drew, to weete what mote it be;   *weete* know
   There he a troupe of Ladies dauncing found
   Full merrily, and making gladfull glee,
And in the midst a Shepheard piping he did see.

11
He durst not enter into th'open greene,
   For dread of them vnwares to be descryde,   *descryde* observed, noticed
   For breaking of their daunce, if he were seene;
   But in the couert of the wood did byde,   *couert* covering, shelter
   Beholding all, yet of them vnespyde.   *vnespyde* unseen, unnoticed
   There he did see, that pleased much his sight,
   That euen he him selfe his eyes enuyde,
   An hundred naked maidens lilly white,
All raunged in a ring, and dauncing in delight.   *raunged* ordered

12
All they without were raunged in a ring,
   And daunced round; but in the midst of them
   Three other Ladies did both daunce and sing,
   The whilest the rest them round about did hemme,   *hemme* border, circle
   And like a girlond did in compasse stemme: *girlond* wreath *stemme* wreathe
   And in the middest of those same three, was placed
   Another Damzell, as a precious gemme,
   Amidst a ring most richly well enchaced,   *enchaced* set with jewels
That with her goodly presence all the rest much graced.

Stanza 9 Venus . . . Cytheron,] Virgil writes in Book I of the *Aeneid* (l. 680) of *alta Cythera* ('high Cythera'), Venus' sacred temple in Cyprus. Spenser's claim here that she preferred Acidale appears to be fanciful.
   11.1–2 He durst not enter . . .] Calidore's hesitation here may recall Pentheus' fear of the Bacchic orgy in Euripides' *Bacchae*.

13
Looke how the Crowne, which *Ariadne* wore
  Vpon her yuory forehead that same day,
  That *Theseus* her vnto his bridale bore,
  When the bold *Centaures* made that bloudy fray
  With the fierce *Lapithes* which did them dismay;
  Being now placed in the firmament,
  Through the bright heauen doth her beams display,
  And is vnto the starres an ornament,
Which round about her moue in order excellent.

14
Such was the beauty of this goodly band,
  Whose sundry parts were here too long to tell:
  But she that in the midst of them did stand,
  Seem'd all the rest in beauty to excell,
  Crownd with a rosie girlond, that right well
  Did her beseeme. And euer, as the crew   *beseeme* befit, suit
  About her daunst, sweet flowres, that far did smell,
  And fragrant odours they vppon her threw;
But most of all, those three did her with gifts endew.

15
Those were the Graces, daughters of delight,
  Handmaides of *Venus*, which are wont to haunt   *wont* accustomed
  Vppon this hill, and daunce there day and night:
  Those three to men all gifts of grace do graunt,
  And all, that *Venus* in her selfe doth vaunt,   *vaunt* boast
  Is borrowed of them. But that faire one,
  That in the midst was placed parauaunt,   *parauaunt* foremost, first
  Was she to whom that shepheard pypt alone,
That made him pipe so merrily, as neuer none.

***Stanza 13* Looke how the Crowne ...**] Ovid records in the *Metamorphoses* (8.169–82) how, after the Cretan princess Ariadne was abandoned by her husband Theseus, Bacchus set her bridal crown among the stars as the constellation Corona Borealis. The centaurs' battle with the Lapithae took place, according to Ovid (*Metamorphoses*, 12.210–535), at the wedding of Pirithous and Hippodame, when the drunken centaur Eurytus attempted to rape the bride.

15.1 ff. **the Graces,**] Aglaia, Euphrosyne and Thalia, usually said to be daughters of Jove and Eurynome, 'from whose eyes as they glanced flowed love that unnerves the limbs: and beautiful is their glance beneath their brows' (Hesiod, *Theogony*, ll. 907–11). Conti discusses usual features of their representation and the import of their symbolism (*Mythologiae*, 4.15).

16

She was to weete that iolly Shepheards lasse,   *to weete* truly, indeed
   Which piped there vnto that merry rout,
   That iolly shepheard, which there piped, was
   Poore *Colin Clout* (who knowes not *Colin Clout*?)
   He pypt apace, whilest they him daunst about.   *apace* quickly, briskly
   Pype iolly shepheard, pype thou now apace
   Vnto thy loue, that made thee low to lout;   *lout* bow, stoop
   Thy loue is present there with thee in place,
Thy loue is there aduaunst to be another Grace.

17

Much wondred *Calidore* at this straunge sight,
   Whose like before his eye had neuer seene,
   And standing long astonished in spright,
   And rapt with pleasaunce, wist not what to weene;   *wist* knew *weene* believe
   Whether it were the traine of beauties Queene,   *traine* retinue
   Or Nymphes, or Faeries, or enchaunted show,
   With which his eyes mote haue deluded beene.
   Therefore resoluing, what it was, to know,
Out of the wood he rose, and toward them did go.

18

But soone as he appeared to their vew,
   They vanisht all away out of his sight,
   And cleane were gone, which way he neuer knew;   *cleane* completely, utterly
   All saue the shepheard, who for fell despight
   Of that displeasure, broke his bag-pipe quight,
   And made great mone for that vnhappy turne.   *turne* event, circumstance
   But *Calidore*, though no lesse sory wight,   *wight* person
   For that mishap, yet seeing him to mourne,
Drew neare, that he the truth of all by him mote learne.   *mote* might

19

And first him greeting, thus vnto him spake,
   Hail iolly shepheard, which thy ioyous dayes

   Stanza 16 that iolly Shepheards lasse,] That jolly shepherd, Colin Clout, is the central figure of Spenser's *The Shepheardes Calender* (1579) and of *Colin Clouts Come Home Againe* (1595), and functions here, perhaps, as Spenser's persona within his own poem – certainly it is tempting to read the appeal to Gloriana in stanzas 25–9 (below) as a personal one. The 'lasse' of which the poem speaks has thus been read as Spenser's new wife, Elizabeth Boyle, to whom he was married in the summer of 1595; but it is not necessary to read this section of the poem as anything more than apparently autobiographical – as always, the consummate myth-maker is most adept at mythologising himself. The gesture toward privacy also has important metaphysical, psychological and political interest.
   18.4–5 the shepheard . . . broke his bag-pipe] Colin Clout also breaks his bag-pipe at the end of the 'Januarye' eclogue in *The Shepheardes Calender*, Spenser's first published work.

Here leadest in this goodly merry make,   *merry make* merry-making, festivity
Frequented of these gentle Nymphes alwayes,
Which to thee flocke, to heare thy louely layes;   *layes* songs
Tell me, what mote these dainty Damzels be,
Which here with thee doe make their pleasant playes?
Right happy thou, that mayst them freely see:
But why when I them saw, fled they away from me?

20

Not I so happy answerd then that swaine,
   As thou vnhappy, which them thence didst chace,
   Whom by no meanes thou canst recall againe,
   For being gone, none can them bring in place,
   But whom they of them selues list so to grace.   *list* desire, please
   Right sory I, (saide then Sir *Calidore*,)
   That my ill fortune did them hence displace.
   But since things passed none may now restore,
Tell me, what were they all, whose lacke thee grieues so sore.

21

Tho gan that shepheard thus for to dilate;   *tho* then *gan* began
   Then wote thou shepheard, whatsoeuer thou bee,   *wote* know
   That all those Ladies, which thou sawest late,
   Are *Venus* Damzels, all with in her fee,   *in her fee* in her service
   But differing in honour and degree:
   They all are Graces, which on her depend,
   Besides a thousand more, which ready bee
   Her to adorne, when so she forth doth wend: *wend* go, journey
But those three in the midst, doe chiefe on her attend.   *chiefe* chiefly

22

They are the daughters of sky-ruling Ioue,
   By him begot of faire *Eurynome*,
   The Oceans daughter, in this pleasant groue,
   As he this way comming from feastfull glee,   *feastfull glee* a festive banquet
   Of *Thetis* wedding with *Æacidee*,
   In sommers shade him selfe here rested weary.
   The first of them hight mylde *Euphrosyne*,   *hight* is called
   Next faire *Aglaia*, last *Thalia* merry:
Sweete Goddesses all three which me in mirth do cherry.   *cherry* cheer, solace, delight

Stanza 22 the daughters of sky-ruling Ioue ...] See above, 15.1–6n. The marriage of Peleus (son of Aeacus) and Thetis is famous not for the conception of the Graces, but for the origins of the Trojan War; it was at this wedding that Ate, Spenser's 'mother of debate', threw a golden apple, inscribed 'for the fairest', among the gods Juno, Minerva and Venus. Their contention led to Paris's judgment for Venus, the rape of Helen, and the mobilisation of the Greek host.

23

These three on men all gracious gifts bestow,
    Which decke the body or adorne the mynde,
    To make them louely or well fauoured show,
    As comely carriage, entertainement kynde,
    Sweete semblaunt, friendly offices that bynde,   *semblaunt* expression, countenance
    And all the complements of curtesie: *complements* perfections,
    They teach vs, how to each degree and kynde   accomplishments
    We should our selues demeane, to low, to hie;   *demeane* behave, comport
To friends, to foes, which skill men call Ciuility.

24

Therefore they alwaies smoothly seeme to smile,
    That we likewise should mydle and gentle be,
    And also naked are, that without guile
    Or false dissemblaunce all them plaine may see,   *dissemblaunce* deceit, dissimulation
    Simple and true from couert malice free: *couert* hidden
    And eeke them selues so in their daunce they bore,   *eeke* also
    That two of them still forward seem'd to bee,
    But one still towards shew'd her selfe afore;
That good should from vs goe, then come in greater store.

25

Such were those Goddesses, which ye did see;
    But that fourth Mayd, which there amidst them traced,
    Who can aread, what creature mote she bee,   *aread* interpret, conjecture, guess
    Whether a creature, or a goddesse graced
    With heauenly gifts from heuen first enraced?   *enraced* implanted
    But what so sure she was, she worthy was,
    To be the fourth with those three other placed:
    Yet was she certes but a countrey lasse,   *certes* certainly, truly
Yet she all other countrey lasses farre did passe.

    ***Stanzas 23–4* These three ... bestow,]** In these stanzas, Spenser closely follows Thomas Cooper's account of the Graces ('Charites') in his *Dictionarium* (sig. F3ʳ).
    ***23.7–9* Ciuility.]** On the relation of 'civility' to 'courtesy', see headnote.
    ***24.6–9* so in their daunce they bore ...]** 'Forward' here means 'in the direction in which the gaze is travelling' – that is, facing away from Calidore. Some past editors have taken this word as a compositor's mistake for 'froward' (thus creating an opposition between 'to' and 'fro', in the words 'froward' and 'toward'), though if so, it remained uncorrected in the 1609 edition. In any case, and especially taken in combination with the equivocal 'then' of 24.9 (which can mean both 'than' and the modern 'then'), Spenser's verse unpacks the paradox of the Graces' symbol of gift exchange.
    ***25.3 ff.* what creature mote she bee,]** See Stanza 16n., above. As E. K. records in the gloss to 'Aprill' (l. 109) of *The Shepheardes Calender*, Homer also includes a fourth Grace, whom Hera (Juno) promises as a wife to Hypnos (Somnus) (*Iliad*, 14.276–7). Her name, Pasithea, may suggest that she contains 'all the divinity' of her fellows.

26
So farre as doth the daughter of the day,
   All other lesser lights in light excell,
   So farre doth she in beautyfull array,   *array* attire, presentation
   Aboue all other lasses beare the bell,   *beare the bell* win the prize
   Ne lesse in vertue that beseemes her well,
   Doth she exceede the rest of all her race,
   For which the Graces that here wont to dwell,
   Haue for more honor brought her to this place,
And graced her so much to be another Grace.

27
Another Grace she well deserues to be,
   In whom so many Graces gathered are,
   Excelling much the meane of her degree;
   Diuine resemblaunce, beauty soueraine rare,
   Firme Chastity, that spight ne blemish dare;   *ne* nor
   All which she with such courtesie doth grace,
   That all her peres cannot with her compare,
   But quite are dimmed, when she is in place.
She made me often pipe and now to pipe apace.

28
Sunne of the world, great glory of the sky,
   That all the earth doest lighten with thy rayes,
   Great *Gloriana*, greatest Maiesty,
   Pardon thy shepheard, mongst so many layes,
   As he hath sung of thee in all his dayes,
   To make one minime of thy poore handmayd,   *minim* a short note, a trifle
   And vnderneath thy feete to place her prayse,
   That when thy glory shall be farre displayd
To future age of her this mention may be made.

29
When thus that shepherd ended had his speach,
   Sayd *Calidore*; Now sure it yrketh mee,
   That to thy blisse I made this luckelesse breach,
   As now the author of thy bale to be,   *bale* evil, grief, sorrow
   Thus to bereaue thy loues deare sight from thee: *bereaue* steal, snatch away
   But gentle Shepheard pardon thou my shame,
   Who rashly sought that, which I mote not see.

Stanza 28] This stanza provides another point of apparent autobiographical contact in this episode: Spenser makes a similar petition to Elizabeth in sonnet 80 of his sonnet sequence *Amoretti* (1595).

Thus did the courteous Knight excuse his blame,
And to recomfort him, all comely meanes did frame.   *comely* appropriate, seemly, fair

30
In such discourses they together spent
   Long time, as fit occasion forth them led;
   With which the Knight him selfe did much content,
   And with delight his greedy fancy fed,
   Both of his words, which he with reason red;   *red* interpreted, construed
   And also of the place, whose pleasures rare
   With such regard his sences rauished,
   That thence, he had no will away to fare,   *fare* travel, go
But wisht, that with that shepheard he mote dwelling share.

31
But that enuenimd sting, the which of yore,   *of yore* long time since
   His poysnous point deepe fixed in his hart
   Had left, now gan afresh to rancle sore,   *rancle* fester
   And to renue the rigour of his smart:
   Which to recure, no skill of Leaches art   *recure* recover, cure
   Mote him auaile, but to returne againe   *him auaile* be of use, profit to him
   To his wounds worker, that with louely dart
   Dinting his brest, had bred his restlesse paine,   *dinting* striking
Like as the wounded Whale to shore flies from the maine.

32
So taking leaue of that same gentle swaine,
   He backe returned to his rusticke wonne,   *wonne* dwelling
   Where his faire *Pastorella* did remaine:
   To whome in sort, as he at first begonne,   *in sort* in the manner
   He daily did apply him selfe to donne,
   All dewfull seruice voide of thoughts impure
   Ne any paines ne perill did he shonne,
   By which he might her to his loue allure,
And liking in her yet vntamed heart procure.

33
And euermore the shepheard *Coridon*,
   What euer thing he did her to aggrate,   *aggrate* please
   Did striue to match with strong contention,
   And all his paines did closely emulate;
   Whether it were to caroll, as they sate

33.1 the shepheard *Coridon*,] Calidore's rustic rival for the love of Pastorella.

Keeping their sheepe, or games to exercize,
Or to present her with their labours late;
Through which if any grace chaunst to arize
To him, the Shepheard streight with iealousie did frize.   *frize* go cold, freeze

34
One day as they all three together went
   To the greene wood, to gather strawberies,
There chaunst to them a dangerous accident;
A Tigre forth out of the wood did rise,
That with fell clawes full of fierce gourmandize,   *gourmandize* voraciousness
And greedy mouth, wide gaping like hell gate,
Did runne at *Pastorell* her to surprize:
Whom she beholding, now all desolate
Gan cry to them aloud, to helpe her all too late.

35
Which *Coridon* first hearing, ran in hast
   To reskue her, but when he saw the feend,
Through cowherd feare he fled away as fast,
Ne durst abide the daunger of the end;
His life he steemed dearer then his frend.   *steemed* esteemed, valued
But *Calidore* soone comming to her ayde,
When he the beast saw ready now to rend   *rend* tear
His loues deare spoile, in which his heart was prayde,   *prayde* taken as a prey or spoil
He ran at him enrag'd in stead of being frayde.

36
He had no weapon, but his shepheards hooke,
   To serue the vengeaunce of his wrathfull will,
With which so sternely he the monster strooke,
That to the ground astonished he fell;
Whence ere he could recou'r, he did him quell,
And hewing off his head, it presented
Before the feete of the faire *Pastorell*;
Who scarcely yet from former feare exempted,   *exempted* delivered
A thousand times him thankt, that had her death preuented.

37
From that day forth she gan him to affect,   *affect* incline to, prefer
   And daily more her fauour to augment;

34.3 ff. a dangerous accident;] An attack by wild beasts is a stock element of pastoral romance, and here Spenser imitates his immediate predecessor, Sir Philip Sidney, who had written a similar scene in *The Countess of Pembroke's Arcadia* (1.19).

But *Coridon* for cowherdize reiect,   *cowherdize* cowardice
Fit to keepe sheepe, vnfit for loues content:
The gentle heart scornes base disparagement.   *disparagement* discredit or dishonour,
Yet *Calidore* did not despise him quight,   especially through marriage to an inferior
But vsde him friendly for further intent,
That by his fellowship, he colour might   *colour* disguise
Both his estate, and loue from skill of any wight.

38

So well he woo'd her, and so well he wrought her,   *wrought* influenced, moved
With humble seruice, and with daily sute,
That at the last vnto his will he brought her;
Which he so wisely well did prosecute,   *prosecute* perform, bring to achievement
That of his loue he reapt the timely frute,
And ioyed long in close felicity: *close* intimate, private
Till fortune fraught with malice, blinde, and brute,
That enuies louers long prosperity,
Blew vp a bitter storme of foule aduersity.

39

It fortuned one day, when *Calidore*
Was hunting in the woods (as was his trade)
A lawlesse people, *Brigants* hight of yore,
That neuer vsde to liue by plough nor spade,   *vsde* practised
But fed on spoile and booty, which they made   *spoile* plunder, stolen livestock or goods
Vpon their neighbours, which did nigh them border,
The dwelling of these shepheards did inuade,
And spoyld their houses, and them selues did murder;
And droue away their flocks, with other much disorder.

40

Amongst the rest, the which they then did pray,
They spoyld old *Melibee* of all he had,
And all his people captiue led away,
Mongst which this lucklesse mayd away was lad,
Faire *Pastorella*, sorrowfull and sad,
Most sorrowfull, most sad, that euer sight,   *sight* sighed, lamented
Now made the spoile of theeues and *Brigants* bad,
Which was the conquest of the gentlest Knight,
That euer liu'd, and th'onely glory of his might.

39.3 ff. Brigants] Ptolemy's second-century map of Europe showed eastern Ireland inhabited by a Celtic tribe called the Brigantes – a detail also recorded by Tacitus (cf. *Annales*, 12.32) and picked up by Cooper's 1565 *Dictionarium*, both of which place this Celtic group in northern England.
    40.2 old Melibee] Pastorella's father and the elder of the pastoral community.

41
With them also was taken *Coridon*,
  And carried captiue by those theeues away;
  Who in the couert of the night, that none
  Mote them descry, nor reskue from their pray,   *pray* captivity, spoiling
  Vnto their dwelling did them close conuay.
  Their dwelling in a little Island was,
  Couered with shrubby woods, in which no way
  Appeard for people in nor out to pas,
Nor any footing fynde for ouergrowen gras.

42
For vnderneath the ground their way was made,
  Through hollow caues, that no man mote discouer
  For the thicke shrubs, which did them alwaies shade
  From view of liuing wight, and couered ouer:
  But darkenesse dred and daily night did houer
  Through all the inner parts, wherein they dwelt.
  Ne lightned was with window, nor with louer,   *louer* louvre, roof lantern
  But with continuall candlelight, which delt
A doubtfull sense of things, not so well seene, as felt.

43
Hither those *Brigants* brought their present pray,
  And kept them with continuall watch and ward,
  Meaning so soone, as they conuenient may,
  For slaues to sell them, for no small reward,
  To merchants, which them kept in bondage hard,
  Or sold againe. Now when faire *Pastorell*
  Into this place was brought, and kept with gard
  Of griesly theeues, she thought her self in hell,
Where with such damned fiends she should in darknesse dwell.

44
But for to tell the dolefull dreriment,   *dreriment* sorrowing
  And pittifull complaints, which there she made,
  Where day and night she nought did but lament
  Her wretched life, shut vp in deadly shade,
  And waste her goodly beauty, which did fade
  Like to a flowre, that feeles no heate of sunne,

    43.8 in hell,] Pastorella's descent underground sets the stage for a rescue that will invoke Christ's three-day harrowing of hell, as well as Orpheus' near-redemption of the dead Eurydice from Hades (cf. Ovid, *Metamorphoses*, 10.1–63).

Which may her feeble leaues with comfort glade. *glade* cheer, sustain
But what befell her in that theeuish wonne,
Will in an other Canto better be begunne.

Canto XI.

The theeues fall out for Pastorell,
Whilest Melibee is slaine:
Her Calidore from them redeemes,
And bringeth backe againe.

1

The ioyes of loue, if they should euer last,
   Without affliction or disquietnesse,
   That worldly chaunces doe amongst them cast, *chaunces* accidents, fortune
   Would be on earth too great a blessednesse,
   Liker to heauen, then mortall wretchednesse.
   Therefore the winged God, to let men weet,
   That here on earth is no sure happinesse,
   A thousand sowres hath tempred with one sweet,
To make it seeme more deare and dainty, as is meet. *meet* fitting, suitable

2

Like as is now befalne to this faire Mayd,
   Faire *Pastorell*, of whom is now my song,
   Who being now in dreadfull darknesse layd,
   Amongst those theeues, which her in bondage strong
   Detaynd, yet Fortune not with all this wrong
   Contented, greater mischiefe on her threw,
   And sorrowes heapt on her in greater throng;
   That who so heares her heauinesse, would rew
And pitty her sad plight, so chang'd from pleasaunt hew. *plight* case, circumstance

3

Whylest thus she in these hellish dens remayned,
   Wrapped in wretched cares and hearts vnrest,
   It so befell (as Fortune had ordayned)
   That he, which was their Capitaine profest, *profest* recognised, acknowledged

Stanza 1 **sowres ... sweet,**] The transience of mortal happiness is the theme of Spenser's first literary venture, translations commissioned for Jan van der Noot's *A Theatre for Worldlings* (1569), and of his 1591 book of short poems, *Complaints*. The compound flavour of love is the subject of Thomalin's emblem at the end of 'Marche' in *The Shepheardes Calender*: 'Of Hony and of Gaule in loue there is store: The Honye is much, but the Gaule is more.'

And had the chiefe commaund of all the rest,
   One day as he did all his prisoners vew,
   With lustfull eyes, beheld that louely guest,   *guest* stranger; captive, hostage
     Faire *Pastorella*, whose sad mournefull hew
Like the faire Morning clad in misty fog did shew.

4
At sight whereof his barbarous heart was fired,
   And inly burnt with flames most raging whot,   *inly* within *whot* hot
   That her alone he for his part desired
     Of all the other pray, which they had got,
     And her in mynde did to him selfe allot.
   From that day forth he kyndnesse to her showed,
   And sought her loue, by all the meanes he mote;
   With looks, with words, with gifts he oft her wowed:
And mixed threats among, and much vnto her vowed.

5
But all that euer he could doe or say,
   Her constant mynd could not a whit remoue,   *a whit* at all, a bit
   Nor draw vnto the lure of his lewd lay,   *lay* song, suit
     To graunt him fauour, or afford him loue.   *afford* give, yield
     Yet ceast he not to sew and all waies proue,   *sew* pursue *proue* try, attempt
   By which he mote accomplish his request,   *request* desire, demand
   Saying and doing all that mote behoue;   *behoue* be fitting, be helpful
   Ne day nor night he suffred her to rest,   *suffred* allowed, permitted
But her all night did watch, and all the day molest.

6
At last when him she so importune saw,   *importune* importunate, persistent
   Fearing least he at length the raines would lend
   Vnto his lust, and make his will his law,
     Sith in his powre she was to foe or frend,   *sith* since
     She thought it best, for shadow to pretend   *for shadow* in appearance
   Some shew of fauour, by him gracing small,   *gracing small* gratifying a little
   That she thereby mote either freely wend,
   Or at more ease continue there his thrall:
A little well is lent, that gaineth more withall.   *withall* therewith

7
So from thenceforth, when loue he to her made,
   With better tearmes she did him entertaine,
   Which gaue him hope, and did him halfe perswade,
     That he in time her ioyaunce should obtaine.   *her ioyaunce* enjoyment of her

But when she saw, through that small fauours gaine,
That further, then she willing was, he prest,
She found no meanes to barre him, but to faine   *faine* pretend
A sodaine sickenesse, which her sore opprest,
And made vnfit to serue his lawlesse mindes behest.   *behest* command, bidding

8
By meanes whereof she would not him permit
   Once to approch to her in priuity,   *in priuity* in private, alone
   But onely mongst the rest by her to sit,
   Mourning the rigour of her malady,   *rigour* extremity
   And seeking all things meete for remedy.
   But she resolu'd no remedy to fynde,
   Nor better cheare to shew in misery,   *cheer* countenance, aspect, expression
   Till Fortune would her captiue bonds vnbynde,
Her sickenesse was not of the body but the mynde.

9
During which space that she thus sicke did lie,
   It chaunst a sort of merchants, which were wount
   To skim those coastes, for bondmen there to buy,   *bondmen* slaves
   And by such trafficke after gaines to hunt,
   Arriued in this Isle though bare and blunt,
   T'inquire for slaues; where being readie met
   By some of these same theeues at th'instant brunt,   *at th'instant brunt* at the first moment
   Were brought vnto their Captaine, who was set   (of their arrival)
By his faire patients side with sorrowfull regret.

10
To whom they shewed, how those marchants were
   Arriu'd in place, their bondslaues for to buy,
   And therefore prayd, that those same captiues there
   Mote to them for their most commodity   *commodity* advantage, benefit
   Be sold, and mongst them shared equally.
   This their request the Captaine much appalled;
   Yet could he not their iust demaund deny,
   And willed streight the slaues should forth be called,
And sold for most aduantage not to be forstalled.   *forstalled* prevented

11
Then forth the good old *Meliboe* was brought,
   And *Coridon*, with many other moe,   *moe* more (in quantity)
   Whom they before in diuerse spoyles had caught:
   All which he to the marchants sale did showe.

Till some, which did the sundry prisoners knowe,   *sundry* various, several
   Gan to inquire for that faire shepherdesse,
   Which with the rest they tooke not long agoe,
   And gan her forme and feature to expresse,
The more t'augment her price, through praise of comlinesse.

12

To whom the Captaine in full angry wize   *wize* manner
   Made answere, that the Mayd of whom they spake,
   Was his owne purchase and his onely prize,   *purchase* conquest
   With which none had to doe, ne ought partake,
   But he himselfe, which did that conquest make;
   Litle for him to haue one silly lasse: *silly* simple; helpless, frail
   Besides through sicknesse now so wan and weake,
   That nothing meet in marchandise to passe.
So shew'd them her, to proue how pale & weake she was.

13

The sight of whom, though now decayd and mard,   *decayd* impaired, ruined *mard* ruined
   And eke but hardly seene by candle-light,   *hardly* with difficulty, scarcely
   Yet like a Diamond of rich regard,   *regard* appearance, value
   In doubtfull shadow of the darkesome night,
   With starrie beames about her shining bright,
   These marchants fixed eyes did so amaze,
   That what through wonder, & what through delight,
   A while on her they greedily did gaze,
And did her greatly like, and did her greatly praize.

14

At last when all the rest them offred were,
   And prises to them placed at their pleasure,
   They all refused in regard of her,
   Ne ought would buy, how euer prisd with measure,
   Withouten her, whose worth aboue all threasure
   They did esteeme, and offred store of gold.
   But then the Captaine fraught with more displeasure,
   Bad them be still, his loue should not be sold;   *bad* commanded, ordered
The rest take if they would, he her to him would hold.

15

Therewith some other of the chiefest theeues
   Boldly him bad such iniurie forbeare;   *iniurie* wrong *forbeare* refrain, abstain from
   For that same mayd, how euer it him greeues,
   Should with the rest be sold before him theare,

To make the prises of the rest more deare.
That with great rage he stoutly doth denay;
And fiercely drawing forth his blade, doth sweare,
That who so hardie hand on her doth lay,
It dearely shall aby, and death for handsell pay.

aby pay the penalty (for)
handsell earnest money, a first instalment

16
Thus as they words amongst them multiply,
   They fall to strokes, the frute of too much talke,
   And the mad steele about doth fiercely fly,
   Not sparing wight, ne leauing any balke,
   But making way for death at large to walke:
   Who in the horror of the griesly night,
   In thousand dreadful shapes doth mongst them stalke,
   And makes huge hauocke, whiles the candlelight
Out quenched, leaues no skill nor difference of wight.

balke miss, exception

skill distinction, ability to discriminate

17
Like as a sort of hungry dogs ymet
   About some carcase by the common way,
   Doe fall together, stryuing each to get
   The greatest portion of the greedie pray;
   All on confused heapes themselues assay,
   And snatch, and byte, and rend, and tug, and teare;
   That who them sees, would wonder at their fray,
   And who sees not, would be affrayd to heare.
Such was the conflict of those cruell *Brigants* there.

assay apply, put to trial, attempt

18
But first of all, their captiues they doe kill,
   Least they should ioyne against the weaker side,
   Or rise against the remnant at their will;
   Old *Meliboe* is slaine, and him beside
   His aged wife, with many others wide,
   But *Coridon* escaping craftily,
   Creepes forth of dores, whilst darknes him doth hide,
   And flyes away as fast as he can hye,
Ne stayeth leaue to take, before his friends doe dye.

wide far and wide, throughout

hye hasten, go

19
But *Pastorella*, wofull wretched Elfe,
   Was by the Captaine all this while defended,
   Who minding more her safety then himselfe,
   His target alwayes ouer her pretended;

target shield *pretended* held out, before

By meanes whereof, that mote not be amended,
He at the length was slaine, and layd on ground,
Yet holding fast twixt both his armes extended
Fayre *Pastorell*, who with the selfe same wound
Launcht through the arme, fell down with him in drerie swound.

                                                            launcht pierced, stabbed

20

There lay she couered with confused preasse   *couered* (disyllabic)
  Of carcases, which dying on her fell.
  Tho when as he was dead, the fray gan ceasse,
  And each to other calling, did compell
  To stay their cruell hands from slaughter fell,   *fell* fierce, savage, mortal
  Sith they that were the cause of all, were gone.
  Thereto they all attonce agreed well,   *attonce* immediately
  And lighting candles new, gan search anone,   *anone* straightaway
How many of their friends were slaine, how many fone.   *fone* foes (arch. plural)

21

Their Captain there they cruelly found kild,
  And in his armes the dreary dying mayd,   *dreary* gory; melancholy
  Like a sweet Angell twixt two clouds vphild:
  Her louely light was dimmed and decayd,   *decayd* diminished
  With cloud of death vpon her eyes displayd;
  Yet did the cloud make euen that dimmed light
  Seeme much more louely in that darknesse layd,
  And twixt the twinckling of her eye-lids bright,
To sparke out litle beames, like starres in foggie night.

22

But when they mou'd the carcases aside,
  They found that life did yet in her remaine:
  Then all their helpes they busily applyde,
  To call the soule backe to her home againe;
  And wrought so well with labour and long paine,
  That they to life recouered her at last.
  Who sighing sore, as if her hart in twaine
  Had riuen bene, and all her hart strings brast,   *riuen* cleft *brast* burst, broken
With drearie drouping eyne lookt vp like one aghast.   *eyne* eyes (arch. plural) *aghast* frightened

23

There she beheld, that sore her grieu'd to see,
  Her father and her friends about her lying,
  Her selfe sole left, a second spoyle to bee

Of those, that hauing saued her from dying,
Renew'd her death by timely death denying:
What now is left her, but to wayle and weepe,
Wringing her hands, and ruefully loud crying?
Ne cared she her wound in teares to steepe,
Albe with all their might those *Brigants* her did keepe. *albe* albeit, although

24

But when they saw her now reliu'd againe,
   They left her so, in charge of one the best
Of many worst, who with vnkind disdaine
And cruell rigour her did much molest;
Scarse yeelding her due food, or timely rest,
And scarsely suffring her infestred wound,
That sore her payn'd, by any to be drest.
   So leaue we her in wretched thraldome bound,
And turne we backe to *Calidore*, where we him found.

25

Who when he backe returned from the wood,
   And saw his shepheards cottage spoyled quight,
And his loue reft away, he wexed wood,   *reft* stolen, taken *wexed* grew
And halfe enraged at that ruefull sight,   *wood* insane, furious
That euen his hart for very fell despight,   *despight* outrage, indignation
And his owne flesh he readie was to teare,
He chauft, he grieu'd, he fretted, and he sight,   *chauft* became (or made himself) angry
   And fared like a furious wyld Beare,   *sight* sighed *fared* behaved
Whose whelpes are stolne away, she being otherwere.   *whelpes* cubs

26

Ne wight he found, to whom he might complaine,
   Ne wight he found, of whom he might inquire;
That more increast the anguish of his paine.
He sought the woods; but no man could see there,
He sought the plaines; but could no tydings heare.
The woods did nought but ecchoes vaine rebound;
The playnes all waste and emptie did appeare: *waste* deserted
   Where wont the shepheards oft their pypes resound,
And feed an hundred flocks, there now not one he found.

27

At last as there he romed vp and downe,
   He chaunst one comming towards him to spy,
That seem'd to be some sorie simple clowne,

With ragged weedes, and lockes vpstarting hye,   *weedes* clothes, garments
As if he did from some late daunger fly,
And yet his feare did follow him behynd: *his feare* that which frightened him
Who as he vnto him approched nye,
He mote perceiue by signes, which he did fynd,   *fynd* discover (in him)
That *Coridon* it was, the silly shepherds hynd.

28
Tho to him running fast, he did not stay
To greet him first, but askt where were the rest;
Where *Pastorell*? who full of fresh dismay,
And gushing forth in teares, was so opprest,
That he no word could speake, but smit his brest,   *smit* beat, struck
And vp to heauen his eyes fast streming threw.
Whereat the knight amaz'd, yet did not rest,
But askt againe, what ment that rufull hew:
Where was his *Pastorell*? where all the other crew?

29
Ah well away (sayd he then sighing sore)   *well away* a sorrowful exclamation
That euer I did liue, this day to see,
This dismall day, and was not dead before,
Before I saw faire *Pastorella* dye.
Die? out alas then *Calidore* did cry: *out alas* an exclamation of grief
How could the death dare euer her to quell?   or abhorrence
But read thou shepheard, read what destiny,   *read* discover, tell, reveal
Or other dyrefull hap from heauen or hell   *hap* chance, occurrence
Hath wrought this wicked deed, doe feare away, and tell.   *doe ... away* quell, master

30
Tho when the shepheard breathed had a whyle,
He thus began: where shall I then commence
This wofull tale? or how those *Brigants* vyle,
With cruell rage and dreadfull violence
Spoyld all our cots, and caried vs from hence?   *cots* cotes, sheep-cotes
Or how faire *Pastorell* should haue bene sold
To marchants, but was sau'd with strong defence?
Or how those theeues, whilest one sought her to hold,
Fell all at ods, and fought through fury fierce and bold.

31
In that same conflict (woe is me) befell
This fatall chaunce, this dolefull accident,
Whose heauy tydings now I haue to tell.

First all the captiues, which they here had hent,   *hent* taken, carried off
Were by them slaine by generall consent;
Old *Meliboe* and his good wife withall   *withall* likewise, along with the rest
These eyes saw die, and dearely did lament:
    But when the lot to *Pastorell* did fall,   *lot* fate, turn
Their Captaine long withstood, & did her death forstall.

32
But what could he gainst all them doe alone:
    It could not boot; needs mote she die at last: *boot* profit, succeed
    I onely scapt through great confusione   *needs mote* it was necessary, inevitable
    Of cryes and clamors, which amongst them past,   *scapt* escaped
    In dreadfull darknesse dreadfully aghast;
    That better were with them to haue bene dead,
    Then here to see all desolate and wast,   *wast* ruined, laid waste
    Despoyled of those ioyes and iolly head,   *iolly head* merriment
Which with those gentle shepherds here I wont to lead.

33
When *Calidore* these ruefull newes had raught,   *raught* obtained, received
    His hart quite deaded was with anguish great,   *deaded* overcome, killed
    And all his wits with doole were nigh distraught,   *doole* sorrow, grief
    That he his face, his head, his brest did beat,
    And death it selfe vnto himselfe did threat;
    Of cursing th'heauens, that so cruell were
    To her, whose name he often did repeat;
    And wishing oft, that he were present there,
When she was slaine, or had bene to her succour nere.   *succour* aid, relieve

34
But after griefe awhile had had his course,
    And spent it selfe in mourning, he at last
    Began to mitigate his swelling sourse,   *sourse* spring, fountain
    And in his mind with better reason cast,
    How he might saue her life, if life did last;
    Or if that dead, how he her death might wreake,   *wreake* revenge
    Sith otherwise he could not mend thing past;
    Or if it to reuenge he were too weake,
Then for to die with her, and his liues threed to breake.

35
Tho *Coridon* he prayd, sith he well knew
    The readie way vnto that theeuish wonne,
    To wend with him, and be his conduct trew

Vnto the place, to see what should be donne.
But he, whose hart through feare was late fordonne,   *fordonne* undone, destroyed
Would not for ought be drawne to former drede,   *drede* object or cause of fear, danger
But by all meanes the daunger knowne did shonne:
Yet *Calidore* so well him wrought with meed,   *meed* reward, bribery
And faire bespoke with words, that he at last agreed.

36
So forth they goe together (God before)
  Both clad in shepheards weeds agreeably,   *agreeably* suitably, conformably
  And both with shepheards hookes: But *Calidore*
  Had vnderneath, him armed priuily.   *priuily* secretly, stealthily
  Tho to the place when they approched nye,
  They chaunst, vpon an hill not farre away,
  Some flockes of sheepe and shepheards to espy;   *espy* perceive, observe
  To whom they both agreed to take their way,
In hope there newes to learne, how they mote best assay.   *assay* make their attempt, assault

37
There did they find, that which they did not feare,
  The selfe same flocks, the which those theeues had reft
  From *Meliboe* and from themselues whyleare,   *whyleare* not long since
  And certaine of the theeues there by them left,
  The which for want of heards themselues then kept.   *heards* herders, shepherds
  Right well knew *Coridon* his owne late sheepe,
  And seeing them, for tender pittie wept:
  But when he saw the theeues, which did them keepe
His hart gan fayle, albe he saw them all asleepe.

38
But *Calidore* recomforting his griefe,
  Though not his feare: for nought may feare disswade;
  Him hardly forward drew, whereas the thiefe
  Lay sleeping soundly in the bushes shade,
  Whom *Coridon* him counseld to inuade   *inuade* set upon, attack
  Now all vnwares, and take the spoyle away;
  But he, that in his mind had closely made   *closely* secretly, privately
  A further purpose, would not so them slay,
But gently waking them, gaue them the time of day.

39
Tho sitting downe by them vpon the greene,
  Of sundrie things he purpose gan to faine;
  That he by them might certaine tydings weene   *weene* conceive, believe

Of *Pastorell*, were she aliue or slaine.
Mongst which the theeues them questioned againe,
What mister men, and eke from whence they were.   *mister* manner (of)
To whom they answer'd, as did appertaine,   *appertaine* befit
That they were poore heardgroomes, the which whylere
Had from their maisters fled, & now sought hyre elswhere.   *hyre* employment, occupation

40

Whereof right glad they seem'd, and offer made
To hyre them well, if they their flockes would keepe:
For they themselues were euill groomes, they sayd,
Vnwont with heards to watch, or pasture sheepe,   *vnwont* unaccustomed *watch* keep watch
But to forray the land, or scoure the deepe.   *forray* ravage, make raids across
Thereto they soone agreed, and earnest tooke,   *earnest* earnest money,
To keepe their flockes for little hyre and chepe: promissory payment
For they for better hyre did shortly looke,
So there all day they bode, till light the sky forsooke.

41

Tho when as towards darksome night it drew,
Vnto their hellish dens those theeues them brought,
Where shortly they in great acquaintance grew,
And all the secrets of their entrayles sought.   *entrayles* heart, soul
There did they find, contrarie to their thought,
That *Pastorell* yet liu'd, but all the rest
Were dead, right so as *Coridon* had taught:
Whereof they both full glad and blyth did rest,   *blyth* happy
But chiefly *Calidore*, whom griefe had most possest.

42

At length when they occasion fittest found,
In dead of night, when all the theeues did rest
After a late forray, and slept full sound,   *forray* raid
Sir *Calidore* him arm'd, as he thought best,
Hauing of late by diligent inquest,   *inquest* search
Prouided him a sword of meanest sort:
With which he streight went to the Captaines nest.
But *Coridon* durst not with him consort,   *with him consort* accompany him
Ne durst abide behind, for dread of worse effort.

43

When to the Caue they came, they found it fast: *fast* locked, barred
But *Calidore* with huge resistlesse might,
The dores assayled, and the locks vpbrast.   *vpbrast* burst open

With noyse whereof the theefe awaking light,
Vnto the entrance ran: where the bold knight
Encountring him with small resistance slew;
The whiles faire *Pastorell* through great affright
Was almost dead, misdoubting least of new   *misdoubting* fearing
Some vprore were like that, which lately she did vew.

44

But when as *Calidore* was comen in,
   And gan aloud for *Pastorell* to call,
   Knowing his voice although not heard long sin,   *sin* since
   She sudden was reuiued therewithall,
   And wondrous ioy felt in her spirits thrall: *thrall* captivity, bondage
   Like him that being long in tempest tost,
   Looking each houre into deathes mouth to fall,
   At length espyes at hand the happie cost,
On which he safety hopes, that earst feard to be lost.   *earst* at first, before

45

Her gentle hart, that now long season past
   Had neuer ioyance felt, nor chearefull thought,   *ioyance* happiness, joy
   Began some smacke of comfort new to tast,
   Like lyfull heat to nummed senses brought,   *lyfull* vital
   And life to feele, that long for death had sought;
   Ne lesse in hart reioyced *Calidore*,
   When he her found, but like to one distraught
   And robd of reason, towards her him bore,
A thousand times embrast, and kist a thousand more.

46

But now by this, with noyse of late vprore,
   The hue and cry was raysed all about;   *hue and cry* alarm
   And all the *Brigants* flocking in great store,   *in great store* in company
   Vnto the caue gan preasse, nought hauing dout
   Of that was doen, and entred in a rout.
   But *Calidore* in th'entry close did stand,
   And entertayning them with courage stout,   *entertayning* confronting, engaging
   Still slew the formost, that came first to hand,
So long till all the entry was with bodies mand.

47

Tho when no more could nigh to him approch,
   He breath'd his sword, and rested him till day: *breath'd* relaxed, rested
   Which when he spyde vpon the earth t'encroch,

Through the dead carcases he made his way,
   Mongst which he found a sword of better say,   *say* assay, temper (of metal)
   With which he forth went into th'open light:
   Where all the rest for him did readie stay,
   And fierce assayling him, with all their might
Gan all vpon him lay: there gan a dreadfull fight.   *lay* i.e. lay strokes

48

How many flyes in whottest sommers day
   Do seize vpon some beast, whose flesh is bare,
   That all the place with swarmes do ouerlay,
   And with their litle stings right felly fare;   *felly* fiercely, cruelly
   So many theeues about him swarming are,
   All which do him assayle on euery side,
   And sore oppresse, ne any him doth spare:
But he doth with his raging brond diuide   *brond* sword
Their thickest troups, & round about him scattreth wide.

49

Like as a Lion mongst an heard of dere,
   Disperseth them to catch his choysest pray;
   So did he fly amongst them here and there,
   And all that nere him came, did hew and slay,
   Till he had strowd with bodies all the way;
   That none his daunger daring to abide,
   Fled from his wrath, and did themselues conuay
   Into their caues, their heads from death to hide,
Ne any left, that victorie to him enuide.   *enuide* begrudged, refused

50

Then backe returning to his dearest deare,
   He her gan to recomfort, all he might,
   With gladfull speaches, and with louely cheare,
   And forth her bringing to the ioyous light,
   Whereof she long had lackt the wishfull sight,
   Deuiz'd all goodly meanes, from her to driue
   The sad remembrance of her wretched plight,
So her vneath at last he did reuiue,   *vneath* scarcely, with difficulty
That long had lyen dead, and made againe aliue.

51

This doen, into those theeuish dens he went,
   And thence did all the spoyles and threasures take,
   Which they from many long had robd and rent,   *rent* stolen

But fortune now the victors meed did make; *meed* prize, reward
Of which the best he did his loue betake;
And also all those flockes, which they before
Had reft from *Meliboe* and from his make, *make* spouse
He did them all to *Coridon* restore.
So droue them all away, and his loue with him bore.

Textual Notes

The base text for these selections from *The Faerie Queene* is the second edition of the poem, printed by Richard Field in 1596, and in particular two volumes held in the Cambridge University Library: CUL Syn.7.59.21 (Part 1, Books I–III) and CUL Syn.7.59.125 (Part 2, Books IV–VI). Because this edition of the poem is in some places defective, it has been necessary to make some alterations to the text, which are summarised below. For the most part, these changes reflect superior readings from the first edition of Books I–III in 1590, printed by John Wolfe (including the list of 'Faults Escaped' (*FE*) appended to all copies in that edition), or from the first full edition of the poem, printed by Matthew Lownes in 1609. In the notes below, the (uncorrected) reading is cited by book, canto, stanza and line number, followed by my (corrected) reading of the 1596 text and, in italics, the warrant (if any) for my correction. Thus, to make an example of the first note, the reader will find the word 'They' in the text above at Book I, canto i, stanza 10, line 4, whereas the 1596 edition of the poem reads 'The' at the same location; my authority for making this change is the 1590 edition of the poem. In the few cases where I have indulged my own common sense, I have signed the note *AZ*.

1.1.10.4 The] They *1590*
1.1.12.5 hardy stroke] stroke *FE*
1.1.17.1 perceiu'ed] perceiu'd *1590*
1.1.21.5 ebbe gins to auale,] spring gins to auale, *FE*
1.1.25.7 wound.] wound, *1590*
1.1.31.2 euill euill] euill *1590*
1.1.32.6 for wearied] forwearied *1590*
1.1.34.8 genlty] gently *1590*
1.1.48.9 her Yuie] her with Yuie *1590*
1.1.50.3 thought haue] thought t'haue *1609*
1.1.50.8 canshe] can she *1590*
1.2.3.4 lusty-hed.] lusty-hed *1590*
1.2.17.5 cruelties] cruell spies *FE*
1.2.29.3 that mounted] ymounted *FE*

160 *The Faerie Queene: A Reading Guide*

1.2.32.9 guitlesse] guiltlesse *1590*
1.2.40.1 Then] Thens *FE*
1.2.41.5 Then] Thens *FE*

2.12.1.6 And this] And that *FE*
2.12.6.1 did see,] doe see, *FE*
2.12.27.3 pittifull] pittifully *1590*
2.12.27.4 through the sea the resounding] through the sea resounding *1609*
2.12.30.6 peasaunt] pleasaunt *1590*
2.12.50.4 grenee,] greene, *1590*
2.12.51.6 crearures,] creatures, *1590*
2.12.52.9 Of *Eden*,] Of *Eden* selfe, *1590*
2.12.54.3 seemed] seemd *1590*
2.12.57.7 no'te] n'ote *AZ*
2.12.62.7 bortom] bottom *1590*

3.11.14.1 cenceiued] conceiued *1590*
3.11.15.6 And least] At least *1590*
3.11.16.2 fruilesse] fruitlesse *1590*
3.11.20.4 vowed] vow'd *1609*
3.11.20.6 for wandred] forwandred *1590*
3.11.23.5 This (quoth he)] This is (quoth he) *1590*
3.11.26.7 and imperious] and with imperious *1590*
3.11.42.8 snaly-locke] snaky-locke *1590*
3.11.44.9 parts,] parts. *1590*
3.11.45.2 he so?] he so?) *1590*
3.11.51.8 weare?] weare, *1590*
3.12.9.3 others] other *1609*
3.12.11.1 cloth'] cloth'd *1590*
3.12.22.5 knigdome] kingdome *1590*
3.12.26.2 note] n'ote *AZ*
3.12.26.7 with that] by the *1590*
3.12.27.3 away] away. *1609* (N.B. *1590* ends: 'nothing did remayne.')
3.12.28.1 their] there *1609*
*3.12.43.4 fuccour,] succour, *FE*

5.Pr.1.3 prime.] prime, *1609*
5.2.Arg.3 *Momera*,] *Munera*, *AZ*
5.2.4.1 she)] hee) *1609*
5.2.7.9 ouersight] ouersight. *1609*
5.2.17.5 *Art egall*] *Artegall AZ*

5.2.18.9 dight] dight. *1609*
5.2.22.2 Gastle] Castle *1609*
5.2.32.4 eare,] earth, *1609*

6.10.5.7 Deuized] Deuiz'd *1609*
6.10.18.7 wight,,] wight, *1609*
6.10.22.5 *AEcidee*] *Æacidee*, AZ (N.B. 1609 reads *Aecidee*)
6.10.31.5 Whch] Which *1609*
6.10.32.6 impare] impure *1609*
6.10.35.9 enraged] enrag'd *1609*
6.10.36.6 *This line is defective*
6.11.9.7 the instant] th'instant *1609*
6.11.37.3 themseles] themselues *1609*

Chapter 3

Contexts and Reception

Texts and intertexts

Spenser and Renaissance *imitatio*

These days, we expect our literary writers to be distinctive, even original. Students taking classes in prose and poetic composition are urged 'to find their own voices', and to seek to differentiate their writing both from what has come before, and from others writing in the same field. A network of social and legal restraints protects and legitimates an author's published writing, so that if others want to repeat or adapt it, they must acknowledge that use openly, and they often have to pay for the privilege. Sixteenth-century English writers, by contrast, faced none of these restraints. On the contrary, in their training they were encouraged to imitate past writers; they were taught to mine other authors' work for apt expressions and choice insights, and to collect them in notebooks for later use; and they often worked collaboratively in ways that can be difficult for us (with our enlightened ideas about authorship and copyright) to understand. Throughout his career Spenser engaged with the writings of other poets, both dead and living, in a way that would, today, certainly land him in court. But we should not make the mistake of assuming that a collaborative or derivative literary work is, by its collaborative or imitative nature, somehow bad; nor should we think Spenser was alone in writing in this way. Shakespeare lifted whole passages from his sources, and some of his greatest plays (e.g. *Hamlet*) are rewritings of existing materials by other playwrights. Instead, we should recognise that our own assumptions about originality and authority are unhistorical and problematic. Early modern ideas about translation, imitation and allusion offered Spenser challenges and artistic opportunities largely unavailable to modern writers.

The nature and causes of the differences between early modern and modern ideas about authorship are complex and variable. Two kinds of context – the material and intellectual contexts – are probably most important to a study of Spenser's works. The printing press remained a comparative novelty even at the end of the sixteenth century. Like many other writers, Spenser continued both to circulate his work in manuscript form, and to think about his authorial status in the context of a much older manuscript tradition. Poetic manuscripts circulated vigorously in Elizabethan cities, towns, educational institutions (like the universities and the Inns of Court) and households: they were read, shared, copied and anthologised, and their constituent texts often altered or adulterated in the process. Writers writing for manuscript circulation knew some of their readers, and could make a pretence of knowing all of them; manuscript texts travelled by social relationships, and remained marked by the social transactions that spread them. Francis Meres could write in 1598, for example, of the circulation of Shakespeare's 'sugred Sonnets among his priuate friends', a description that links the sonnets' special tastiness with their private, manuscript status.[1] Writers who expected their works to be copied out by readers could, similarly, expect their readers to be intimately familiar with a shared literary tradition and with the wider contemporary literary culture. In the short term, Spenser wrote for a readership that knew his sources and analogues probably about as well as he himself did. When he first published *The Faerie Queene* in 1590, it was printed with a letter addressed to Sir Walter Ralegh, an apparently ideal reader to whom Spenser's letter explains his 'whole intention in the course of this worke'; but the first edition also included two commendatory poems written by Ralegh, which compare Spenser to Petrarch and Homer, and use the figure of Philomela, the nightingale, to allude both to Ovid and, probably, to a factional struggle for the Queen's favour at court in 1590.[2] In other words, the first printing of *The Faerie Queene* carefully advertises the poem's earlier circulation in manuscript, while insisting on its first readers' intimate knowledge not only of literary history, but of the intricacies of a shared social and political culture. In this context, Spenser could afford to translate, adapt and allude to other works – works originally written in Greek, Latin, Italian, French and English – with considerable freedom, trusting that his readers would recognise many, if not all, of his various debts.

The intellectual culture of the age, particularly as it was transmitted through humanist pedagogy, emphasised what the Latin rhetorical teachers had called *imitatio*, imitation. From an early age, grammar school students were encouraged to develop their grammatical and rhetorical skills by reading, analysing, extracting from and finally imitating the works of Latin, and later Greek, writers. The pedagogical writings of the humanist scholar and educator Desiderius Erasmus, for example, insist on the importance of a 'commonplace book of systems and topics', in which a boy may, 'wherever something noteworthy occurs ... write it down in the appropriate column'.[3] This book will have headings for moral virtues and vices, as well as commonplace or proverbial positions or arguments (e.g. 'he gives twice who gives readily,' 'the married is preferable to the single life,' and so on), each carefully subdivided to allow the student to accommodate a range of disparate material: authors, examples, sententious sayings. 'So our student', Erasmus writes, 'will flit like a busy bee through the entire garden of literature, will light on every blossom, collect a little nectar from each, and carry it to his hive.'[4] Similarly, the English scholar and teacher Roger Ascham suggests that boys should from the earliest age be required to parse Latin and Greek sentences, identifying their grammatical structure and classifying the senses in which the important words are used: literal, figural, metaphorical, and so on. Students were then to practise writing in various modes – as Erasmus has it, 'praise, censure, mythology, simile, comparison; sometimes with a figure of speech, or description, division, impersonation, rhetorical question and answer, signification'. In these exercises they might take directions from Aphthonius' *Progymnasmata*, a collection of exercises in various modes and genres, the mastery of which would lead to a complete style. Finally, Erasmus suggested that 'from time to time they should imitate in vocabulary and style a letter of Pliny or Cicero';[5] and he insisted that the teacher should mix exercises with ongoing reading 'so that the pupils always have material for imitation'.[6]

Spenserian intertextuality

The humanist pedagogical emphasis on commonplacing and on *imitatio* suggests how sixteenth-century English writers like Spenser developed a writing practice more readily susceptible than our own to conscious adaptations, borrowings, citations, allusions, and other forms of intertextual reference to earlier and contemporary works. In a famous study of Bakhtin's account of Rabelais, Julia Kristeva coined the term 'intertextuality' to refer to the phenomenon of a text's permeation by other, prior texts, the result of unconscious processes in which the author acts as a conduit for the re-expression of digested, re-assembled morsels from earlier reading experiences.[7] Kristeva's intertextuality describes a structural condition of writing that, following Bakhtin, she alleges characterises all authors and works: 'any text is constructed as a mosaic of quotations; any text is the absorption and transformation of another. The notion of *intertextuality* replaces that of intersubjectivity, and poetic language is read as at least double.'[8] Whether or not one accepts her claims, there is no doubt that sixteenth-century writers like Spenser were aware of this potential – indeed, their grammatical training and their commonplacing habits insisted upon it – and they were keen to exploit it consciously where possible. A letter to Spenser's friend Gabriel Harvey from one 'E. K.' – possibly another friend of Spenser's, or Spenser himself, writing under assumed initials – was published as a preface to Spenser's eclogues in *The Shepheardes Calender* in 1579. In this letter E. K. introduces Spenser's new poetry and defends some contentious aspects of his style, and particularly his archaic language:

> And firste of the wordes to speake, I graunt they be something hard, and of most men vnused, yet both English, and also vsed of most excellent Authors and most famous Poetes. In whom whenas this our Poet hath bene much traueiled and throughly redd, how could it be, (as that worthy Oratour sayde) but that walking in the sonne although for other cause he walked, yet needes he ought be sunburnt; and hauing the sound of those auncient Poetes still ringing in his eares, he mought needes in singing hit out some of theyr tunes.[9]

E. K. acknowledges the unconscious structural conditions of reading and writing which are Kristeva's focus, but in a coyly ambiguous way: he introduces two metaphors to describe the way in which Spenser assimilated and unconsciously imitated the style of his models, but the first of these metaphors (sunburn) he attributes (explicitly) to 'that worthy Oratour', Cicero. The reference to Cicero is immediately followed by another version of the same metaphor (singing), which he borrows (but not explicitly) from a classical tradition that extends back to Quintilian's discussion of *imitatio* in the *Institutes of Oratory*.[10] In other words, E. K. claims that Spenser's text is permeated by intertexts, but he makes the argument with two intertexts of his own, one conscious and the other apparently not. The force of his presentation seems to suggest that Spenser's own imitations may be persistently ambiguous – perhaps conscious, perhaps not.

When we turn to some examples of Spenser's translations, imitations, allusions and intertexts, we discover not only a full range of different degrees of relation to other texts and generic traditions, but also the way in which these different species of citation result in diverse effects. Possibly the simplest and most obvious type of intertextual citation in *The Faerie Queene* comes in moments of direct translation or adaptation from classical or continental works. In the opening stanza of the poem, for example, Spenser quotes from four lines of Virgilian verse once thought to be the authentic beginning of the *Aeneid*:

> *Ille ego, qui quondam gracili modulatus auena*
> *Carmen . . .*
>   *. . . at nunc horrentia Martis*
> *Arma virumque cano . . .*[11]

Spenser's translation of these lines ('Lo I the man . . .', from *FQ* I.Pr.1) simultaneously puts *The Faerie Queene* in the generic tradition of the *Aeneid*, and constructs Spenser's poetic career – as a pastoral poet who has now graduated to epic – on the model of Virgil's original. Spenser achieves a similar kind of effect – this time appealing to Homer's *Odyssey* – when he describes the banquet held for Britomart, the knight of chastity, and Sir Paridell at the house of Malbecco, in the middle of Book III:

> Now when of meats and drinks they had their fill,
>   Purpose was moued by that gentle Dame,
>   Vnto those knights aduenturous, to tell
>   Of deeds of armes, which vnto them became,
>   And euery one his kindred, and his name. (III.ix.32.1–5)

Homer repeatedly resorts to a similar formula throughout the *Odyssey*, as in this instance from the third book, when Telemachos visits the court of Nestor at Pylos:

> But when they had put from them the desire of food and drink, the horseman, Nestor of Gerenia, spoke first among them: "Now verily is it seemlier to ask and enquire of the strangers who they are, since now they have had their joy of food. Strangers, who are ye? Whence do ye sail over the watery ways?[12]

It is a formula to which Homer frequently returns, sometimes with the words, αὐτὰρ ἐπεὶ τάρπησαν ἐδητύος ἠδὲ ποτῆτος ('but when they had enough of food and drink').[13] It is fitting that Malbecco's wife Hellenore – 'that gentle Dame' – should use a Homeric formula at this point in *The Faerie Queene*, because she is shortly to elope with the knight Paridell in an imitation of Helen's flight from Sparta with the Trojan prince Paris. Moreover, Spenser imitates not only the words themselves, echoing Homer's syntax, but also the particulars of the Homeric hospitality which the form of words preserves; it was crucial to the sacred custom of hospitality during the Homeric period, as Nestor observes above, that a host should not demand the identity of his guests until they had been fed. Spenser imitates this tradition in his account of Malbecco's feast to parodic effect, for we have only just seen, in the preceding four stanzas (III.ix.28–31), that Hellenore has already fallen in love with the still-anonymous Paridell. In this context, it is particularly funny that she should borrow her Homeric phrasing from a unique instance in the *Odyssey* (5.201), one in which the goddess Calypso attempts to prevent Odysseus from returning home to his wife Penelope. His marital fidelity in that episode, with his desire to fulfil his *nostos* ('homecoming'), stands as a comic foil to Hellenore's indiscriminate lasciviousness and imminent elopement. Spenser's use of Homer, like his translation of pseudo-Virgil, puts his poem in an epic tradition; but it also wittily burlesques that tradition.

These debts to classical writers – and there are many more across Spenser's works, ranging from short phrases thieved from Theocritus to whole pages pinched from Plutarch – help Spenser to configure his poetry's relations to its Greek and Latin models. Similar effects dominate Spenser's use of material from his continental models, and above all Ariosto's *Orlando Furioso* and Tasso's *Gerusalemme Liberata*. Spenser mentions both Ariosto and Tasso in his *Letter of the Authors*, where he discusses the architecture of their moral and political allegory. But his debts to both writers are vast. For example, to Ariosto Spenser was indebted for his refinement of the narrative technique of *entrelacement*, whereby a poet alternates independent narrative strands, ultimately weaving them together into an allegorically suggestive structure. In Books III and IV of *The Faerie Queene* – the most Ariostan sections of Spenser's poem – he adapts Ariosto's narrative techniques to produce a dizzy tapestry of histories interlaced in complex fashion. A typical example is the way in which Spenser launches the history of the maiden Florimell, who first appears at *FQ* III.i.15, tearing through a wood, hotly pursued by a 'griesly Foster'. Several knights chase after her, including Prince Arthur, but we hear nothing further of this chase until canto iv (at stanza 45). Even then we learn only the history of Arthur and his squire Timias, who fights the foster but fails to recover Florimell herself. Their failure to overtake her is the poem's failure, too, as Spenser throws obstacle after obstacle in our way; for example, though we briefly sight Florimell at a witch's house in canto vii, soon afterwards the witch creates a false Florimell to take her place (III.viii.5–9), further deferring the resolution of Florimell's narrative. Her flight is not ultimately concluded, nor her narrative resolved, until the final canto of Book IV. Spenser has created a masterpiece of Ariostan *entrelacement*; it is fitting, then, that the entire history of Florimell's flight is based on the opening episode of *Orlando Furioso*, in which the maid Angelica similarly flees the French princes Rinaldo and Orlando.

Spenser's imitation of Ariosto's narrative technique gives his own poem a special status; because Ariosto's epic romance was considered one of the richest literary fruits of the Italian Renaissance, Spenser's studied improvement on Ariosto's own signature technique gives *The Faerie Queene* – and English as a literary language – pre-packaged credibility. Spenser's imitations of Tasso add a similar lustre to his poem, for much the same reasons. Tasso's reputation as *the* pre-eminent modern epic poet had been secured by the publication in 1581 of *Gerusalemme Liberata*, a poem which combined allegorical and historical complexity, strict classical purity in diction and structure, and – crucially – an explicitly Christian subject. But Spenser's imitation of Tasso's poem constitutes more than an attempt to stand on Tasso's giant shoulders; it also becomes the ground of a careful, contestatory revision by which Spenser re-writes – and eventually deconstructs – the epic genre in polemically Protestant terms. Tasso was a devout Catholic and a client of the d'Este family of Ferrara, a family that included cardinals and dukes in its number. His poem ultimately rehabilitates its central villain, the enchantress Armida, and reintegrates the wayward knight Rinaldo – along with the high-blooded passions he represents – into the Christian moral triumph of the poem's conclusion. Although he borrowed the name for his own Book II enchantress from Trissino, Spenser created in Acrasia a witch very like Tasso's Armida, and the parallels between her bower and that of Tasso's Armida are so close that, for long stretches in canto xii of Book II of *The Faerie Queene*, Spenser virtually translates Tasso's Italian.[14] These close imitations, however, only heighten the radical divergence in Spenser's conclusion to the Legend of Sir Guyon; when he finally penetrates Acrasia's enchanted bower at the end of canto xii, Guyon and his companion, the Palmer, capture the witch and destroy her paradise, root and branch. There is no place in Spenser's Protestant moral scheme for a garden of delight, or the worldly, sensuous appetites that it excites.

English models

Spenser's adaptations of and allusions to earlier English writers work to slightly different ends. Upon the publication of the first three books of *The Faerie Queene* in 1590, Spenser was immediately recognised as the heir to England's first great poet, Geoffrey Chaucer. The identification of Spenser and Chaucer was based mostly on the apparent archaism of Spenser's diction. Words like 'eftsoones', 'mote', 'whilome', 'forthy', 'blent' and 'eke' were considered to carry a distinctive Chaucerian twang, and Spenser deployed other Chaucerian elements – such as the past participle prefix y- in such words as 'yclad' – with strategic force. Spenser constructed himself as Chaucer's heir more directly by grafting his own poem on to the frayed remains of Chaucerian fragments, as at *FQ* IV.ii–iii where Spenser's narrative continues and completes the unfinished 'Squire's Tale' from *The Canterbury Tales*. The Chaucerian elements foregrounded in *The Faerie Queene* only perpetuate an association between the two poets cultivated in Spenser's first published work, *The Shepheardes Calender*, in which Spenser's persona Colin Clout is frequently compared to 'Tityrus', a name by which Spenser refers to both Virgil and Chaucer. In assuming a Chaucerian mantle Spenser doubtless intended to write himself into English literary history, but he also seems to have been participating in a distinctively Protestant self-fashioning. Chaucer's reputation among reformed English Protestants of the 1570s and 1580s was high, in part because he was thought to have been a Lollard sympathiser and the author of a dialogue, under the name of Jack Upland, which criticised friars; he was also reputed to have written the spurious 'Plowman's Tale', a Lollard poem known to Chaucer's first Tudor editor, William Thynne, and regularly printed in Chaucer's works between 1545 and 1775.[15] In addition, the reformist theology of Protestant apologists like Thomas Parker (Archbishop of Canterbury in Spenser's youth) and John Jewel (prolific bishop of London) stressed that English Protestantism was not an innovation, but – like Spenser's archaisms – a return to the practices of a pristine, unsullied age. Spenser's assumption of a Chaucerian stylistic veneer thus placed his poem in a native Protestant tradition.

Another key English touchstone for Spenser was the poet John Skelton, on whom both Oxford and Cambridge had conferred laureate status (in 1490 and 1495, respectively). Skelton had in 1521–2 composed a satirical verse attack on Lord Chancellor Cardinal Wolsey called *Collyn Clout*, in which the eponymous, supposedly guileless narrator relates to the reader the many scurrilous, often enigmatic, criticisms of Wolsey ostensibly circulating in London at this time. Skelton's poem, with its yokel-cam and anti-clerical stance, inspired Spenser to adopt the persona of Colin Clout as a figure for the author in his anti-clerical pastoral eclogues of 1579, *The Shepheardes Calender*. By 1596 this persona was so closely identified with Spenser that he could appear in its guise within *The Faerie Queene*, too, thereby to admonish and instruct his own knight of courtesy, Calidore (see *FQ* VI.x.5–30). While Spenser's use of the figure of Colin Clout cannot be called an imitation of Skelton's poetry, it represents yet another way in which – and another end to which – Spenser cited and adapted his predecessors. Colin provides Spenser with a kind of pastoral shorthand for the poet of complaint, the anti-court satirist whose plain-dealing innocence is (supposedly) his natural virtue. But even as Spenser cited Skelton in the figure of Colin Clout, he also appropriated him, re-inscribing his own meanings both literary and extra-literary on Skelton's rhetorical *prosopon* ('mask'). Skelton, for example, was no Protestant poet; Spenser's Colin may speak from just that reformed conviction.

Allusiveness and Englishness: folk traditions and the Bible

Two special kinds of allusiveness are particularly important to the encyclopedically intertextual fugue of *The Faerie Queene*, though unlike these earlier examples their transmission was likely not strictly or simply textual. First of all, folk traditions – stories, common proverbs, traditional entertainments, superstitions – play a substantial role in a poem so explicitly concerned with fairy lore and traditional chivalric narratives. An obvious example of this influence is the history of the knight of holiness, Redcrosse, in Book I of the poem. The traditional elements of the St George story, as it was performed in pageants and mumming plays, all feature in Spenser's narrative; a virgin princess, leading a milk-white lamb, is delivered from a venomous dragon by the hero, who then turns down her hand in marriage before setting off on further adventures. While Spenser seems to have assimilated some details of the St George narrative from the *Legenda Aurea* of Jacopus de Voragine, and others from Mantuan's *Georgius* (translated into English in about 1515 by Alexander Barclay), folk traditions clearly played a part not only in his composition but in the early reception of his poem. A similar survival of folk tradition in *The Faerie Queene* is Spenser's incorporation of the Mr Fox (or Bluebeard) legend in the narrative of Britomart's delivery of the virgin Amoret in Book III (cf. the headnote to the third selection, above); the psychosexual anxiety of the virgin bride, central to the legend, is infused into Britomart's quest when she repeatedly discovers the words 'bee bold' above the doors of Busirane's house. No written record of the Mr Fox legend survives from this period, but common features cited in various contemporary texts suggest that it was circulating orally in much the same form in which it was eventually printed in the eighteenth and nineteenth centuries.[16] Spenser's adaptation of these and other folk elements participates in the overall encyclopedic impact of his densely allusive text; but these folk elements also serve both to nationalise his poem, and to layer it – possibly ironically – with a popular woof that undercuts the more scholarly warp of his learned imitations.

Also central to the intertextual structure of *The Faerie Queene* – as to much English literary writing of this period – is the influence of the Bible. Spenser's assimilation of biblical narratives, figures and phraseology is often precisely turned; but in other cases it seems almost passive, the unconscious intertextual perfusion (in the Kristevan sense) of a much-read and fully absorbed text. When in her fight with Redcrosse the monster Errour spews out books and papers from her 'filthie maw', her vomit is full of 'bookes and papers', as well as 'loathly frogs and toades, which eyes did lacke' (I.i.20, in selection 1, above). The combination of books and frogs may at first seem odd, but makes sense if it is read as an allusion to the book of Revelation as printed in the Geneva Bible of 1583. Here we read (in Revelation 16) of a great dragon, and of a beast, and of a false prophet, who will prepare the way for Armageddon, and from whose mouths frogs will issue: 'And I sawe three vncleane spirits like frogs come out of the mouth of the dragon, and out of the mouth of the beast, and out of the mouth of the false Prophet' (16:13).[17] So far the frogs. But Spenser's image of Errour also has a precise relation to this particular edition of the Bible, which includes a gloss explaining these amphibian terrors:

> That is, a strong number of this great deuill the Popes ambassadours which are euer crying and croking like frogges and come out of Antichrists mouth, because they should speake nothing but lyes, and vse all maner of craftie deceit to maintaine their rich Euphrates against the true Christians.[18]

The pope's ambassadors will 'speake', naturally, through their written works: works on doctrine, church government and even temporal affairs, penned on paper. Here Spenser's allusion to a particular page of the Geneva text of the Bible itself participates in the material textuality of the allusion, foregrounding its own specificity. The allusion appears to establish the Protestant credentials of Spenser's poem, inasmuch as Errour can now be read as a figure for Roman Catholic polemicists, and Redcrosse as a good Protestant defender of the true faith. But if we think further, these easy identifications break down. For one thing, it was the reformed Protestant position that everything necessary to salvation was contained in Scripture, a position that put new emphasis on 'bookes and papers'; moreover, it is Spenser's poem, by virtue of its own materialist allusivity, that throws up the need for many books. Are these frogs the ambassadors of Antichrist, or symbols for the ungovernable intertextuality of Spenser's own poem?

Countless other examples of Spenser's recourse to scripture might be cited – from the sorceress Duessa's triumphant entrance astride the beast of Revelation (*FQ* I.vii.16–18, viii.6), to Guyon's temptations in the delve of Mammon (an analogue to Christ's harrowing of hell; see *FQ* II.vii.3–66), to Artegall's Solomonic judgment of Sir Sanglier (V.i; see selection 4, above). Each of these intertextual references is framed by its own unique set of concerns, and provokes a unique resonance from the scriptural original; but, as in the case of Errour's frog-vomit, it is safe to say that Spenser's allegory often remains obscure unless the very precise details of his allusions are known or can be traced. This is a general insight true of Spenser's allegorical method generally; his recruitment of the words and works of his predecessors, and of the standard theological and mythological sources (both written and oral) of his age, along with his detailed engagement with historical chronicle and even current events, mark him as one of the pre-eminent encyclopedic poets of his era. This encyclopedic impression of *The Faerie Queene*, this sense of its intertextual density, is – paradoxically – occasioned by a kind of emptiness. Spenser's spare and often visual writing relies on reference to other texts to complete – or at least complicate – its meaning. To read Spenser without heeding his constant calls for extratextual conferral is to leave his meaning at the most superficial and dreamlike level. His allegorical construction is thus so firmly embedded in its literary, mythological, theological and historical contexts that it is nothing without them; but with them, *The Faerie Queene* functions almost as a meta-text, a text that controls and confers all others. Whether this constitutes a gesture of humility or a stunning display of hubris may depend on the reader.

History and prophecy

Fashioning the reader: exemplary history

Spenser's is a book that probably needs to be judged – at least in the first instance – by its cover. The title page of *The Faerie Queene* in all its early editions is distinctive for saying not only what the poem *is*, but what it *does*: 'THE FAERIE QVEENE. Disposed into twelue books, Fashioning XII. Morall vertues'. What does it mean to 'fashion' moral virtues? Clearly the books of the poem are here said to shape or create these virtues, but where – on the page or in the reader? In Spenser's *de facto* preface to the poem, the 'Letter of the Authors . . . to Sir Walter Raleigh', this word appears again, this time very clearly with reference to the reader:

> The generall end therefore of all the booke is to fashion a gentleman or noble person in vertuous and gentle discipline: Which for that I conceiued shoulde be most plausible and pleasing, being coloured with an historicall fiction, the which the most part of men delight to read, rather for variety of matter, then for profite of the ensample: I chose the historye of king Arthure, as most fitte for the excellency of his person, being made famous by many mens former workes, and also furthest from the daunger of enuy, and suspition of present time.[19]

Spenser here alludes to a theory of poetry as a thing both *utile* (profitable) and *dulce* (sweet, delightful), a view of poetry that goes back to the Latin poet and critic Horace.[20] The moral purpose of writing and reading poetry – Spenser's 'vertuous and gentle discipline' – is part of a tradition that we have, since the Romantics, tended to suppress, even in our encounters with poets who, like Spenser, explicitly inform us that their work is to be read for 'profite'. By contrast, for the Elizabethan poets, the moral purpose of poetry was not only a facet of their work, but its animating and rationalising principle. Spenser's contemporary Philip Sidney argues in his Aristotelian *Defence of Poetry* (c. 1580–2) that the arts and sciences, though 'they have each a private end in themselves,' are

> all directed to the highest end of the mistress-knowledge, by the Greeks called ἀρχιτεκτονική, which stands (as I think) in the knowledge of a man's self, in the ethic and politic consideration, with the end of well-doing and not of well-knowing only.[21]

Poetry, Sidney claims, out-performs all other branches of learning or endeavour – and particularly history and philosophy – by leading the reader to an ethical and political understanding of the self that issues in virtuous action. This is the core, too, of Spenser's 'fashioning'; like Sidney, Spenser insists from the first on the morally propulsive power of poetry.

Spenser declares in his 'Letter of the Authors' that he has chosen the history of King Arthur both 'for variety of matter' and 'profite of the ensample'; in other words, this traditional English mythic history will provide an entertaining and an instructive backbone for his poem. A modern academic historian would probably snort at Spenser's claim that Arthur's life qualified as a kind of 'historye', but this would be to overlook fundamental differences in the concept of history between the Elizabethan period and our own. For a historian like Jacques Amyot, the Frenchman who translated Plutarch's *Lives of the Noble Grecians and Romans* from Greek in 1559, history is 'an orderly register of notable things said, done, or happened in time past, to mainteyne the continuall remembrance of them, and to serue for the instruction of them to come.'[22] Early modern historiographers like Amyot (and his translator, Sir Thomas North, who Englished Amyot's Plutarch in 1579) put a strong emphasis on the instructive power of history-writing, so strong in fact that the first selection of 'notable things' – the very genesis of the historical project – was driven by the impulse to inculcate in readers a particular set of virtuous ideals. For fortitude, whose life was like Mark Antony's? For constancy, who like Brutus? To tell these lives out of Plutarch was to instruct the reader in a particular virtue or cluster of virtues. Historiographers celebrated their craft for its special efficacy in communicating virtuous learning, which it achieved through example. Instead of delineating to the analytical and rational mind the nature, parts and occasions of a virtue, and then contrasting it with its concomitant vices, the exemplary history showed a virtuous man or woman exercising that virtue in a social and political context. The history thus provided a narrative pattern ready for the reader's imitation. As Amyot argues:

> These things [history] doth with much greater grace, efficacy, and speede, than the bookes of morall Philosophie doe: forasmuch as examples are of more force to moue and instruct, than are the arguments and proofes of reason, or their precise precepts, bicause examples be the very formes of our deedes, & accompanied with all circumstances. Whereas reasons and demonstrations are generall, and tend to the proofe of things, and to the beating of them into vnderstanding: and examples tende to the showing of them in practise and execution, bicause they doe not only declare what is to be done, but also worke a desire to do it, aswell in respect of a certaine naturall inclination which all men haue to follow examples, as also for the beawtie of vertue, which is of such power, that wheresoeuer she is seene, she maketh her selfe to be loued and liked.[23]

Spenser, like Amyot, values the historical fiction because it is the nature of examples to incite their readers to imitative action; moreover, the exemplary history, 'accompanied with all circumstances', gives readers a complete blueprint for the performance of virtuous deeds within the complex social and political contexts in which real people act. Philosophy might well teach the understanding of virtue; but for the fashioning of virtuous readers, who themselves will fashion virtuous actions, history is both more palatable and more effective.

Narrative and image in *The Faerie Queene*

The use of narrative as an instrument for moral instruction thus lies at the heart of Spenser's claim, in the 'Letter of the Authors', to follow 'all the antique Poets historicall' from Homer and Virgil right up to Ariosto and Tasso. His emphasis on morally exemplary narratives is everywhere evident in the poem, from Redcrosse's errant misprisions in Book I and Guyon's 'rigour pitilesse' in the destruction of the Bower of Bliss (see II.xii, above), to Artegall's legal judgments in Book V (see V.i–ii, above) and the Ovidian fable of Faunus and Molanna that structures the *Two Cantos of Mutabilitie*. In all of these areas of the poem, as in many others, we see allegorical figures taking on the persona of everyman as they negotiate difficult ethical, social and political problems. Redcrosse's abandonment of Una at I.ii.7 furnishes a good example of how narrative participates in the moral meaning of the poem. We know that Redcrosse has been deceived in his midnight visions of Una's seedy underbelly, but from Redcrosse's own perspective, he has been exceptionally careful and deliberate in his ultimate resolution to leave his lady. The enchanter Archimago tempts him first at I.i.47–55, when he sends Redcrosse a false dream of Una's looseness, and then teases him with a lecherous double. But Redcrosse shows caution:

> All cleane dismayd to see so vncouth sight,
>   And halfe enraged at her shamelesse guise,
>   He thought t'haue slaine her in his fierce despight:
>   But hasty heat tempring with sufferance wise,
>   He stayde his hand, and gan himselfe aduise
>   To proue his sense, and tempt her faigned truth. (I.i.50.1–6)

Redcrosse's 'sufferance wise' is further tested, though, at the start of the ensuing canto, when Archimago himself summons the bleary knight to witness his lady's exertions *in flagrante delicto*. This time, Redcrosse is unable to 'temper' his heat but, burning 'with gealous fire', he nearly lashes out at the two sprites before him. From Redcrosse's perspective, his patience has been sorely tried, and he has shown a caution that, on the face of it, much improves upon his earlier hastiness in the contest with the monster Errour (cf. Redcrosse 'full of fire and greedy hardiment' at I.i.14.1). But the narrative situation of Redcrosse's judgment here opposes his apparent caution against another kind of rashness; although he resists anger until Archimago shows him the ocular proof, nonetheless Redcrosse rashly trusts far too confidently in his own senses. Though he hesitates, he does not hesitate to trust his own eyes. This episode excites the reader's passionate response, as Redcrosse precipitously and unjustly abandons his lady, and the narrative thus aligns our disgust and disappointment with Redcrosse's mistake. But the narrative situation of Redcrosse's judgment also shows how a moral precept like that against rashness must be 'accompanied with all circumstances' to be of any practical value.

Spenser gives history and narrative pride of place in his prefatory letter to *The Faerie Queene*, and in this sense his poem earns its seat in the tradition of epic writing – historical poems like Virgil's *Aeneid* that chronicle the exemplary exploits of some famous hero. But Spenser's poem is also allegorical, and it exploits various devices conventional to allegorical writing in order to paint virtues and vices in more visual and cognitive terms. Obvious examples of this technique in the first two books include the description of the monster Errour (I.i.11–27, above), the pageant of the seven deadly sins (I.iv.16–38), the description of the House of Holinesse (I.x), Spenser's account of the house of Medina (II.ii.12–46), Guyon's and Arthur's view of the castle of Alma (II.ix.17–60), and the description of the Bower of Bliss (II.xii, above). These passages of the poem use personification and visual emblems to detail the substance, parts, circumstances and other aspects of various virtues and, similarly, to picture the nature and circumstances of their associated vices. Lechery, for example, rides 'vpon a bearded Gote' with 'whally eies (the signe of gelosy)'. His face – 'rough, and blacke, and filthy' – makes him an 'vnseemely man to please faire Ladies eye', and yet 'he of Ladies oft was loued deare, | When fairer faces were bid standen by' (I.iv.24). The glaring ('whalley') eyes of the jealous man attend Lechery because his vice occasions suspicion, while his shaggy hair indicates his luxuriousness. His dual aspect, both 'filthy' and desirable, gestures at his hypocrisy, and gestures too at the sickness in those who prefer his vice to the virtue of others. In the following stanza, Spenser suggests how this hypocrisy works:

> In a greene gowne he clothed was full faire,
>   Which vnderneath did hide his filthinesse,
> And in his hand a burning hart he bare,
>   Full of vaine follies, and new fanglenesse;
>   For he was false, and fraught with ficklenesse,

> And learned had to loue with secret lookes,
> And well could daunce, and sing with ruefulnesse,
> And fortunes tell, and read in louing bookes,
> And thousand other waies, to bait his fleshly hookes. (I.iv.25)

The green of his gown invokes the ever-fresh appetite of the lusty man, whose insatiable desire recurrently expends itself on new objects of love and lust. Key to his success is the concealment of his 'filthinesse' under the cover of this freshness – a visual detail that suggests a paradiastole[24] ('he is no fickle Lothario; he is an impressionable romantic!') – and under the cover of his 'secret lookes'. Spenser then gives us a set of social markers that will denote this vice: dancing, singing, fortune-telling, romance and lyric reading. This kind of pictorial or emblematic writing helps the reader to understand the nature, parts and occasions of the vice being described. In other places, Spenser's allegorical representations work through a hybrid combination of visual description, like this, and narrative combination, as when Britomart delivers Amoret from the house of Busirane to the embrace of the knight Scudamour in the 1590 version of the conclusion of Book III. The erotic jealousy dividing Scudamour from Amoret (pictured in the masque of Cupid in III.xii.1–27, above) must here be controlled by the ordering influence of chastity, symbolised by Britomart's presence; only thus can the lovers be reliably reunited. While Spenser's narrative examples give pleasure and incite the reader's imitation, visual and composite allegories like these inform the understanding.

The relationship between narrative and illustrative modes of moral investigation in Spenser's poetry is complex and varies from instance to instance. But broadly speaking, Spenser's conflation of these two modes, sometimes antagonistic but at other times complementary, seems to derive from his reading of Aristotle's *Nicomachean Ethics*. Aristotle's major work on ethics (like his *Politics*) was, both in its Latin translation and increasingly in the Greek original, a standard element in both grammar school and university teaching, and surfaces ubiquitously in Elizabethan writing. It is to this work that Spenser refers in 'A Letter of the Authors', when he notes that his poem's moral scheme will be based on the 'twelue priuate morall vertues, as Aristotle hath deuised'.[25] In the *Nicomachean Ethics* Aristotle argues that genuine ethical understanding requires knowledge of the universal ideal as well as accurate knowledge of the particular circumstances in which that ideal is to be applied. The proper relation between universal and particular kinds of knowledge he frames as a syllogism, in which the universal principle of ethical action is expressed as the major premise (e.g. 'All good people should avoid jealousy') and the individual circumstances of the particular situation are contained in the minor premise ('This situation would plunge me into jealousy'), such that the necessary ethical conclusion follows ('As a good person I must avoid this situation').[26] Once the student of ethics has absorbed the universal principles of ethical action, Aristotle argues, she or he must practise making the syllogistical transition from these universal positions to individual judgments in particular practical cases, learning to avoid logical faults ('it's not jealousy if I turn out to be right!'), sensory misperceptions ('he is such a loyal ensign'), and the interference of emotional or appetitive imperatives ('I love too well to love wisely'). In many cases, too, what at first sight seem simple ethical judgments can become clouded by conflicting universal codes for behaviour ('To fall in love with what she feared to look on!'). Spenser's alternation between narrative and illustrative representations of the same and related virtues furnishes the reader with just this sort of practice in the transition between ostensibly unimpeachable universal ethical and political ideals, and the messy circumstances of practical ethical and political judgment, where compromise is often required.

Prophetic time

According to the Sidneian scheme (from *The Defence of Poesy*), then, *The Faerie Queene* thus seems to divide between elements which present a narrative, historical exemplification of virtues and vices, and elements of a visual and emblematic nature, which present complex philosophical analyses of those virtues and vices. This is the divide, in short, between the moral educative powers of history, to one side, and to the other, philosophy. Another way of figuring and understanding this opposition is by considering it from a temporal perspective. The *exempla* furnished by the poem in its human histories of knights – and above all, Prince Arthur – pursuing adventures in the completion of an overarching quest, are historical events that take place diachronically (through time). The reader follows these histories with narrative appetite, and indeed many of these histories shadow (as we will see in a moment) historical personages and events of the near Elizabethan past. By contrast, the emblematic 'cores' of *The Faerie Queene*, delivered in vivid and luxurious *ekphraseis* and in the formal, architectural order of masques, pageants and trials, do not 'take place', but exist synchronically (with or in time) before us, like any visual artwork. The eye may travel in time over these visions of beauty and order, but the very movement of the eye across them is the index of their stability and perdurability. This is a lesson that Calidore, the knight of courtesy, learns the hard way in canto x of Book VI, when he attempts to approach the timeless, circular beauty of the dance of the Graces on Mount Acidale (*FQ* VI.x.5–30); he can glimpse their 'order excellent' (13.9) so long as he remains 'astonished in spright' and 'rapt with pleasaunce' (17.3–4), but the moment he 'resolu[es] ... to know' who the Graces are, they disappear. The critic Angus Fletcher has encouraged us to see these moments in Spenser's allegorical work as instances of 'prophecy', not in the popular but the true sense of the word. A prophet for Fletcher is a seer whose apperceptions and utterances are not bounded by the temporal, but are timeless, even though they exist in and are grounded in that temporal moment in which they are had and made. As Fletcher writes, 'the paradox may be resolved if we think that the prophet utters an eternal truth that is immanent in the daily affairs of men.'[27] Indeed, as we have seen, the synthesis of universal or eternal truth (what Sidney following Aristotle calls *gnosis*, 'recognition') with a historical moment of *praxis* ('action') constitutes exactly that proper configuration of self to absolute that Aristotle considered the essence of ethical virtue.

Although Spenser claims that his book will 'fashion' a reader in ethical and political discipline, his poem is not the dusty didactic landscape likely, through much plodding, to result in a bunion. On the contrary, it is the dynamic, often sceptical play of history and prophecy in *The Faerie Queene* that animates and grounds its philosophical subject. While the poem is instructive and 'fashions' its reader in moral discipline, it would be wrong to suppose that Spenser's poetry takes a clear, coherent and consistent line on any one ethical or political ideal, and communicates this to the reader, 'fashioning' her or him on its design. Instead the poem invites the reader into a kind of sceptical play between universal principles and the particular circumstances, both of individual narratives recounted in the poem, and of real historical characters and events shadowed behind these narrative screens. The process of conferral, application, revision, adjustment and accommodation provoked by Spenser's patterned superimpositions and analogies ultimately leads the reader not to a given position, or set of positions, on ethics or politics; instead it instructs the reader (as he says) in the discipline of these moral sciences, creating the skills necessary for ethical and political judgment and action.

In a landmark study of the Bower of Bliss, Stephen Greenblatt has noticed that Guyon's destruction of the bower is marked by a rigour and extremity apparently inconsistent with Spenser's earlier emphasis in Book II on temperance as a mean between the extremes of deficiency and profligacy, slackness and severity. Instead, Greenblatt suggests, Guyon's destructive actions look like Elizabethan encounters with New World peoples, Elizabethan practices in the brutal military theatres of sixteenth-century Ireland, and Elizabethan reformist attacks on the traditional iconography of the medieval Christian church.[28] Greenblatt's situation of the bower's destruction within these historical contexts is helpful, as is his argument that, in destroying the bower, Guyon attacks the very fabric of the poem, which like the bower is an artwork built on *sprezzatura* – that is, an artwork that conceals its own artistry[29] – but Greenblatt's Spenser emerges as an imperialist Puritan zealot whose temperance recalls not Aristotle (virtue is a mean) but Calvin (meanness is a virtue). Greenblatt's reading is important because it suggests a challenge to the dynamic relationship between history and prophecy in Spenser's work for which I have been arguing here. Is that all there is to Spenserian temperance? Of course not; but instead of taking Guyon's action as *the* expression of Spenser's view on temperance, we might read it as the means by which he poses a question to the reader. A key to how we might articulate that question lies in the name of Spenser's intemperate enchantress, Acrasia; ἀκρατῆς is Aristotle's word for 'unrestraint', a word derived from κράτος, 'strength', and one that shares a close similarity to ἄκρατος (from the verb κεράννυμι, 'to mix'), meaning 'unmixed, pure, absolute'. Both stems eventually issued in the noun form ἀκρασία, differing only in the length of the medial vowel, which could therefore act as a near-pun meaning both 'absoluteness, unmixedness' and 'incontinence, unrestraint'. In the passages of the *Nicomachean Ethics* where Aristotle uses ἀκρατῆς to mean 'unrestraint', he is arguing that the temperate person should achieve a more certain relation between universal principles and particular judgments – that is how this person can show ἐγκρατῆς ('self-restraint') and achieve virtue. In Aristotle's view, then, unrestraint occurs when the universal ethical principle is not applied in the particular circumstance: that is, when the ethical subject does not allow him or herself to conform to the universal ethical principle. Spenser makes an elaborate joke when, after capturing Acrasia and her lover Verdant, Guyon binds her:

> They tooke them both, & both them strongly bound
> In captiue bandes, which there they readie found;
> But her in chaines of adamant he tyde;
> For nothing else might keepe her safe and sound;
> But *Verdant* (so he hight) he soone vntyde,
> And counsell sage in steed thereof to him applyde. (II.xii.82.4–9)

Guyon's double binding of Acrasia puts him in a double-bind. His excessive rigour shows him to be as unmoderated and absolute as Acrasia, precisely as – and because – he binds her so thoroughly. Unlike Tasso's handling of Armida, as we have seen, Spenser's treatment of Acrasia is severe and unremitting. If Greenblatt is correct that Guyon's rigour invokes not one but several historical contexts, we see Guyon abandoning the Aristotelian conception of temperance – as an admixture or mean between two extremes

– just at that moment at which three historical particulars thrust themselves conspicuously into view. The confrontation with Acrasia, therefore, makes Guyon guilty of ἀκρασία, allowing the particular to overmaster the universal; and yet she remains bound, and that with adamant. Spenser's playful erudition gives the lie to Greenblatt's two-dimensional view of Spenser's purpose here. What is more, this instance of interpretative play in the poem, by dint of its reference to Aristotle's discussion of universals and particulars, concerns exactly that vexed relation of history to prophecy which it exemplifies.

Politics and historical allegory

As Greenblatt reminds us, another sort of history and prophecy also matters to *The Faerie Queene*. This is the sort of history and the prophecy that we normally imagine when we use these words: history as the 'orderly register of notable things said, done, or happened in time past', and prophecy as the inspired foretelling of things to come. Spenser's poetry is remarkable among that of Elizabethan writers not for its engagement with topical political and religious events, but for the intensity of that engagement. Nearly every narrative strand in Spenser's poem seems to betray, upon the least pressure, some careful and pointed allusion to a salient or defining moment in the political and religious history of the English nation under Elizabeth's reign. So thick do these historical allegories fly – particularly in Book V – that the work sometimes feels nothing more than a tissue of memorials to the councillors, judges and royal favourites, and the plots, trials and battles of the late Tudor polity. Obvious examples litter the text, from the defeat of the Spanish Armada shadowed in Redcrosse's fight with the dragon (I.xi), to the trial of Mary Queen of Scots, only thinly veiled in the history of Mercilla's trial and execution of Duessa (V.ix.22–x.4). Key figures from Elizabeth's government also figure in Spenser's narrative, from the clear allusions to Robert Dudley, Earl of Leicester in Sir Guyon, to the close associations between Artegall, the knight of justice, and Arthur Lord Grey of Wilton, Spenser's one-time employer and patron in Ireland. Similarly, the extended history of the love between Arthur's squire, Timias, and the chaste huntress Belphoebe, which spans Books III and IV, transparently allegorises the vagaries of Sir Walter Ralegh's fortunes at court in the early 1590s. Equally important, though less conspicuous, are the acutely turned, but lesser, historical allegories that lurk in minor episodes. Such, for example, is that expounded by René Graziani, who in a seminal article has shown how the knight of chastity, Britomart, passes through a series of linked episodes in Book V that recall the fine details of contemporary treason trials and conspiracies to murder Queen Elizabeth.

Not only, Graziani argues, do the details of Britomart's allegorical vision at Isis Church (V.vii.12–17) recall very similar visual allegories in the seditious 'political prophecies' prepared for and trusted by senior members of the powerful Howard family; but Britomart's narrow escape at the house of Dolon – where her bed falls through the floor in the night, nearly plunging her to her death – also recalls a plot laid for Elizabeth by one William Stafford, who claimed to have conspired with the French ambassador to blow up the Queen, using gunpowder, while she lay in her bed.[30] These minute and detailed historical memorials operate on readers in various ways, but probably most importantly they transform Spenser's epic into a national poem, a poem that constructs its readers as a community of sharers in a common history of war, religious strife, factional politics, court intrigues, assassinations and executions, and so on.

If the poem records and memorialises key personages and events from recent Elizabethan history – so giving the lie to Spenser's claim that he would eschew 'suspition of present time' – *The Faerie Queene* also engages in pointed experiments in political and religious prophecy. The defeat of the dragon in canto xi of Book I memorialises one victory – that over Spain in 1588 – but it also foretells a promised victory in a larger struggle with Catholic Europe in the years to come. More specifically, one of Spenser's most inspired seers, the wizard Merlin, delivers to Britomart in III.iii, as a prophecy, the entire (mythical) history of her descendants, culminating in a virgin queen whose reign very clearly invokes that of Elizabeth (III.iii.49). The use of this temporal device – situating prophecies in the historical past (here, the mythical past) as a means of avoiding the usual uncertainties of oracular apprehension – nonetheless has important consequences for our thinking about temporality in *The Faerie Queene*. The certainty and specificity of Merlin's predictions endow his prophecies with a providential security, one that prepares us to read other instances of prophecy proper – though they are necessarily more vague – with a sense of optimism and conviction. The prophetic overtones of the marriage of the Thames and Medway (IV.xi), for example, encourage readers to see England's imperial future as intrinsically involved with its naval and merchant strength. Similarly, Calidore's extermination of the brigants in Book VI, in a pastoral landscape that looks conspicuously like rural Ireland, surely suggests the establishment of a settled and peaceful English government there – a cherished dream for a hardworking colonialist planter like Spenser, but one that did not come to pass in his lifetime, or ever. Here, as in the *Two Cantos of Mutabilitie*, Spenser's poetry shares considerable ground with the plots and provisions articulated by the seasoned political observer, Irenius, in Spenser's 1596 prose tract on Irish reform, *A view of the present state of Ireland*.

Allegory and philosophy

The dark pleasure of allegory

Spenser informs Walter Ralegh in 'A Letter of the Authors' that *The Faerie Queene* is 'a continued Allegory, or darke conceit', the kind of poem that does not say exactly what it seems to say. By the time Spenser came to it in the sixteenth century, the figure *allegoria* had a long history in the theory and practice of rhetoric. Although Aristotle left no comment on it, Quintilian in his *Institutes of Oratory* offers in several places a rich discussion of this figure and practice. In general, as he says, '*Allegory*, which is translated in Latin by *inversio*, either presents one thing in words and another in meaning, or else something absolutely opposed to the meaning of the words.'[31] This general description of allegory follows its Greek etymology, from ἄλλως ἀγορεύειν, 'to speak otherwise, to speak so as to imply something other than the literal sense'. Quintilian connects *allegoria* to the *poeticae fabulae*, or 'fictions of the poets', observing that these homely stories

> are specially attractive to rude and uneducated minds, which are less suspicious than others in their reception of fictions and, when pleased, readily agree with the arguments from which their pleasure is derived. Thus Menenius Agrippa is said to have reconciled the plebs to the patricians by his fable of the limbs' quarrel with the belly.[32]

The persuasive force of allegory derives, for Quintilian, from the pleasure natural to its literal meaning, which by an unconscious process induces unsophisticated readers to accept arguments implied by the allegory's hidden meaning; thus Menenius Agrippa could persuade a revolting citizen to return to his starving home, simply by explaining that it was natural in Rome's civic body that the leading men (the belly) should be given the available food, while its tradesmen and artisans (its outer limbs and extremities) should go without. Allegory emerges from Quintilian's influential treatment as a technique of persuasion that works by pleasure, suitable for duping peasants, for trifling, and for embellishing arguments where a little looseness is not unseemly.

Other writers offer a very different account. Among extant classical works, the first to discuss allegory is that attributed to Demetrius, *On Style* (*Peri hermeneias*), a Greek treatise probably dating from the second century B.C. Demetrius appears to think of allegory as a figure – that is, an artificial form of thought or words that gives beauty or impact to an expression. For Demetrius, the value of allegory lies in the dignity and power it confers on the speaker:

> Allegory is also impressive, particularly in threats, for example that of Dionysius, 'their cicadas will sing from the ground.' If he had said openly that he would

ravage the land of Locris, he would have shown more anger but less dignity. As it is, he has shrouded his words, as it were, in allegory. What is implied always strikes more terror, since its meaning is open to different interpretations, whereas what is clear and plain is apt to be despised, like men who are stripped of their clothes. This is why the mysteries are revealed in allegories, to inspire the shuddering and awe associated with darkness and night. In fact allegory is not unlike darkness and night.[33]

Dionysius, the fourth-century tyrant of Syracuse, is here commended for his use of allegory in threatening the inhabitants of Locris, in central Greece; his resort to allegory reflects his dignity and power, for even his meaning, as it were, is muffled in grandeur. It was from this passage of Demetrius' treatise that Torquato Tasso, the poet of the *Gerusalemme Liberata*, derived his view on the special import of allegory for heroic poems: 'Allegory', he writes, 'has rightly been said to resemble night and darkness; it is therefore to be used in mysteries and in poems full of mystery like the heroic.'[34] Spenser, in turn, probably had Tasso before him when he composed 'A Letter of the Authors', for he too associates allegory with 'darke conceit', and later acknowledges that his poem is 'clowdily enwrapped in Allegoricall deuises.'[35] The tradition stretching back through Tasso to Demetrius is important, for it suggests that Spenser wished his first readers to register a more awful, more mysterious potential in allegory, a potential more closely linked to terror and threat than to pleasure and pastime.

Consistent with his view of allegory as the medium of serious philosophical and religious truth, Tasso tends to see allegorical meaning as prescriptive and determinate; while Tasso's heroic poem may encode mysterious truths, the recovery of those meanings from his allegory is a process that, when pursued with knowledge, care and intelligence, will yield definite and not accidental insights. It is possible to read Tasso correctly. Tasso himself acknowledges this in his comments on the allegory of Dante's *Divina Commedia*:

[Dante] tells us that the meaning is fourfold: literal, moral, allegorical [i.e. historical allegorical], and anagogic [i.e. mystical, metaphysical]. The first of these is simple enough and easily understood; the second aims at teaching moral habit; the other two are directed rather to the intellect, the third conducing to speculation on lower, the fourth on higher matters, and both serving to excuse the poet's mistakes in imitating. But if the defence involves some fault in the first meaning and is combined with a fault in decorum, some ugliness or unseemliness in the things imitated, it is neither good nor commendable. That is why Aristotle did not list it among other defences; and indeed if allegory were an accidental perfection in the poem, it could not reasonably make defects of art excusable, these being intrinsic defects.[36]

For Tasso, the structure of a poem's allegorical meanings must not be accidental, but carefully inscribed and signalled to the reader in the first, surface layer of the poem's literal sense. Where the poet makes 'mistakes' in imitating (that is, in writing a plausible narrative that, as Aristotle has it in his *Poetics*, imitates the nature of things as they should be), these 'mistakes' can be permitted only where they are necessary to make possible, or to signal, some insight in the (historical) allegorical or anagogic levels of the poem's meaning. Implicit in this view of the poem's literal and higher senses is Tasso's view that the artist must *mean* – that is to say, he must be a skilled artificer of – each level of the allegory. The reader will have confidence in the poet's allegorical intentions if, and only if, the poet can produce a seamless, tight construction, in which each level of the allegory is excellent and coherent both in itself, and in its relations to the other levels. The reader of such a poem, like the Locrians before Dionysius, will retire in dread and awe.

Spenser's residual allegory

To recognise Spenser's debt to Tasso and Demetrius is not, however, to discount the importance of the fabular strand in Spenser's allegorical weave. In keeping with his own fabular emphasis on allegory, Quintilian hesitates to identify allegory completely with irony, a figure by which the speaker clearly means one thing, something not said, which is the opposite of what she says. Quintilian marshals the figures of irony under the titles of σαρκασμός, ἀςτεϊσμός, ἀντίφρασις and παροιμία (sarcasm, urbane wit, antiphrasis or contradiction, and the use of proverbs), each of which clearly indicates a specific meaning distinct from what has been said. But he cautions:

> There are, however, some writers who deny that these are species of *allegory*, and assert that they are actually *tropes* in themselves: for they argue shrewdly that allegory involves an element of obscurity, whereas in all these cases our meaning is perfectly obvious. To this may be added the fact that when a *genus* is divided into *species*, it ceases to have any peculiar properties of its own: for example, we may divide tree into its species, pine, olive, cypress, etc., leaving it no properties of its own, whereas allegory always has some property peculiar to itself. The only explanation of this fact is that it is itself a species. But this, of course, is a matter of indifference to those that use it.[37]

By a logical argument worthy of Aristotle, Quintilian reasons that allegory cannot be a genus from which ironic figures depend as species, for the allegorical expression is never exhausted by its interpretation, but retains 'some property peculiar to itself'. If it did not, of course, the allegorical expression could not delight, for its significance would be consumed in its reference to its true meaning. (Note that, *pace* Demetrius, it *could* still inspire awe in the Tassonian style; the grandeur of Dionysius' threat to the Locrians lies in the dead certainty of his meaning.) Quintilian implies that the peculiar delight of allegory lies in its obscurity, the failure of perfect fit between the fable and its supposed meaning. In allegory, there is tree to spare.

Spenser makes it clear in the opening canto of *The Faerie Queene* that he has Dante, Tasso and Quintilian all firmly in mind; and, indeed, the opening canto seems to provide a kind of instruction in construing Spenserian allegory. Like the figure of Dante, who finds himself at the opening of *Inferno* in a *selva oscura* (obscure wood), Redcrosse and Una begin their adventures by seeking 'couert' from a storm in a 'shadie groue' (I.i.7.1–2). This place is defined by its darkness, so overcast with leafy canopy that it is 'Not perceable with power of any starre' (I.i.7.6), but the same trees that block out the light also offer occasion for delight:

> And foorth they passe, with pleasure forward led,
>   Ioying to heare the birdes sweete harmony,
>   Which therein shrouded from the tempest dred,
>   Seemd in their song to scorne the cruell sky. (I.i.8.1–4)

Are the trees then a source of Tassonian darkness, or the shady perch for birds which sing, to a tune by Quintilian, the pleasure of allegory's residual obscurity? It is at this moment that Spenser cracks one of his most academic jokes. With Quintilian's discussion of the genus and species of trees fresh in his mind, Spenser has his knight of holiness take a sudden interest in arboriculture:

>   Much can they prayse the trees so straight and hy,
>   The sayling Pine, the Cedar proud and tall,
>   The vine-prop Elme, the Poplar neuer dry,
>   The builder Oake, sole king of forrests all,
> The Alpine good for staues, the Cypresse funerall.
>
> The Laurell, meed of mightie Conquerours
>   And Poets sage, the Firre that weepeth still,
>   The Willow worne of forlorne Paramours,
>   The Eugh obedient to the benders will,
>   The Birch for shaftes, the Sallow for the mill,
>   The Mirrhe sweete bleeding in the bitter wound,
>   The warlike Beech, the Ash for nothing ill,
>   The fruitfull Oliue, and the Platane round,
> The caruer Holme, the Maple seeldom inward sound. (I.i.8.5–9.9)

Spenser's catalogue of trees plays a joke on the proverb 'you can't see the wood, anymore, for the trees'; this is presumably why Redcrosse and Una suddenly find themselves to be lost. But the proverb only expresses Quintilian's point about how species can exhaust genus, and so we recognise that, from at least one perspective, Redcrosse and Una here discover how obscure and terrifying allegory can be. It is Tasso's mystery, a place of night and darkness. However, instead of just showing us trees, Spenser shows us also the properties of trees. The comic force of Spenser's catalogue lies in the simple fact that the properties of the individual species of tree are entirely irrelevant to the function of the (genus) tree in this episode; Redcrosse and Una find themselves beguiled by a specialisation in trees that distracts them from the darkness and obscurity of the trees' shady covering, but that specialisation does not exhaust the darkness and obscurity. Spenser's comment on Tasso and Quintilian here is riven by an irony: it is the residual obscurity of the allegorical element, the tree, that proves allegory to be not only grave and mysterious, but delightful.

Impossible visions

Spenser's handling of the wandering wood shows that his poem entertains two opposed ideas about allegory at once. It is both grave and mysterious, a vehicle for high truths and threatening awe; and trifling and rustic, a toy suitable for orators only on off days. It is not Spenser's first joke at Tasso's expense. The first comes in the opening stanzas of canto i, and it helps to explain how these contradictory dynamics in Spenserian allegory will function, and to what end. In the first stanzas of the canto, we are shown a knight 'pricking on the plaine' (I.i.1.1), a 'louely Ladie' riding 'him faire beside' (I.i.4.1), and a lagging dwarf, 'that lasie seemd in being euer last' (I.i.6.2). The visual absurdity of this presentation was first noticed by John Upton, Spenser's first scholarly editor, who in 1758 attached this note to the passage:

> That expression *pricking on the plaine*, the reader may see explained in the Glossary: it means always riding in career by pricking or spurring the horse: but I must acknowledge this interpretation carries with it no small inaccuracies; for the lady, who attends upon a slow asse, *rides him fair beside*. Shall we apologize for our poet as for painters, who usually draw their knights in full career, notwithstanding any subsequent improprieties? or shall we look for another explanation? shall we say that *pricking on the plaine* means no more than riding on the plain, without any reference to the manner, whether slow or fast? or rather shall we assign some other meaning to the passage, as it stands here?[38]

As Upton observes, a galloping knight, a lady pacing on an ass and a short-legged dwarf struggling under a heavy pack cannot travel together for very long; indeed, they cannot exist in the same frame for more than a moment. Upton is right to suggest that we must 'assign some other meaning' to the passage, and that meaning is, as he also suggests, emblematic. Redcrosse is shown to be galloping because the posture indicates his nature, which is courageous and heroic, but rash. Una paces on an ass because she is humble and, as we soon learn, consumed with care; moreover, that ass is white because she is pure. The dwarf, by contrast, must travel by foot and must lag lazily because, as the representation of the knight's and the poem's 'needments', he fails to keep up with his master's ambition. By the time we hit stanza 6 of the first canto, Spenser very clearly intends us to realise that all is not well with Redcrosse's quest and all is not well with the poem. Spenser here uses the opening of his epic to stick his finger in Tasso's eye; Redcrosse's racy pricking tears a gash through the literal sense of the poem, even as the pun on 'prick' (penis) creates an intolerable 'ugliness or unseemliness'.

A gap opens and widens, here, between the impossible surface of the poem, on the one hand, and on the other its possible interpretations. The effect of this rupture is to deprecate the literal surface of the poem, suggesting to the reader that it is little more than dross to be transcended in the apprehension of a valuable import lying behind it. From one way of thinking, this makes perfect sense of the passage's clear preoccupations with Christian iconography. Redcrosse bears on his armour and shield the cross of St George, 'the deare remembrance of his dying Lord' (I.i.2.2), and we learn in ensuing stanzas that he is charged with redeeming Una's royal parents from the 'infernall feend', a dragon that has 'expeld' them from their kingdom (I.i.5.7–8). As a Protestant poet writing in the first generation of the Elizabethan settlement, Spenser could be expected to take at best an ambivalent view of the traditional iconography of saints, dragons and veiled virgins; these were symbols that had, in his lifetime, been razed in parish churches across the country. By extension, it would be plausible to suppose that the entire fabric of the literal sense of his poem – like the visual iconography it contains – has been written simply to be discarded. Instead, the reader is encouraged to reach for those all-important allegorical and, above all, anagogic meanings. This is probably how Milton construed *The Faerie Queene* when, in his *Areopagitica*, he called Spenser 'sage and serious', and admitted he thought him 'a better teacher then *Scotus* or *Aquinas*', for, 'describing true temperance under the person of *Guion*, [he] brings him in with his palmer through the cave of Mammon, and the bowr of earthly blisse that he might see and know, and yet abstain.'[39] Spenser does not shy from offering us his poem, another bower of pleasurable bliss, but, as Milton has it, he may expect us to abstain.

It is a neat argument, and as strong as Milton is – which is pretty strong. But there are flaws, and in those flaws inhere those very qualities that, though they may prevent *The Faerie Queene* from achieving the greatness of *Paradise Lost*, nonetheless give it a philosophical power, as well as a common humility, far beyond what either Tasso or Milton achieved. In the opening stanzas of Book I, canto i, we may be tempted to abstain from the romance pleasures of the knight, the lady and the dwarf, setting out on their glorious adventure. But other aspects of Spenser's representation encourage us to pause before we jettison the surface of things. Redcrosse wears a suit of armour that, the poem informs us, is much older and more battle-hardened than he is. It is not necessarily a Catholic icon, either, but, as Spenser insists in 'A Letter of the Authors', 'the armour of a Christian man specified by Saint Paul v. Ephes[ians]'.[40] Meanwhile, we know as little of the 'clownish person' inside the armour as he does of himself. Una, too, is veiled. It may be that, when Redcrosse finally does get a glimpse of the New Jerusalem (at I.x.55–64) and learns by just how much it supersedes the earthly paragon of glory, Cleopolis – that is, infinitely – we may feel as smug as Milton in our rejection of the poem's chivalric narrative. But we should note that, even though Spenser allows Redcrosse this vision of a heaven of meaning behind the poem's romance surface, he subscribes it with deferrals. Not only does Redcrosse's aged guide, Contemplation, send him back into the world of the poem to fight the dragon (I.x.63), but even after that victory Redcrosse prefers his vow to Gloriana to his new union with Una:

> Yet swimming in that sea of blisfull ioy,
> He nought forgot, how he whilome had sworne,
> In case he could that monstrous beast destroy,
> Vnto his Farie Queene back to returne:
> The which he shortly did, and *Vna* left to mourne. (I.xii.61.5–9)

The demands of Spenser's iconoclastic Protestant poetics cannot, it seems, wholly divert him from his own diversion. There is yet tree to spare.

Critical and creative engagements

The seat of Spenser's philosophical power in *The Faerie Queene* lies in this residuality of the poem's allegorical structure. Moreover, the great allegorical cores of the poem all turn on the indisseverable conjugation of the poem's surface, lively with its varied incident and secular philosophy, and the transcendent spiritual visions that these surfaces permit. Critical and creative engagements with this conjugation have – since the first years of *The Faerie Queene*'s publication – repeatedly struggled to privilege one or another element of the poem's material, its philosophical ambition or its spiritual intensity, leading to some of the greatest literature and literary criticism in our language. For example, among the first and most remarkable of these interventions is the long 1628 commentary written by Sir Kenelm Digby, the seventeenth-century natural philosopher and gentleman, on a stanza from Book II of *The Faerie Queene*. The canto as a whole relates Arthur's and Guyon's visit to the House of Alma, an allegory for the human body and the various intemperate sensual dangers that threaten it. Digby takes as his subject the twenty-second stanza of canto ix, in which Spenser describes the mathematical basis of the human body:

> The frame thereof seemd partly circulare,
>   And part triangulare, O worke diuine;
> Those two the first and last proportions are,
>   The one imperfect, mortall fœminine;
> Th'other immortall, perfect, masculine,
> And twixt them both a quadrate was the base,
> Proportioned equally by seuen and nine;
> Nine was the circle sett in heauens place,
> All which compacted made a goodly *Dyapase*. (II.ix.22)

To Digby's mind, this stanza reveals 'the profoundest notions that any Science can deliver us', revealing Spenser to be 'thoroughly verst in the Mathematicall Sciences, in Philosophy, and in Divinity'.[41] With painstaking detail, he exposes how the geometries of the male circular – a complete and perfect figure that imitates divine motion, and here stands for the immortal soul – is joined to the female triangular, here an allegorical figure for the *materia*, or mother-stuff, out of which all things (including us) are made. Joining the disparate geometries of the male soul and the female body is the 'quadrate' base, representing the four humours (choler, blood, phlegm and melancholy), all of which are governed by the seven planets and the nine hierarchies of angelic substance, making a cosmic 'diapase' or harmony.

Even in this inadequate epitome of Digby's commentary, it is clear how his account of this stanza ranges across geometry, metaphysics, physiology, cosmology, music and divinity. This conjugation of disparate matter Digby considers God's, and Spenser's, chiefest work:

> Certainly of all Gods works, the noblest and perfectest is Man, and for whom indeed all others were done. For, if we consider his *soul*, it is the very Image of God. If his *bodie*, it is adornd with the greatest beautie and most excellent symmetry of parts, of any created thing: whereby it witnesseth the perfection of the Architect, that of so drossie mold is able to make so rare a fabrick: If his *operations*, they are free: If his end, it is eternall glory. And if you take *all together*, Man is a little world, and of God himself. But in all this, me thinks, the admirablest work is the joyning together of the two *different* and indeed *opposite* substances in Man, to make one perfect compound; the *Soul* and the *Body*, which are of so contrary a nature, that their *uniting* seems to be a Miracle.[42]

Digby's confidence in Spenser's deep philosophical and religious purpose in this stanza makes of him a maker of this little world, in parallel to God the maker of the cosmos – so much so that the identity of the 'Architect' is left yawningly open. But Spenser's combination of the mortal feminine and immortal masculine in this stanza is further charged with at least two other elements, both of which exert a decidedly bathetic influence on Digby's Renaissance optimism. First, the stanza clearly alludes to the myth of the hermaphrodite as related by Aristophanes in Plato's *Symposium*, a tongue-in-cheek story that imagines metaphysical transcendence as the result of a hermaphroditic sexual union between male and female.[43] This is a subtext to the stanza which is given decided weight by Spenser's consummate pun on 'dyapase' – or 'die apace', the immediate orgasm one might expect from a cosmic union this spectacular. Digby is certainly correct to draw out at such length Spenser's 'compacted' meaning in this stanza; but his philosophical wishfulness makes him deaf to the possibility that universal conjugation might be a naughty, playful sort of coitus.

The centuries following the publication of *The Faerie Queene* witnessed a range of imitative appropriations of Spenser's allegorical methods and poetic techniques. Phineas Fletcher, who like Digby was fascinated by Spenser's House of Alma, again anatomised the body in *The Purple Island* (1633), while Milton experimented with Spenserian allegory – and especially the snaky folds of Errour – in his representation of Sin and Death in *Paradise Lost* (II.648–790). Milton's special sterility leads to a humourless flattening of Errour's Nile-like irrigatory power; not so the sustained engagement of the Romantic poets with Spenser's thought and allegorical strategies. In his *Eve of St Agnes*, for example, John Keats adopts Spenser's stanza form, but owes a greater debt than this to Spenser in his cultivation of a distributed, sensuous materiality of passion. Music, fabric, carved images, cold stone, soft hues, costly perfumes and exotic commodities confusedly, but for all that compactly, create the experience of Madeline's union with her lover Porphyro, in an 'elfin-storm from faery land' (stanza 39). Keats, like many of his near-contemporaries, saw in Spenser's allegory a richly variegated material surface, a literal sense remarkable for its pregnant capacity not merely to signify, but to *contain* a heady range of cognitive and affective psychic states. In the hands of the Romantic poets, Spenser's tendency to transferred epithet – the figure that allows his lovers to languish on 'drowsy couches' (cf. II.iii.1) and his knights to challenge one another with 'cruel steel' (cf. I.v.9) – became the basis for the creation of a sumptuous sensual landscape of human feeling. Keats and his contemporaries put the pace back in Digby's diapase.

In the twentieth century, critical fashion has tended to swing back toward the philosophical reach of Spenser's allegory – what Tasso, following Dante, called the anagogic. This emphasis – or perhaps we should coldly call it bias – has naturally deprecated both the poem's moral sense (an outdated mode teaching largely irrelevant values) and its historical sense (what, borrowing a phrase from Shakespeare, C. S. Lewis blisteringly condemned as 'the glistering of this present'). As it sheds its constituencies, *The Faerie Queene* has come to be embraced primarily by critics who can publicly justify their fondness for Spenser by appealing to, and in some sense perhaps creating, his deep intellectual reach. Typical of these studies is the seminal work of Isabel MacCaffrey in her reading of *Spenser's Allegory: The Anatomy of Imagination*. For MacCaffrey, 'imagination is the generator of images, and allegory gives us insight into the life-processes of those images'; by means of allegory, 'the mind turns inward in order that it may return with a more powerful sense of identity and purpose to its own experience in a bewildering universe, which may yet be remade in the image of the heart's desire.'[44] Thus when MacCaffrey turns to Spenser's description of the Garden of Adonis (III.vi.29–50), she finds him dealing 'with a kind of meaning that is both deeper and higher, or more general, than the direct mirroring of the mind's desires reflected in mimetic fantasies and exemplified in the Bower of Bliss'. Spenser reveals in the Garden an 'inarticulate life-force, the Freudian Eros at its eternal war with Thanatos'.[45] As a *locus amoenus* (or blessed place), the Garden of Adonis is charged for MacCaffrey with a sexual energy that transcends simple materiality, engaging the imagination to extend its reach into the furthest abstractions of Platonic analogy.

Spenser's presentation of the Garden is equal to the reading MacCaffrey gives it. Adonis, 'Father of all formes', dwells forever in the garden, 'ioying his goddesse' Venus, as the two of them bring substance forever into contact with form, through which it passes, is changed and emerges again (see III.vi.37–8). But, as so often, in the loftiest pitch of his philosophical seriousness Spenser finds a way to bring his transcendent vision crashing down in pieces. To an Athenian in the time of Plato, a 'Garden of Adonis' was a pot planted with seeds left to germinate and then wither, probably as part of a ritual observance of the ephemerality of human endeavour. Moreover, these Gardens of Adonis were proverbial for triviality, a sense in which Socrates cites them at the end of Plato's dialogue *Phaedrus* – a work, ironically enough, that concerns the nature of rhetoric and of love.[46] Socrates questions the value of the written word as a vehicle for philosophical truth, arguing instead that philosophers must preserve the vigour and clarity of their insights by realising them in live conversation and debate. The written record of a philosophical investigation, he says, would be like a Garden of Adonis – cheap, ephemeral and insubstantial, something someone would do only for the sake of amusement (παιδιᾶς χάριν). Plato is being coy, of course, for 'Socrates' makes this argument within a written work; but the point of the passage appears to be that the reader must take care, when interpreting Plato's written dialogues, to read them in a spirit of truly sceptical balance, as opportunities for reflection and not as sources of authority. Spenser's appropriation of the Garden of Adonis functions, I think, to the same end: it undercuts the passage's philosophical pretensions, but also insists upon an ongoing openness to deliberation between the various possible referents of Spenser's allegorical images. If we are not careful, our reading of *The Faerie Queene* risks degenerating into παιδιή, 'childish play'.

In the foregoing discussion, I have stressed some of the key historical and intellectual contexts of the composition of *The Faerie Queene*, as well as some of the more important ways in which, over the last four hundred years, it has been read. If any one thread is to emerge from this discussion, it must be that Spenser's allegorical epic is a poem of longing, a poem that requires of us an exhaustive capacity for readerly play, ethical and political experimentation, and philosophical deliberation. But one of the consequences of this longing in the poem is the way in which, having demanded our engagement, *The Faerie Queene* slips the hold and leaves us exposed; no matter how many properties we name, there is always more tree to spare. In a recent short study of the *Two Cantos of Mutabilitie*, Gordon Teskey reminds us that Mutabilitie's attempt against Jove is very like our interpretative attempt against the poem; it is a bid for mastery:

> Poetry confers a visionary firmness, an identity, on the fleeting world of experience. But if we try to use poetry to pursue the truth too far, as Mutabilitie does, then Nature's words to Mutabilitie may be applied to the project of *The Faerie Queene* as well: 'thy decay thou seekst by thy desire'. But we find that this is only partly true. For what could be more in the nature of the materials of poetry ... than for those materials always to long to turn into something other and better than themselves, such as the truth, even as they continually return to themselves?[47]

Mutabilitie is 'whist', or hushed, silenced – like a child guilty of παιδιή. Probably Spenser's greatest achievement in *The Faerie Queene* was to produce a poem that creates no end of longing for meaning. Before its exhaustive capacity for renewal, we grow wise only to discover that we have become, once again, only children.

Notes

1. Francis Meres, *Palladis Tamia* (London: Cuthbert Burbie, 1598), fol. Oo1^v-Oo2^r.
2. Steven May has proposed that Ralegh's reference to 'Philumena' may allude to a poem by the Earl of Essex, written at about this time, which attacks Ralegh as a cuckoo that

has attempted to oust the nightingale (presumably Essex). See Steven May, *Sir Walter Ralegh* (Boston: Twayne, 1989), p. 36.
3. Desiderius Erasmus, *De ratione studii*, in *Collected Works of Erasmus*, vol. 24: *Literary and Educational Writings 2*, ed. Craig R. Thompson (Toronto: University of Toronto Press, 1978), p. 672.
4. Erasmus, *De copia*, in *Collected Works of Erasmus*, vol. 24: *Literary and Educational Writings 2*, ed. Craig R. Thompson (Toronto: University of Toronto Press, 1978), p. 639. In the metaphor of the bee, Erasmus is echoing Seneca's *Epistulae Morales*, no. 84, which likens imitative reading to the activity of a bee collecting nectar, and imitative composition to the production of honey.
5. Erasmus, *De ratione studii*, p. 679.
6. Erasmus, *De ratione studii*, p. 679.
7. Julia Kristeva, 'Word, Dialogue, and Novel', in *Desire in Language: A Semiotic Approach to Literature and Art*, ed. Leon S. Roudiez, trans. Thomas Gora, Alice Jardine and Leon S. Roudiez (Oxford: Basil Blackwell), pp. 64–6.
8. Kristeva, 'Word, Dialogue, and Novel', p. 66.
9. E. K., epistle 'To ... Mayster Gabriell Haruey', in *The Shepheardes Calender*, pp. 7–8.
10. Quintilian, *Institutio Oratoria*, 10.2.2.
11. I quote from the 1580 edition of the *Aeneid* published in *Opera P. Virgilii Maronis* (London: Henry Middleton for John Harrison), p. 137.
12. Homer, *Odyssey*, ed. and trans. A. T. Murray (London: Heinemann, 1919), 3.67–71.
13. Homer uses this formula in the *Iliad* at 11.780 and in the *Odyssey* at 5.201. Elsewhere he uses the similar formula, 'αὐτὰρ ἐπεὶ πόσιος καὶ ἐδητύος ἐξ ἔρον ἕντο' ('but when they had been released from the desire of food and drink'); cf. e.g. *Iliad* 1.469, 2.432, 7.323, etc., and *Odyssey*, 1.150, 3.67, 3.474, etc.
14. A typical example of Spenser's fidelity to his model here is his translation of Tasso's verses describing a bird singing in Armida's garden (*Gerusalemme Liberata*, XVI.14–15). In Spenser's version the song is sung by 'some one' – perhaps even by Tasso himself (*FQ* II.xii.74–5). For a fuller treatment of Spenser's various responses to, and adaptations of, Tasso's work, see Graham Hough, *A Preface to* The Faerie Queene (London: Duckworth, 1962), pp. 59–81.
15. In his *Actes and Monuments* (London: John Daye, 1583) – commonly known as the *Book of Martyrs* – the Elizabethan Protestant publicist John Foxe includes Chaucer, along with Hocclve and Gower, in a list of 'faythfull witnesses in the time of *Iohn Wickleffe*' (fol. *5v). For the dialogue by 'Jack Upland', see pp. 262–4. The 'Plowman's Tale' was first printed among Chaucer's works in the 1545(?) third edition based on Thynne's text; Spenser would probably have known it from Stowe's edition of *The workes of Geffrey Chaucer* (London: J. Kingston for J. White, 1561).
16. Cf. Benedick's allusion to this legend in *Much Ado About Nothing*: 'Like the old tale, my lord – it is not so, nor 'twas not so, but indeed, God forbid it should be so' (1.1.203–4).
17. See *The Bible. Translated according to the Ebrew and Greeke, and conferred with the best translations in diuers languages* (London: Christopher Barker, 1583).
18. *The Bible* (1583), against Rev. 16:13 (f. 135r of the New Testament).
19. See 'A Letter of the Authors', in Edwin Greenlaw et al., eds, *The Works of Edmund Spenser: A Variorum Edition* (Baltimore: Johns Hopkins University Press, 1932–45), I, p. 167.
20. See Horace, *Ars Poetica* (*Art of Poetry*), ll. 343–4: '*Omne tulit punctum qui miscuit utile dulci, | lectorem delectando pariterque monendo*' ('He wins every point who mixes profit with pleasure, delighting and at the same time instructing the reader').
21. Philip Sidney, *A Defence of Poetry*, in *Miscellaneous Prose of Sir Philip Sidney*, ed. Katherine Duncan-Jones and Jan van Dorsten (Oxford: Clarendon Press, 1973),

pp. 82–3. Much of Sidney's argument derives from a close reading of the early chapters of Aristotle's *Poetics*.
22. 'Amiot to the Readers', in Sir Thomas North, *The Lives of the Noble Grecians and Romanes* (London: Thomas Vautroullier, 1579), sig. *iij^v.
23. 'Amiot to the Readers', sig. *iiij^r.
24. *Paradiastole* is the figure of 'rhetorical redescription' or extenuation, by which something vicious is redescribed in positive terms, often in order to flatter or curry favour.
25. See 'A Letter of the Authors', *Variorum*, I, p. 167.
26. See Aristotle, *Nicomachean Ethics*, ed. and trans. H. Rackham (Cambridge: Harvard University Press, 1926), VII.iii.1–14. In these sections Aristotle discusses the concepts of ἐγκρατῆς (self-restraint) and ἀκρατῆς (unrestraint), the latter of which furnishes the name of the enchantress of Book II of *The Faerie Queene*, Acrasia. Self-restraint and unrestraint are concepts that make sense only when an ethical subject knows the correct course of action.
27. Angus Fletcher, *The Prophetic Moment: An Essay on Spenser* (Chicago: Chicago University Press, 1971), p. 38.
28. See Stephen Greenblatt, *Renaissance Self-Fashioning from More to Shakespeare* (Chicago: University of Chicago Press, 1980), pp. 157–92 (esp. 179–89).
29. Greenblatt, *Renaissance Self-Fashioning*, pp. 189–90.
30. See René Graziani, 'Elizabeth at Isis Church', *PMLA*, 79 (1964), 376–89 (pp. 384–5, 388–9).
31. Quintilian, *The Institutes of Oratory (Institutio Oratoria)*, trans. by H. E. Butler, 4 vols (Cambridge, MA: Harvard University Press, 1920), VIII.vi.44.
32. Quintilian, *The Institutes of Oratory*, V.xi.17
33. Demetrius, *On Style*, ed. and trans. by Doreen C. Innes (Cambridge, MA: Harvard University Press, 1995), 99–101. Aristotle, in his *Rhetoric* (II.xxi.8, III.xi.6), twice attributes this allegorical saying to Stesichorus.
34. Torquato Tasso, *Discourses on the Heroic Poem*, trans. by Mariella Cavalchini and Irene Samuel (Oxford: Clarendon Press, 1973), p. 151.
35. See 'A Letter of the Authors', *Variorum*, I, p. 168.
36. Tasso, *Discourses on the Heroic Poem*, pp. 153–4.
37. Quintilian, *Institues of Oratory*, VIII.vi.57–8.
38. John Upton, ed., *Spenser's Faerie Queene. A New Edition with a Glossary, and Notes explanatory and critical* 2 vols (London: J. & R. Tonson, 1758), II, p. 335.
39. John Milton, *Areopagitica*, in the *Complete Prose Works of John Milton*, 7 vols (New Haven, CT: Yale University Press, 1959), II, p. 516.
40. See 'A Letter of the Authors', *Variorum*, I, p. 169.
41. Sir Kenelm Digby, *Observations on the 22. Stanza in the 9th. Canto of the 2d. Book of Spencers Faery Queen* (London: Daniel Frere, 1643), pp. 3–4.
42. Digby, *Observations*, pp. 10–11.
43. See Plato, *Symposium*, ed. H. N. Fowler (Cambridge, MA: Harvard University Press, 1925), 189c-193e.
44. Isabel G. MacCaffrey, *Spenser's Allegory: The Anatomy of Imagination* (Princeton: Princeton University Press, 1976), pp. 31–2.
45. MacCaffrey, *Spenser's Allegory*, p. 260.
46. See Plato, *Phaedrus*, trans. H. N. Fowler (Cambridge, MA: Harvard University Press, 1925), 276b-d.
47. Gordon Teskey, 'Night Thoughts', in Jane Grogan, ed., *Celebrating Mutabilitie: Essays on Edmund Spenser's Mutabilitie Cantos* (Manchester: University of Manchester Press, 2010), p. 37.

Chapter 4
Teaching the Text

One of the chief strengths of a long poem is the ample canvas it gives the poet to build structure in narrative and imagery through careful repetition and differentiation. Another key advantage of long works lies in their ability to grasp at totality of vision, in various respects; Spenser explicitly acknowledges his aim to engage with all of moral science, for example, and we have seen how the poem also strives to chronicle the political history of its age, and to act as a platform for the perception of universal metaphysical and even mystical truths. The problem for us today is that such complex operations require long evenings and not a little re-reading. It is unfortunate for Spenser that modern Western lifestyles tend to involve books – when they involve books at all – as consumables; once read, the book can be passed on or put on a shelf as a kind of trophy. By contrast, we are often content to listen to music, whether popular or more traditional, over and over again. This may perhaps be because music retains the whiff of freshness conferred upon it by its production, so that we think of music as something performed, and a text as something inert. Nothing could be further from the truth. If we are to take pleasure from great literature like *The Faerie Queene*, and perhaps some day to become masters in (not of!) it, we must listen to it – not once, but many times. It took great skill for Spenser to construct so productively significant a poem; he challenges us to teach, and re-teach, ourselves to read it, every time we try.

This penultimate section of the *Guide* is designed to help the reader of *The Faerie Queene* teach the poem, in just this sense. I use schemes and ideas like the following to teach others, but also to teach myself; and so I hope they will be useful not only to instructors leading classes on *The Faerie Queene*, but to all of us readers who conduct critical conversations within the closed circuit of our own contemplations. From these suggestions it should be abundantly clear that *The Faerie Queene*, perhaps pre-eminently among English works of literary imagination, is capacious; it admits and supports different temporalities and modes of reading, from high musical sensitivity or abstracted visualising cognition, to meticulous syntactical and rhetorical analysis. Among its many potential preoccupations, readers will find the whole range of historical, philosophical, psychological, social and literary problems upon which this *Guide* has already touched.

In what follows, I mention the work of well-known Spenserian critics, most of which can be traced in the 'Resources' cited in the next chapter. I also suggest some specific readings in different contexts; these proposed readings are widely available, either in print copies in libraries, or in digitised form through online providers. All of Spenser's texts are now available through online providers, both by subscription (e.g. early editions on Early English Books Online (EEBO), or the *Variorum* text of Spenser's works, via Chadwyck-Healy's Literature Online) and via free sites.

1. Seminar: interactive reading

The first and most important thing to learn about *The Faerie Queene* is that it is anything but inert. Many critics have commented on the way in which Spenser's poem feels like a live, or at least a moveable thing. Here I call this phenomenon 'interactivity', a word that may suggest the way in which the reader can change the poem, even as the poem transforms the reader. When we think of a literary work, we are not thinking of patterns of ink laid out on pages bound into a book, or indeed of patterns of darkness sprayed across an illuminated screen. Instead we are thinking loosely of the significance of those marks. All texts require us to become involved in enabling, even creating, the significance of those marks, by bringing to bear our own understanding of the words and concepts that those marks seem to signify. Spenser's poetry requires a higher level of literacy than most, in part because his language (i.e. both his use of English words and his conceptual language) is very dated, but in part too because he writes allegorically, demanding that his readers supply meanings remote from his expression. The poem thus provides scope for intense interactivity. The poem's structure, too, promotes a kind of interactivity. For example, some critics – above all, James Nohrnberg – have stressed the importance of the *structure* of Spenser's verse, both at local levels and in larger movements. Analogical patterning between books, episodes, smaller narrative elements, emblematic imagery and allegorical figures helps us to see two or more things in combination, either as instances of one another or as alternatives. The play of sameness and difference – both intensively, between two elements of a pair, and extensively across many such pairs – leads to moments of interpretative crisis and judgment, on matters of ethical, political, psychological and metaphysical importance. A rich allegory invites deep (vertical) play but Spenser's poem is more than an allegory; it is a 'continued' allegory, and thus it also demands broad (horizontal) play.

In addition, we also constantly have to make decisions about the mode in which we read a given part of the work. For example, Britomart sometimes seems to be a human subject, capable of passions and interiority, and at these moments we tend to try to empathise with her in her narrative predicament; but at other moments, she seems more clearly a vehicle for an idea, such as an ideal of chastity. At yet other moments, both of these modes are overtaken by a sense that she is a protrusion from another literary work (for example, when she enacts a scene from Chaucer's *Franklin's Tale* at III.iv.5–11), or even by the sense that she is an extrusion of another allegorical figure's own predicament (for this sea-side Chaucerian moment connects her to Florimell, who actually experiences the sea-captivity of which Britomart only thinks; cf. III.viii.20–43). The choices we make about how to view figures, emblems and narratives determine how we construct interpretative arrays from them, whether consciously or unconsciously. Similarly, our attitudes to elements or aspects of the poem – is the pageant of seven deadly sins a piece of sententious religious instruction or a hilarious deconstruction of out-of-date medieval religious ideology? – will affect what we notice, how we construe it, and thus what the poem *is*.

The Spenserian passages below all present figures for Spenser's allegory and for Spenser as allegorist – Archimago is an image-maker, Duessa and Acrasia are poet-like enchantresses, Errour represents the principle upon which much of Spenser's narrative and allegorical divagation is constructed, and Lucifera's palace is a storehouse for the moral *exempla* of which *The Faerie Queene* is constructed; not only does she stage allegorical pageants, but she has classical and Biblical heroes and villains locked in her basement.

From *The Faerie Queene*	I.i–ii (Redcrosse and Errour, Redcrosse at Archimago's); I.iv–v (Lucifera and the house of Pride); II.xii (the Bower of Bliss)
Reading	Gordon Teskey, 'Allegory', in *The Spenser Encyclopedia*, ed A. C. Hamilton (Toronto: University of Toronto Press, 1990), 16–22.
	Harry Berger, Jr, 'Archimago: Between Text and Countertext', *Studies in English Literature 1500–1900*, 43 (2003), 19–64.
	James Nohrnberg, *The Analogy of* The Faerie Queene (Princeton: Princeton University Press, 1976), 89–135.

- A. D. Nuttall, 'Spenser and Elizabethan Alienation', *Essays in Criticism*, 55 (2005), 209–25.
- Stephen Greenblatt, 'To Fashion a Gentleman', in *Renaissance Self-Fashioning from More to Shakespeare* (Chicago: University of Chicago Press, 1980), 157–92.

Questions for consideration

- These passages from the poem present multiple versions of image-makers, as well as some striking images – some violent, hybrid and repulsive, others alluring and seductive. How should our experience of Errour, Archimago, Duessa, Lucifera and Acrasia inflect our reading of Spenserian allegory?
- Gordon Teskey argues that allegory 'is a convention or rule governing information around a circuit', and shows how Spenser invites the reader not to achieve stable meanings, but to engage in pleasurable interpretative play. A. D. Nuttall, by contrast, sees *The Faerie Queene* as a poem disgusted with its own texture, and Stephen Greenblatt suggests that Guyon's destruction of the Bower is, too, a destruction of the poem itself. Do you think the poem is capable of these thoughts and attitudes, or are they traces of the poet's (or his early readers') attitudes, no longer relevant to our readings? What kind of tone do you think the poem strikes in relation to its surface texture and its allegorical meaning?
- Harry Berger, Jr, contends that the 'Archimago virus' infects not only the hero of Book I but its narrator, and shows how the corrections (*epanorthoses*) marking the conclusion of canto xii raise questions about the security of our vision of holiness. If Berger is right, how do these flaws in Spenser's moral scheme square (if at all) with your understanding of Spenser's allegorical structure in the opening book?

Follow-up reading

- Gordon Teskey, *Allegory and Violence* (Ithaca: Cornell University Press, 1996), especially chs 1 ('Personification and Capture: Francesca da Rimini') and 8 ('Spenser's Mutabilitie and the Authority of Forms'), 1–31, 168–88.
- Jonathan Goldberg, *Endlesse Worke: Spenser and the Structures of Discourse* (Baltimore: Johns Hopkins University Press, 1981).

2. Study plan: signifying and significance

The discovery in 1966 of Carew Ralegh's copy of the 1617 edition of Spenser's *Works* reminded us of something important about how early modern readers read Spenser.[1] In the margins of his copy, Ralegh and his mother, Elizabeth Throckmorton, made a number of annotations, the most interesting of which are interesting because they are so *un*interesting. On those pages corresponding to Book V, canto ix, for example, where Mercilla tries and then executes Duessa, Ralegh has identified Mercilla as Elizabeth, Duessa as the Queen of Scots, and Belge (who appears in the canto argument) as the states of Holland; on page 291, Ralegh identifies the villain Gerioneo as the Spaniard, and his monster Popery, or the Roman Catholic faith.[2] Later, against the relevant lines from *Mother Hubberds Tale* (1591), which contains a satirical attack on William Cecil, Lord Burghley, and his son Robert Cecil, Lady Ralegh has identified the beast fable's prime villain, the fox, as 'Burly', and his sidekick the ape as Robert Cecil, Earl of Salisbury.[3] These annotations are important because it is easy for modern readers to forget how preoccupied Spenser's contemporaries were with the topical historical allegory of his poems. And, indeed, one of our primary critical problems in addressing the allegory of *The Faerie Queene* must be to understand how the historical allegory is to be assimilated in our understanding of the poem's meaning more largely. These historical allusions are often only too painfully evident, as some critics have had cause to complain; they show Spenser's allegory signifying at its most 'naive' level. But are they significant?

One of the best ways to stimulate questions about Spenser's historical allegory – and to begin to provoke answers – is to compare a conspicuously historical passage of *The Faerie Queene* with one of its sources or analogues. Certainly among the most famous of these passages is Mercilla's trial and execution of Duessa in Book V (*FQ* V.ix.7–x.5), which only very thinly veils Elizabeth's 1586 trial and execution of Mary Queen of Scots. The complete history of Mary's life – with special attention to her trial and execution – was recorded by the antiquarian William Camden in his *Annales rerum Anglicarum et Hibernicarum regnante Elizabetha* (London, 1615), an account based on the manuscript sources and personal witness that also informed Spenser's account. Camden's record of Mary Queen of Scots was translated and later published as a separate volume as *The historie of the life and death of Mary Stuart Queene of Scotland* (London, 1624); pages 180–237 of this edition, now widely available through Early English Books Online (see Chapter 5), provide a curious counterpart to Spenser's allegorisation of the trial in *The Faerie Queene*. Compare these two texts. How does Spenser's allegorisation transform history – what Elizabethans called 'antiquities' – into moral history? Spenser's version of the trial may seem unapologetically ideological, as Mary has become falsehood itself, and stands accused of treason, irreligion, murder, sedition, incontinence and adultery – even while Elizabeth, as Mercilla, is described in terms that all but deify her in her righteous majesty. How do the clear links between Duessa's and Mary's trials inform our understanding of justice as an ethical and political virtue? Do these links sully our view of Spenser's representation of justice, or glorify his account of Elizabeth's reign of justice – or both? To follow up this comparison, try looking at Richard McCabe's fascinating account of James VI's 1596 response to reading this passage of *The Faerie Queene*, in 'The Masks of Duessa: Spenser, Mary Queen of Scots, and James VI', *English Literary Renaissance*, 17 (1987), 224–42. As McCabe shows, King James very quickly recognised the ideological force of Spenser's historical allegory.

Similar to the problems posed by historical allegory are those presented by the dynastic, chronicle and chorographic passages of *The Faerie Queene*. These passages carried substantial ideological and aesthetic weight with Spenser's first readers, and both showed and transmitted an impressive historical and geographical knowledge in an age where most of the sources of such knowledge remained the preserve of wealthy readers of Latin. These passages do not simply record cultural memory; they create it, and do so in a way strongly inflected by ideological pressures – for example, those exerted by concepts and practices such as royal sovereignty, primogeniture, merchant trading and colonial plantation. Typical of these passages is the tenth canto of Book II, in which Arthur and Guyon read chronicle accounts of the British and Faery realms. The British material derives from several sources, the most important of which is Geoffrey of Monmouth's *Historia Regum Britanniae*, a twelfth-century (mythical) history of the Celtic and Anglo-Saxon kings of England. Geoffrey's history of early Britain was particularly important to Tudor monarchs because of its strong emphasis on the Welsh origins of medieval English kings, an emphasis that supported the Welsh Tudors in their claim to the throne. Geoffrey's *Historia* is widely available in English translation – not only in print, but in several online editions. Compare the first six books of the *Historia* with this canto of *The Faerie Queene*. This will not only offer an opportunity to reflect on Spenser's selective attention to the mythic history – what does he adapt, what does he omit, what does he alter? – but will also prompt questions about how he frames the chronicle history of British kings within an allegorical narrative about temperance. Further, the pairing of this chronicle stuff with a clearly fanciful history of Elvish emperors (concluding in Spenser's Gloriana) raises further questions about the fanciful elements in Geoffrey's history, as well as its ideological slant, particularly in the hands of Tudor propagandists.

Spenser's historical matter and his historical allegory have been the focus of some of the most interesting critical engagements with *The Faerie Queene*, especially in recent years. The work of René Graziani, Frank Kermode, Stephen Greenblatt, Andrew Hadfield, Bart van Es and Richard McCabe, among others, has stressed the importance of attending to Spenser's careful synthesis and manipulation of historical sources, and his participation in the construction of an idea of history, often with distinctively political import. These studies can be traced in the bibliography provided in the next chapter of the *Guide*.

3. Seminar: word and image

Spenser has always been considered an especially visual poet. In part this critical commonplace stems from his early experimentation with sixteenth-century emblem books: both the 1569 *Theatre for Voluptuous Worldlings* (which contains poems translated by the teenage Spenser) and his pastoral masterpiece, *The Shepheardes Calender* (1579), set Spenser's poetry alongside emblematic woodcuts that both illustrate and complicate the meaning of his written words. But in *The Faerie Queene*, too, Spenser conspicuously adopts a visual style, consistent with his emphasis on personification, pageant and masque. In the readings suggested below, we see Spenser at his visual best, in descriptive passages and visual *tableaux* ranging from the pageant of the seven deadly sins to the otherworldly dance of the Graces on Mount Acidale. In collating these passages, the reader will inevitably be curious about how Spenser's visual writing accomplishes such different effects in different contexts. For example, the emblematic descriptions of the seven deadly sins are flat and closed, each visual detail corresponding obviously to its underlying ethical referent; so Gluttony (I.iv.21–3), for example, rides a 'filthie swyne' because his voracious and indiscriminate hogging defiles him. By contrast, the procession of fears and anxieties that crowd the Masque of Cupid (III.xii.1–27) shimmer, writhe and teem, perhaps because Spenser leaves these figures visually incomplete. In the readings below, too, we see Spenser's experiments with two ways of pairing words with images: *ekphrasis*, in which the poet describes a visual artwork (here, Busirane's Ovidian tapestries); and the curious scene in Book VI where Colin Clout, Spenser's poetic persona, explains to Sir Calidore the full meaning of the divine vision he has just witnessed.

One of the most important contexts for understanding and evaluating Spenser's visual writing is, of course, the English Reformation. Between Henry VIII's break with Rome in 1534 and Elizabeth's accession in 1558, many English churches endured successive waves of iconoclasm, including the defacing of paintings and the destruction of ornate wood and stone carving. The doctrinal stance of Elizabeth's famous 'settlement' stressed the sufficiency of Scripture – of the written word of the Bible – to human salvation. As the years of her reign wore on, Elizabeth witnessed a slow transformation of the landscape of religious experience in England, as the old images were decommissioned, put away and eventually destroyed. In their place came words: books and, above all, preaching. Spenser's visual poetry occupies a fraught position within this profound social and doctrinal shift.

From *The Faerie Queene*	I.iv.1–38 (Lucifera's palace and the pageant of the seven deadly sins); III.vi (the Garden of Adonis); III.xi–xii (the Masque of Cupid and the house of Busirane); IV.x (the rape of Amoret); V.ii.29–54 (the giant with the scales); VI.x.1–31 (the dance of the Graces)
Reading	S. K. Heninger, 'Words and Meter in Spenser and Scaliger', *Huntington Library Quarterly*, 50 (1987), 309–22.
	Judith Anderson, 'Frozen Words' and 'Weighing Words', in *Words that Matter: Linguistic Perception in Renaissance English* (Stanford: Stanford University Press, 1996), 7–42, 167–231.
	Harry Berger, Jr, 'Spenser's Gardens of Adonis: Force and Form in the Renaissance Imagination', in *Revisionary Play: Studies in the Spenserian Dynamics* (Berkeley: University of California Press, 1988), 131–53.
	Isabel MacCaffrey, 'Mirrors of Fiction: The Ecphrastic Image' and '"Good Love": The Garden of Adonis and Belphoebe's Bower', in *Spenser's Allegory: The Anatomy of Imagination* (Princeton: Princeton University Press, 1976), 104–29, 254–70.
	John N. King, 'Spenserian Iconoclasm' and 'Spenser's Royal Icons', in *Spenser's Poetry and the Reformation Tradition* (Princeton: Princeton University Press, 1990), 47–147.
Questions for consideration	Judith Anderson sees Artegall's encounter with the giant in *FQ* V.ii as an example of the strain in Spenser's works 'between metaphorical and material dimensions of meaning, between concept and history, or between words and things'. Does the absurdity of the giant's argument make him a fall guy for Spenser's allegorical method? Are we always in danger of treating words as signs, thus

Teaching the Text 203

as objects, and thus as things? How might this help us to understand Spenser's supposed Protestant ambivalence to iconic materiality?

- For Isabel MacCaffrey, the Garden of Adonis is doubly figurative, both as a symbol, and as a model. Harry Berger, by contrast, sees how 'the various maternal and erotic images [of Venus in] the first six cantos have been gathered up into a single form which controls and redefines the erotic force; yet this form is not static ... but understood only within the dynamic field of the tableau, in relation to Adonis, the boar, Cupid, and Psyche – a field in which each figure is in some sense part of all the others.' How do the dynamics of, and tensions between, linguistic and visual meaning help us to understand form in *The Faerie Queene*?

- John N. King argues for the 'ambiguous status of the imagination' in the late Elizabethan period, contending that Spenser in *The Faerie Queene* attacks only the abuse of art, and not art itself. The space left open by the destruction of Catholic icons, he suggests, was at least partly filled by a new appetite for royal iconography. Collating your readings of Lucifera's palace, the House of Busirane and the dance of the Graces, do you think Spenser is sympathetic to the materiality of any of his icons or ideas? How important is Busirane's charactered spell, or Colin Clout's piping, to your judgment?

Follow-up reading

- Linda Gregerson, 'Emerging Likeness: Spenser's Mirror Sequence of Love', in *The Reformation of the Subject: Spenser, Milton, and the English Protestant Epic* (Cambridge: Cambridge University Press, 1995), 9–47.
- Darryl J. Gless, *Interpretation and Theology in Spenser* (Cambridge: Cambridge University Press, 1994).

4. Exercise: rhetoric and versification

One of the best ways to probe and understand Spenser's rhetorical and prosodic techniques in *The Faerie Queene* is to imitate them. Over the last four hundred years, most English poets of any note or ambition have tried their hands at Spenser's stanza form: nine iambic lines, rhyming *ababbcbcc*, the first eight of which are pentameter, and the ninth an alexandrine, or hexameter. Students often find the stanza at first remarkably welcoming but ultimately difficult to turn well. Spenser's lines tend to be mellifluous, often airy, their cogs working glibly on the grease of monosyllabic verb auxiliaries such as 'can', 'could', 'gan', 'mote' and 'will'; mobile adverbs and adverbial phrases; and words of pliable pronunciation, which can be compressed or extended to suit the foot (e.g. 'euery', which can be both di- and trisyllabic, or 'endewed', which can also be written 'endew'd' or 'endu'd'). Spenser makes constant use of alliteration (as of the false Florimell at *FQ* V.iii.22: 'But some fayre Franion, fit for such a fere, | That by misfortune in his hand did fall'), and frequently employs common rhetorical figures such as ploce, anaphora, anadiplosis, hypallage (transferred epithet), zeugma, syllepsis, metonymy, synecdoche and epanorthosis. Spenser often breaks the stanza into two halves, pausing after the fifth (or less often the sixth) line, and occasionally reserves the alexandrine for a summing-up, a moral or a kind of punchline. Other recurrent and extraordinary features of his rhetorical and prosodic construction can be observed and noted, in preparation for this exercise.

In setting an exercise in Spenserian stanza-writing, care should be taken to encourage the student to study and imitate not only the stanza form, but also Spenser's rhetorical and syntactic techniques for achieving that form. This is difficult to achieve in modern English, which is much less tolerant than Spenser's of the syllabic deformations, periphrastic distensions and syntactic inversions that make his verse run smoothly. For this reason, it may be best to offer students of the poem the opportunity of writing not only formal imitation, but also (perhaps limited) pastiche, giving them the licence to play – as Spenser himself did – with archaic words, pronunciations and patterns of speech. These antique elements will afford more opportunities for the kind of rhetorical play that serially studs Spenser's expression. Help with Renaissance rhetoric is most conveniently to be had from the third book of George Puttenham's 1589 *Arte of English Poesie*, available on EEBO or in several modern editions, most recently that edited by Frank Whigam and Wayne Rebhorn; or from the *New Princeton Encyclopedia of Poetry and Poetics*. This exercise works best when the imitative stanza or stanzas can be written *into* the poem – that is, when they are devised not only the model of Spenser's own verse, but also as a supplement to some part of the poem that will admit of a digression, a visual description, a mythological elaboration, and so on. For example, a student might be asked to compose an additional or substitute epic simile to describe the fight between Redcrosse and Errour (cf. *FQ* I.i.23), or that between Arthur and Maleger (cf. *FQ* II.xi.32–3); or, for a slightly longer exercise, to describe what happens when the seagods' physician comes to attend on Marinell at *FQ* III.iv.43.

5. Seminar: gender, sexuality and power

Throughout *The Faerie Queene*, female figures like Mutabilitie occupy, aspire to or are thrown from positions of power; Duessa, Malecasta, Poeana, Radigund and Mirabella are only some of the other queens and ladies whose ambitious or arrogant pretensions are summarily crushed. But the poem has, too, its successful images of female power – Una, Alma, Belphoebe, Britomart, Mercilla. An older critical tradition saw these figures as versions of Elizabeth, and their narratives straightforward celebrations, or criticisms, of her royal power. Recent criticism has sought to understand how Spenser received and perhaps modulated the conventional misogynies of the intellectual tradition, with its gendered pairings of the male with form (*pattern*), and the female with matter (*materia*). In critical accounts of desire, voyeurism, genre and poetic authority, these studies have demonstrated just how fundamental sexual difference is to Spenser's conception of art and power in *The Faerie Queene*.

From *The Faerie Queene*	II.x (the House of Alma); III.vi (the Garden of Adonis); III.xi–xii (Britomart in the House of Busirane); V.vii.24–45 (Britomart defeats Radigund); V.ix (Mercilla's trial of Duessa), VII.vi–vii (the tale of Faunus and Molanna, and Mutabilitie's plea)
Reading	Katherine Eggert, 'Genre and the Repeal of Queenship in Spenser's *Faerie Queene*', in *Showing Like a Queen: Female Authority and Literary Experiment in Spenser, Shakespeare, and Milton* (Philadelphia: University of Pennsylvania Press, 2000), 22–50.
	Theresa M. Krier, *Gazing on Secret Sights: Spenser, Classical Imitation, and the Decorums of Vision* (Ithaca: Cornell University Press, 1990).
	Louis Montrose, 'Spenser and the Elizabethan Political Imaginary', *English Literary History*, 69 (2002), 907–46.
	David Lee Miller, 'Gender, Justice, and the Gods in *The Faerie Queene*, Book 5', in *Reading Renaissance Ethics*, ed Marshall Grossman (New York: Routledge, 2007), 19–37.
	Clare Carroll, 'The Construction of Gender and the Cultural and Political Other in *The Faerie Queene* and *A View of the Present State of Ireland*: The Critics, the Context, and the Case of Radigund', *Criticism*, 32 (1990), 163–92.

Questions for consideration

- David Lee Miller judges Britomart's glory, and dynastic destiny, to be purchased at the cost of her person; like her double, Amoret, following her betrothal to Artegall she slips unseen from the poem. Is Britomart's strange evanescence a consequence of her chastity? Her justice?

- Louis Montrose points us to the curious moment in *FQ* II.iii where Braggadocchio, the braggart knight, encounters Belphoebe – a parody, as he notes, of Aeneas' first meeting with Dido, but also a rewriting of Actaeon's intrusion upon Diana. Aeneas mistook a mortal for a goddess, (famously) crying, 'O dea certe' ('you are surely a goddess!'), while Actaeon mistook this goddess for a woman, and was torn to pieces for his misprision. The intertextual pivot of Braggadocchio's meeting with Belphoebe suggests the instability and binarism of female power in *The Faerie Queene*. Is it always the case that the poem's men must either fulfil their destinies by forsaking women, or in submission be destroyed?

Follow-up reading

- Edmund Spenser, *Amoretti and Epithalamion* (1595).
- Sheila T. Cavanagh, *Wanton Eyes and Chaste Desires: Female Sexuality in The Faerie Queene* (Bloomington: Indiana University Press, 1994).
- Elizabeth Fowler, 'Architectonic Person and the Grounds of the Polity in *The Faerie Queene*', in *Literary Character: The Human Figure in Early English Writing* (Ithaca: Cornell University Press, 2003), 179–244.
- David Lee Miller, *The Poem's Two Bodies: The Poetics of the 1590 Faerie Queene* (Princeton: Princeton University Press, 1988).

6. Study plan: conquest, law and empire

It is an uncomfortable fact for modern readers that Spenser's moral purpose in *The Faerie Queene*, and the apparently playful openness of his poem's allegorical structure, sit very uneasily against his participation in the violent colonial project of English rule in Elizabethan Ireland. Many critics of *The Faerie Queene* have insisted that, in reading the poem, we must take notice of Spenser's Irish experience, as well as his 1596 dialogue on social, political and military reform in the 'New English' administration there. Recent studies include work by Annabel Patterson, Elizabeth Fowler, Andrew Hadfield,

Patricia Palmer, Julia Reinhard Lupton, Willy Maley, Richard McCabe and Brian Lockey. These critics reconsider Spenser's moral and allegorical project in relation to his poem's engagement with law, force and conquest, and ideas about sovereignty and imperialism. Just because Spenser's poem begins, from Book V, to concern itself with oppressive violence and repressive political power, of course, does not mean that his allegory and ethical enquiry are tainted by it. But the increasing encroachment into his poem of topical historical reference, much of it occupied with English imperial adventures in the New World, Europe and Ireland, reminds us that this was a poem written and read within a period distinctive for its highly charged political and martial tensions. War, famine, threat of invasion, and the succession problem plagued England in the 1590s; critics of Elizabeth's European policy in the 1590s considered the stakes of inaction, or of careless action or of wrong action, to be high. If the 'ending end' of poetry was for Spenser, as for Sidney, ethical and political knowledge, and if that knowledge consisted not only in well *knowing*, but also in well *doing*,[4] the reader may justly fret about what Spenser thought his poem might induce her to do.

Two obvious means of accessing this important context for Spenser's moral and allegorical meaning in *The Faerie Queene* lie in the two manuscript sources that describe Spenser's experience in Ireland, and his response to that experience. In Spenser's *Selected Letters and Other Papers*, edited by Christopher Burlinson and Andrew Zurcher (see the bibliography in Chapter 5), students of the poem can find first-hand accounts of Lord Grey's massacre at Smerwick in November 1580, his military campaigns in Ulster and Wexford, and the devious political machinations that defined New English politics in Dublin during these years. These letters are all in other men's voices – mostly that of Lord Grey – but each of them passed through Spenser's hands, and many of them were documents he copied out in his own elegant 'secretary' handwriting. They provide an unparalleled witness of the brutality and often desperate conditions of Spenser's life in Ireland, and of the high stakes of moral and political action in a place where ideals all too frequently had to be compromised for the sake of security and survival. Students of *The Faerie Queene* may be particularly interested in Grey's letter to the Queen from his siege of Spanish and papal forces at Smerwick, dated 12 November 1580 (pp. 13–27), and in his letter to the Privy Council of 10 June 1581, detailing his military campaign against the O'Byrnes, O'Tooles, and other 'rebels' of Wicklow and Wexford (pp. 76–89). Both of these letters show the combination of ruthless violence and politic stratagem peculiar to the English 'reformation' of Ireland during this period, and provide a provocative historical context for *FQ* VI.x–xii (see selection 5, above), which narrates Calidore's battle with the Brigants and restoration of Pastorella to her courtly origins.

Other fruitful comparisons might be made between Artegall's recall from Irena's reformation (V.xii) and Grey's frank letter to Walsingham of 24 April 1581 (pp. 56–63); or between Mutabilitie's trial of 'titles and best rights' in the *Cantos of Mutabilitie* (*FQ* VII.vii) and MacWilliam Eighter's submission to Elizabeth (pp. 38–44).

In *A view of the present state of Ireland* (1596), we see Spenser's interlocutors Irenius and Eudoxus 'discoursing' on the legal, political and military abuses that have led to Ireland's decline (as Spenser has it) into incivility and rebellion, along with urgent proposals for reform. There are many – scarcely numerable – points of contact between Spenser's treatise on Irish affairs and his allegorical poem, from their shared use of metaphor and allegory – for example, their common figuration of the polity as a garden and as a body – to very specific shared allusions to historical events in the Elizabethan struggle to govern the island. Particular attention, though, might be given to civility and savageness (Cf. the *Variorum* text of *A view*, ll. 941–1942 and *FQ* I.vi.1–33, VI.iii.20–VI.iv.16, VI.viii.31–51 and VI.ix–xii); fostering (*A view*, ll. 1943–2133 and *FQ* VI.iv); folkmotes and assemblies (*A view*, ll. 2390–478 and *FQ* V.ii, VII.vii); the relationship between law and power (*A view*, ll. 64–1124 and *FQ* V.ii.1–28, VI.i and VI.vi.17–VI.viii.30, VII.vii); the role of violence in creating or maintaining ethical and political order (*A view*, ll. 134–297, 2899–3433 and *FQ* II.xi–xii, IV.ii.32–IV.iii, IV.x, V.xii); and dialogic balance in interpretation and meaning, especially in connection to political theory (cf. Spenser's use of the dialogue in *A view*, *passim*, against examples of allegorical indeterminacy in *FQ* such as V.ix.20–V.x.5, VI.ix–xii and VII.vi–vii).

Notes

1. See Walter Oakeshott, 'Carew Ralegh's Copy of Spenser', *The Library*, 26 (1971), 1–21.
2. Oakeshott, 'Carew Ralegh's Copy of Spenser', p. 19.
3. Oakeshott, 'Carew Ralegh's Copy of Spenser', pp. 6–7.
4. See Philip Sidney's *Apologie for Poetrie* (London: James Roberts for Henry Olney, 1595), sig. D1ʳ, from which I paraphrase here.

Chapter 5
Resources for Study

Early editions

The Faerie Queene. Disposed into twelue books, Fashioning XII. Morall vertues (London: John Wolfe for William Ponsonby, 1590).
The first quarto edition of the poem, including only Books I–III.

The Faerie Queene. Disposed into twelue bookes, Fashioning XII. Morall vertues, 2 pts (London: Richard Field for William Ponsonby, 1596).
The second quarto edition of the poem, including a slightly revised text of Books I–III and the first printing of Books IV–VI.

The Faerie Queene (London: Humphrey Lownes for Matthew Lownes, 1609).
The first posthumous edition of the poem, printed in folio format and including *Two Cantos of Mutabilitie* (provenance unknown).

The Faerie Queen: The Shepheards Calendar: Together with the Other Works of England's Arch-Poët, Edm. Spenser (London: Matthew Lownes, 1611–17).
The famous first folio edition of Spenser's complete works – also the first folio edition of a modern English poet produced in the period.

Modern editions

The Works of Edmund Spenser: A Variorum Edition, ed. Edwin Greenlaw, Charles Grosvenor Osgood, Frederick Morgan Padelford, et al., 11 vols (Baltimore: Johns Hopkins University Press, 1932–45).
A complete text of Spenser's collected works, with *The Faerie Queene* in six volumes. Each volume includes the text, a survey of critical approaches (to c. 1940), and useful appendices on formal, biographical and historical matters. Available through LION (see below).

The Faerie Queene, ed. Thomas P. Roche, Jr (London: Penguin, 1978).

This no-frills edition of the poem is based on the 1596 text (corrected, with paratexts from 1590 and the *Cantos of Mutabilitie* from 1609), accompanied by a light commentary printed at the back of the volume. The closest thing to a pocket *Faerie Queene*.

The Faerie Queene, ed. A. C. Hamilton, Hiroshi Yamashita and Toshiyuki Suzuki (London: Pearson Education, 2001).
An excellent if not flawless text of the poem, joined to Hamilton's exhaustive commentary on matters poetical, historical, philosophical and critical. This large-format edition helpfully prints the notes alongside the text.

The Faerie Queene, ed. Carol Kaske, Erik Gray, Dorothy Stephens, Abraham Stoll and Andrew Hadfield, 5 vols (Indianapolis: Hackett, 2006–7).
A complete text of the poem with running, if slightly uneven, same-page commentary. The text of the poem is unfortunately cluttered by footnote references.

Other works by Spenser

The Shorter Poems, ed. Richard McCabe (London: Penguin, 1999).
A complete edition of the shorter poems (including Latin verse), providing an excellent text and judicious notes.

A view of the present state of Ireland, ed. Andrew Hadfield and Willy Maley (Oxford: Blackwell, 1997).
Based on the 1633 (flawed) text of Spenser's dialogue, printed by Sir James Ware in Dublin. This edition includes a brief introduction and helpful textual and critical appendices.

Edmund Spenser, Selected Letters and Other Papers, ed. Christopher Burlinson and Andrew Zurcher (Oxford: Oxford University Press, 2009).
A selection of manuscript materials associated with Spenser's service in Ireland between 1580 and 1589.

Critical approaches and reference works

(Studies marked with * are especially recommended to new readers.)

* Paul J. Alpers, *The Poetry of The Faerie Queene* (Princeton: Princeton University Press, 1967).
* Judith Anderson, *Reading the Allegorical Intertext: Chaucer, Spenser, Shakespeare, Milton* (New York: Fordham University Press, 2008).
* Harry Berger, Jr, *Revisionary Play: Studies in the Spenserian Dynamics* (Berkeley: University of California Press, 1988).
Kenneth Borris, *Allegory and Epic in English Renaissance Literature: Heroic*

Form in Sidney, Spenser, and Milton (Cambridge: Cambridge University Press, 2000).
* Colin Burrow, *Epic Romance: Homer to Milton* (Oxford: Clarendon Press, 1993).
Colin Burrow, *Edmund Spenser* (Plymouth: Northcote House, 1996).
Sheila T. Cavanagh, *Wanton Eyes and Chaste Desires: Female Sexuality in The Faerie Queene* (Bloomington: Indiana University Press, 1994).
Donald Cheney, *Spenser's Image of Nature: Wild Man and Shepherd in the Faerie Queene* (New Haven, CT: Yale University Press, 1966).
Patrick Cheney, *Spenser's Famous Flight: A Renaissance Idea of a Literary Career* (Toronto: University of Toronto Press, 1993).
Helen Cooper, *The English Romance in Time: Transforming Motifs from Geoffrey of Monmouth to the Death of Shakespeare* (Oxford: Oxford University Press, 2004).
R. M. Cummings, *Spenser: The Critical Heritage* (London: Routledge & Kegan Paul, 1971).
* Katherine Eggert, *Showing Like a Queen: Female Authority and Literary Experiment in Spenser, Shakespeare, and Milton* (Philadelphia: University of Pennsylvania Press, 2000).
Robert Ellrodt, *Neoplatonism in the Poetry of Edmund Spenser* (Geneva: Droz, 1960).
Angus Fletcher, *Allegory: The Theory of a Symbolic Mode* (Ithaca: Cornell University Press, 1964).
Elizabeth Fowler, 'The Failure of Moral Philosophy in the Work of Edmund Spenser', *Representations*, 51 (1995), 47–76.
Richard C. Frushell and Bernard J. Vondersmith, *Contemporary Thought on Edmund Spenser, With a Bibliography of Criticism of The Faerie Queene, 1900–1970* (Carbondale: Southern Illinois University Press, 1973).
Darryl Gless, *Interpretation and Theology in Spenser* (Cambridge: Cambridge University Press, 1994).
* Jonathan Goldberg, *Endlesse Worke: Spenser and the Structures of Discourse* (Baltimore: Johns Hopkins University Press, 1981).
* Stephen Greenblatt, *Renaissance Self-Fashioning: From More to Shakespeare* (Chicago: University of Chicago Press, 1980).
* Linda Gregerson, *The Reformation of the Subject: Spenser, Milton, and the English Protestant Epic* (Cambridge: Cambridge University Press, 1995).
Kenneth Gross, *Spenserian Poetics: Idolatry, Iconoclasm, and Magic* (Ithaca: Cornell University Press, 1985).
Andrew Hadfield, *Edmund Spenser's Irish Experience: Wilde Fruit and Salvage Soyl* (Oxford: Oxford University Press, 1997).
* Andrew Hadfield, ed., *The Cambridge Companion to Spenser* (Cambridge: Cambridge University Press, 2001).
* A. C. Hamilton, ed., *The Spenser Encyclopedia* (Toronto: University of Toronto Press, 1990).

Elizabeth Heale, *The Faerie Queene: A Reader's Guide* (Cambridge: Cambridge University Press, 1987; 2nd edn 1999).
Richard Helgerson, *Self-Crowned Laureates: Spenser, Jonson, Milton, and the Literary System* (Berkeley: University of California Press, 1983).
Graham Hough, *A Preface to The Faerie Queene* (London: Duckworth, 1962).
Carol Kaske, *Spenser and Biblical Poetics* (Ithaca: Cornell University Press, 1999).
John N. King, *Spenser's Poetry and the Reformation Tradition* (Princeton: Princeton University Press, 1990).
Theresa M. Krier, *Gazing on Secret Sights: Spenser, Classical Imitation, and the Decorums of Vision* (Ithaca: Cornell University Press, 1990).
C. S. Lewis, *The Allegory of Love* (Oxford: Oxford University Press, 1936).
Julia Reinhard Lupton, 'Mapping Mutability: Or, Spenser's Irish Plot', in *Representing Ireland: Literature and the Origins of Conflict, 1534–1660*, ed. Brendan Bradshaw, Andrew Hadfield and Willy Maley (Cambridge: Cambridge University Press, 1993), 43–59.
Richard McCabe, *Spenser's Monstrous Regiment: Elizabethan Ireland and the Poetics of Difference* (Oxford: Oxford University Press, 2002).
Richard McCabe, ed., *The Oxford Handbook of Edmund Spenser* (Oxford: Oxford University Press, 2010).
*Isabel MacCaffrey, *Spenser's Allegory: The Anatomy of Imagination* (Princeton: Princeton University Press, 1976).
Waldo F. McNeir and Foster Provost, *Edmund Spenser: An Annotated Bibliography, 1937–1972* (Pittsburgh: Duquesne University Press, 1975).
Willy Maley, *A Spenser Chronology* (Houndmills: Macmillan, 1994).
Willy Maley, *Salvaging Spenser: Colonialism, Culture and Identity* (London: Macmillan, 1997).
David Lee Miller, 'Spenser's Vocation, Spenser's Career', *English Literary History*, 50 (1983), 197–231.
David Lee Miller, *The Poem's Two Bodies: The Poetics of the 1590 Faerie Queene* (Princeton: Princeton University Press, 1988).
*Louis Montrose, 'Spenser and the Elizabethan Political Imaginary', *English Literary History*, 69 (2002), 907–46.
Louis Montrose, *The Subject of Elizabeth: Authority, Gender, and Representation* (Chicago: University of Chicago Press, 2006).
James Nohrnberg, *The Analogy of* The Faerie Queene (Princeton: Princeton University Press, 1976).
*Patricia Parker, *Inescapable Romance: Studies in the Poetics of a Mode* (Princeton: Princeton University Press, 1979).
Thomas P. Roche, Jr, *The Kindly Flame: A Study of the Third and Fourth Books of Spenser's Faerie Queene* (Princeton: Princeton University Press, 1964).
Gordon Teskey, 'Mutabilitiy, Genealogy and the Authority of Forms', *Representations*, 41 (1993), 104–22.
*Gordon Teskey, *Allegory and Violence* (Ithaca: Cornell University Press, 1996).

Rosemond Tuve, *Allegorical Imagery: Some Mediaeval Books and Their Posterity* (Princeton: Princeton University Press, 1966).
Bart Van Es, *Spenser's Forms of History: Elizabethan Poetry and the 'State of the Present Time'* (Oxford: Oxford University Press, 2002).
Bart Van Es, ed., *A Critical Companion to Spenser Studies* (Basingstoke: Palgrave Macmillan, 2006).
Kathleen Williams, *Spenser's Faerie Queene: The World of Glass* (London: Routledge & Kegan Paul, 1966).
Susanne Lindgren Wofford, *The Choice of Achilles: The Ideology of Figure in Epic* (Stanford: Stanford University Press, 1992).
Jewel Wurtsbaugh, *Two Centuries of Spenserian Scholarship (1609–1805)* (Baltimore: Johns Hopkins University Press, 1936).
Andrew Zurcher, *Spenser's Legal Language: Law and Poetry in Early Modern England* (Cambridge: D. S. Brewer, 2007).

Web resources
Early English Books Online (EEBO) – http://eebo.chadwyck.com
A complete collection of facsimiles (digitised from microfilms) of books printed in England, Scotland, Ireland and Wales, and of English books printed abroad, in the years 1475 to 1700. This is an unrivalled portal for the study of early modern literature, history, philosophy and religion, and culture.

Literature Online (LION) – http://lion.chadwyck.co.uk (and http://lion.chadwyck.com)
A comprehensive selection of English literature from the early modern period. The texts are not always perfectly transcribed, but the coverage is staggering, and the database also includes copious and increasing scholarly content.

The International Spenser Society – http://www.english.cam.ac.uk/spenser/society
The website of the only academic society dedicated to the support of Spenser studies worldwide, including the electronic edition of the *Spenser Review*.

Edmund Spenser: World Bibliography – http://bibs.slu.edu/spenser/index.html
An indispensable reference tool for Spenser studies, including abstracts of virtually all scholarship published on Spenser between 1974 and 2003.

Index

NB: The index does not record references to the figures, places, or other elements of Spenser's poetry, either as summarised in the 'Map of The Faerie Queene' (pp. 5–14) or in the selections from the text of the poem that follow (pp. 16–161). The headnotes and commentary to the selections, however, have been indexed; where reference is made to the poem commentary, the relevant page number is accompanied by the note reference, in parentheses.

Alighieri, Dante, 5, 22n. (7.2), 24n. (14.6–9), 183, 185, 190–1
allegory, theory of, 178, 180–92, 196–7
Amyot, Jacques, 173–4
Anderson, Judith, 202
Aphthonius, *Progymnasmata*, 164
Apollodorus, *The Library*, 56n. (stanzas 22–4), 63n. (45.9), 84nn. (31.2, 33.6), 87n. (43.4–7), 93n. (7.5–9), 107n. (5.6–9)
Apollonius Rhodius (Apollonius of Rhodes), *Argonautica*, 60n. (stanzas 35–6), 62n. (stanzas 44–5), 93n. (7.5–9), 113n. (stanza 12)
Ariosto, Ludovico, *Orlando Furioso*, 3, 5, 18n. (1.1–5), 26n. (stanza 23), 44n. (stanzas 28–45), 50n. (Arg.4), 62n. (stanzas 42–52), 77n. (7.3ff.), 167, 174
Aristotle, *Nicomachean Ethics*, 49, 50–1n. (stanzas 3–8), 111–12n. (7.1–5), 127n. (32.9), 176–80, 182–4, 194nn.26, 33
Ascham, Roger, 14n.6, 164

astronomy (and astrology), 36n. (1.1–5), 107nn. (4.6ff, 5.6–9), 108nn. (6.1–4, stanza 7, 8.1–7, 8.8–9), 113n. (11.5–6)

Bakhtin, Mikhail, 164
Barclay, Alexander, 170
Berger, Harry, Jr, 198, 203
Bible, 20n. (1.2), 25n. (20.7), 40n. (stanza 13), 48n. (43.3–5), 104n. (*44.7–9), 105, 117n. (26.3–5), 128n. (38.1–5), 169–71, 188, 202
Boiardo, Matteo, *Orlando Innamorato*, 3
Bourchier, Sir John, Lord Berners, *Huon of Bourdeux*, 51n. (4.2)
Boyle, Elizabeth, 138n. (stanza 16)
Bryskett, Lodowick, 3
Burlinson, Christopher, 207
Burton, Robert, *The Anatomy of Melancholy*, 32n. (42.7)

Camden, William, 2, 14n.5, 199
Cartwright, Thomas, 2–3

Index 215

Cecil, Robert, earl of Salisbury, 199
Cecil, William, Lord Burghley, 3–4, 14, 15n.13, 199
chastity, 74–5, 176, 197
Chaucer, Geoffrey, 5, 9–10, 22n. (8.5–9.9), 36n. (1.6), 168–9, 193n.15, 197
Cicero (Marcus Tullius Cicero), 2, 164–5
Conti, Natale, *Mythologiae*, 38n. (7.4), 64n. (48.2), 83n. (30.4), 84n. (31.2), 110n. (stanza 2), 111n. (5.4), 137n. (15.1ff.)
Cooper, Thomas, *Dictionarium Historicum & Poeticum*, 30n. (37.8), 34n. (48.9), 140n. (stanzas 23–4), 144n. (39.3ff.)
Cork (city), co. Cork, 1–2, 4
courtesy, 132–3

de Bry, Theodore, 93n. (8.1–4)
Demetrius, *On Style (Peri Hermeneias)*, 182–3, 185
Devereux, Robert, earl of Essex, 192–3n.2
Digby, Sir Kenelm, 188–90
Diodorus Siculus, *Library of History*, 110n. (stanza 2)
Dudley, Robert, earl of Leicester, 1

ekphrasis, 177, 201
Elizabeth (I), Queen of England, 4, 13, 14n.6, 19n. (4.1–4), 49, 109n. (stanza 11), 141n. (stanza 28), 163, 180–1, 199–202, 205, 207–8
entrelacement, 167
Erasmus, Desiderius, 163–4, 193n. 4
Euripides
  Alcestis, 86n. (39.1)
  Bacchae, 136n. (11.1–2)
  Helen, 84n. (32.2)
  Medea, 62n. (stanzas 44–5), 63n. (45.9)

Fletcher, Angus, 178
Fletcher, Phineas, 190
folktales, 75, 90–1n. (54.6–8), 169–70
Foxe, John, 193n.15
Fowler, Elizabeth, 206

Geoffrey of Monmouth, *Historia regum Britanniae*, 106n. (Title), 200
Gerard, John, *The Herbal*, 47n. (40.7)
Gesner, Konrad, *Historia Animalium*, 56n. (stanzas 22–4)
Graziani, René, 180–1, 201
Greenblatt, Stephen, *Renaissance Self-Fashioning*, 178–80, 198, 201
Grey de Wilton, Arthur, Baron, 1, 3–4, 180, 207–8
Grindal, Edmund, Bishop of London and Archbishop of Canterbury, 2–3

Hadfield, Andrew, 201, 206
Hariot, Thomas, *A briefe and true report of the new found land of Virginia*, 93n. (8.1–4)
Harvey, Gabriel, 3, 14, 15n.12, 165
Henry VIII, 201
Herodotus, *The Histories*, 108n. (8.1–7)
Hesiod, *Theogony*, 24n. (14.6–9), 84n. (33.1), 112n. (stanza 9), 137n. (15.1ff.)
history, Renaissance theory of, 172–4, 200
Homer, 2, 19n. (2.7), 26n. (stanza 23), 34n. (48.2), 38n. (7.1–3), 39n. (10.3–4), 50nn. (Arg.4, 3.1), 50–1n. (stanzas 3–8), 55n. (stanzas 18–33), 57n. (stanzas 27–33), 61nn. (stanzas 39–41, 41.3), 62n. (stanzas 42–52), 72n. (81.3–5), 74n. (85.5), 75, 85n. (35.1), 87n. (42.1), 140n. (25.3ff.), 163, 166, 174, 193n.13
Horace (Quintus Horatius Flaccus), 2, 61n. (41.3), 84n. (31.2), 172, 193n.20

humanism, and education, 2, 163–4; see also imitation
hypallage, 190, 204

imitation (*imitatio*), 162–72
intertextuality, 164–5
Ireland, vii, 1–4, 110n. (4.1), 144n. (39.3), 178, 180–1, 206–8

Jewel, John, 169
Jonson, Ben, 2, 5
justice (incl. equity), 105, 106n. (Title), 109n. (stanza 11), 111–12n. (7.1–5), 113n. (stanza 12), 115n. (19.8–9), 127n. (32.9), 132–3, 180, 200, 206

K., E., 34n. (48.9), 140n. (25.3), 165
Keats, John, 190
Kermode, Frank, 201
Kilcolman, co. Cork, 1–2, 4, 13
King, John N., 203
Kristeva, Julia, 164–5

Langland, William, 5, 24n. (14.6–9), 28n. (29.2ff.), 105, 121n. (9.9)
Lewis, C. S., 191
Livy (Titus Livius), 18n. (2.5)
Lockey, Brian, 207
Lupton, Julia Reinhard, 207
Lydgate, John, 5

McCabe, Richard, 201, 207
MacCaffrey, Isabel, 191, 203
MacWilliam Eighter (Richard Ynyren Burke), 208
Maley, Willy, 207
Malory, Sir Thomas, 5
Mantuan (Baptista Mantuanus), 170
Marlowe, Christopher, 5, 63n. (47.2–9)
Martial, *Epigrams*, 135n. (8.9)
Mary, Queen of Scots, 180, 199–200
May, Steven, 192–3n. 2
Merchant Taylors' School, London, 1–2, 4
Meres, Francis, 163

Miller, David Lee, 206
Milton, John, 5, 24n. (14.6–9), 187–8, 190
Montrose, Louis, 206
moral virtue, and poetry, 172–7
Mulcaster, Richard, 2, 14n.6, 14n.10
Munster plantation, Ireland, 1

Nine Years' War (1594–1603), Ireland, 1
Nohrnberg, James, 196
North, Sir Thomas, 173–4
Nuttall, A. D., 198

O'Neill, Hugh, earl of Tyrone, 4
Ovid (Publius Ovidius Naso), vi, 2, 5, 9, 13, 26n. (21.1), 30n. (36.3), 32n. (43.2–3), 34n. (48.9), 36n. (1.1–5), 39n. (10.3–4), 53n. (stanza 13), 58n. (31.2), 62n. (stanzas 44–5), 65nn. (52.1–3, 52.4–5, 52.6–7), 71n. (77.7), 75, 83nn. (stanzas 29–46, 30.5, 30.6), 84nn. (31.2, 32.2), 85nn. (34.3, 34.4, 35.1, 35.2–4, 36.7, 37.2), 86nn. (38.2, 39.1), 87nn. (41.9, 42.2–5, 43.4–7), 106n. (stanza 2), 107n. (5.6–9), 109n. (stanza 9), 111n. (5.4), 137n. (stanza 13), 145n. (43.8), 163, 174

Palmer, Patricia, 207
paradiastole, 176, 194n.24
Parker, Thomas, 169
patronage, 3–4
Patterson, Annabel, 206
Pausanias, *Description of Greece*, 58n. (31.2)
Pembroke College, Cambridge, 1–3
Petrarch (Petrarca), Francesco, 163
Plato (and pseudo-Plato)
  Minos, 113n. (stanza 12)
  Phaedrus, 191–2
  Symposium, 190
Pliny the Elder, 164

Plutarch, 43n. (24.1–3), 63n. (47.2–9), 74n. (86.6–87.8), 167, 173
Pope, and the papacy, 25n. (20.7), 40n. (stanza 13), 42n. (22.7–9), 171, 199
Protestantism, 2–3, 21n. (5.3–6), 43n. (24.1–3), 167–68, 171, 187, 193n.15
Puttenham, George, *The Arte of English Poesie*, 204

Quintilian (Marcus Fabius Quintilianus), *The Institutes of Oratory (Institutio Oratoria)*, 165, 182, 184–6

Ralegh, Carew, 199
Ralegh, Sir Walter, 14, 163, 180, 182, 192–3n.2
Rebhorn, Wayne, 203
Lord Roche, Maurice, Viscount of Fermoy, 4

secretaryship, 4, 207–8
Seneca (Lucius Annaeus Seneca), 2, 193n.4
Shakespeare, William, 5, 53n. (12.5), 162–3, 191, 193n.16
Sidney, Sir Philip, 3, 15n.12, 143n. (34.3ff.), 172–3, 178, 193–4n.21, 207
Skelton, John, 5, 169
Smerwick, co. Kerry, 4
Smith, Sir Thomas, 3
Spenser, Edmund
    Amoretti and Epithalamion, 1–2, 35n. (52.1–2), 141n. (stanza 28)
    Complaints, 1, 146n. (stanza 1)
    Colin Clouts Come Home Againe, 138n. (stanza 16)
    The Faerie Queene
        Acidale, 177–8, 201
        Acrasia, 49, 168, 179–80, 194n.26, 197–8
        Alma, 175, 189–90, 205
        Amoret, 6, 75, 170, 176, 206

Archimago 17, 174–5, 197–8
Artegall 105, 133, 171, 174, 180, 202, 206, 208
Arthur, Prince, 167, 172–3, 175, 177, 180, 189, 200, 204
Belge, 199
Belphoebe, 180, 205–6
Blatant beast, 132–3
the Bower of Bliss, 49, 168, 174–5, 178–9, 191, 193n.14
Britomart, 74–5, 166, 170, 176, 180–1, 197, 205–6
Busirane, 75, 170, 176, 201, 203
Calidore, 132–3, 169, 177–8, 181, 201, 207
Colin Clout, 133, 168–9, 201, 203
Duessa, 17, 171, 180, 197–200, 205
Errour, vi, 17, 170–1, 175, 190, 197–8, 204
Faunus, 174
Florimell, 6, 167, 197, 204
the Garden of Adonis, 191–2, 203
Gerioneo, 199
Gluttony, 201
Guyon, 49, 168, 171, 174–5, 178–80, 189, 198, 200
Hellenore, 75, 166
House of Holinesse, 175
Lechery, 175–6
Lucifera, 197–8, 203
Malbecco, 75, 166
Malecasta, 205
Maleger, 204
Mammon, 171, 187
Marinell, 204
Medina, 175
Mercilla, 180, 199–200, 205
Merlin, 181
Molanna, 174
Paridell, 75, 166
Pastorella, 133, 207
Poeana, 205
Redcrosse, vi, 17, 49, 169–71, 174–5, 180, 185–8, 204
Sanglier, 105, 171

Scudamour, 75, 176
Thames and Medway, 181
Timias, 167, 180
Una, vi, 17, 174, 185–8, 205
life, 1–5
The Shepheardes Calender, 1, 3, 34n.
  (48.9), 133, 138nn. (stanza 16,
  18.4–5), 140n. (25.3ff), 146n.
  (stanza 1), 165, 168–9, 201
A Theatre for Worldlings, 1, 146n.
  (stanza 1), 201
A view of the present state of Ireland,
  181, 208
Stafford, William, 181
syllogisms, 176–7

Tacitus (Publius Cornelius Tacitus), 34n.
  (48.9), 144n. (39.3ff.)
Tasso, Torquato
  Gerusalemme Liberata, 3, 5, 50n.
    (Arg.4), 61n. (stanzas 39–41),
    62nn. (stanzas 42–52, stanzas
    44–5), 66n. (58.8–9), 67n.
    (stanzas 60–9), 70n. (stanzas
    74–5), 77n. (7.3ff.), 167–8, 174,
    179, 183–8, 190, 193n.14
  Rinaldo, 77n. (7.3ff.)
Terence (Publius Terentius Afer), 2
Teskey, Gordon, 192, 198
Theocritus, 167
Throckmorton, Elizabeth, 199
Thynne, William, 169
Trinity College, Cambridge, 2–3
Trissino, Giangiorgio, 49

Upton, John, 20n. (1.1–7), 21n. (4.1–2),
  186

van der Noodt, Jan, 1
van Es, Bart, 201
Virgil (Publius Vergilius Maro), vi, 2, 5,
  18n. (1.1–5), 22nn. (7.2, 8.5–
  9.9), 30n. (36.3), 31n. (40.1–3),
  38n. (7.4), 44n. (stanzas 28–45),
  60n. (stanzas 35–6), 61n. (41.3),
  85n. (34.4), 135n. (8.9), 136n.
  (stanza 9), 165–6, 168, 174,
  175
de Voraigne, Jacques, *Legenda Aurea*,
  170

Walsingham, Sir Francis, 208
Whigham, Frank, 204
White, John, 93n. (8.1–4)
Whitgift, John, Master of Trinity
  College and Archbishop of
  Canterbury, 3
Whitney, Geoffrey, *Choice of Emblemes*,
  97n. (22.1)
Wither, George, *A Collection of
  Emblemes, Ancient and Moderne*,
  115n. (19.8–9)
Wolsey, Thomas, Lord Chancellor
  and Archbishop of Canterbury,
  169

Young, John, Master of Pembroke
  College and Bishop of
  Rochester, 1, 3